# PRIZE RECIPES
From
## GREAT RESTAURANTS
THE SOUTHERN STATES
& THE TROPICS

# PRIZE RECIPES
## From
## GREAT RESTAURANTS

### THE SOUTHERN STATES
### & THE TROPICS

COMPILED BY

## James Stroman

**PELICAN PUBLISHING COMPANY**

GRETNA 1983

**Library of Congress Cataloging in Publication Data**
Main entry under title:

Prize recipes from great restaurants.

Includes indexes.
Contents: [1] The Western States.—[2] The Southern
States and the tropics.
1. Cookery, American.   2. Cookery, International.
TX715.P94227        641.5        78-27415
ISBN 0-88289-293-2 (v. 2)        AACR2

Manufactured in the United States of America

Published by Pelican Publishing Company, Inc.
1101 Monroe Street, Gretna, Louisiana 70053

I proudly dedicate this book to my aunt, Vera Reese of Kingston, Oklahoma . . . the best culinary artist I have ever known. She is capable of making a masterpiece from practically nothing. Cookbooks are not needed when she enters her modest kitchen. A pinch of this, a little of that, and, presto, you have a feast fit for kings.

# Contents

# The Southern States

## TARTAR SAUCE

To two cups of mayonnaise, add 2 tablespoons tarragon vinegar, 2 tablespoons dill pickle relish, 2 teaspoons onion chopped very fine; and 2 teaspoons chopped parsley chopped very fine. Mix well. Refrigerate. Will keep a long time. Delicious with most seafood.

## CLAMS CASINO

1 doz. clams on half shell
1 tsp. butter
1 pimento
1 small onion
1/2 green pepper
2 slices bacon, cooked slightly

Chop all ingredients finely, combine, and cover clams with mixture. Place under broiler for 5 minutes.

## CHEESECAKE

1 lb. cream cheese
8 oz. cottage cheese (blend til smooth before adding)
1/2 cup sugar
4 eggs
3 tbsp. flour
1 cup sour cream
2 tsp. vanilla
dash salt
juice and grated rind of 1 lemon

## GLASGOW ARMS RESTAURANT
## Glasgow

*This grand restaurant has been serving the finest quality food for almost half a century. Its six dining rooms are tastefully decorated with fine antiques and artwork. The Murphy family has continuously operated this outstanding restaurant since it opened in 1937.*

Mix all ingredients until smooth. Line bottom and sides of pie pan with graham cracker crumbs and bake at 285° for about 30 minutes until firm but not brown. Remove from oven and spoon on a mixture of 1 tablespoon lemon juice, 1 teaspoon vanilla, 3 teaspoons sugar, and 1 cup sour cream. Bake 5 minutes more.

## SEAFOOD NEWBURG

Sauté 3 cups mixed seafood (shrimp, king crab, crabmeat, scallops, etc.) in 1/4 cup butter; add 1 cup cream, salt and white pepper to taste. Cook a minute or two, then add 2 tablespoons sherry and 2 beaten eggs. Stir a few minutes over low heat until mixture thickens. Serve immediately on toast points or patty shell. Serves four.

## CRAB SOUP MARYLAND

chopped vegetables, as desired (onions, leeks, carrots, celery, green peppers)
salt and pepper to taste
3 qts. water
2 cups diced potatoes

Sauté vegetables in butter until transparent, not brown. Add water and cook for 15 minutes. Add potatoes. When they are cooked, add 1/2 pound white crabmeat and 1/2 pound claw meat. Cracked claws may be added. Serves eight.

## BACKFIN CRABMEAT AU GRATIN

1/4 cup butter
1 cup flour
1 qt. milk
salt and pepper to taste
1 cup cheddar cheese, shredded
backfin crabmeat

Make white sauce with first three ingredients; add salt and pepper to taste, then add 1 cup shredded cheddar cheese. Add crabmeat, place in casseroles, and put under broiler until sauce bubbles. (Oysters can also be prepared this way.)

## BLUE COAT OPEN-FACED CRAB BROIL SANDWICH

2 slices cracked wheat bread
4 oz. backfin crabmeat
2 tbsp. salad dressing or mayonnaise
juice of 1 lemon
2 slices American cheese

Toast and trim crust from bread. Spread salad dressing or mayonnaise on one side of each slice and put one-half the amount of crabmeat on each. Drizzle lemon juice over crabmeat. Top with cheese. Place on cookie sheet and bake in 350° oven until cheese is hot and bubbly. Serve quickly, garnished with fresh parsley.

## BACON BAKED OYSTERS

**BUTTER MIX**
3 tbsp. melted butter
2 tbsp. lemon juice
dash pepper
dash salt

Combine and mix well.

**BACON-CRUMB MIX**
1/2 cup fresh bread crumbs
1/2 cup fresh crumbled crisply fried
    bacon
2 tbsp. bacon grease

Mix together and toss well.

Open 1 dozen fresh oysters and leave in half shell. Settle each half shell into crumpled foil on baking sheet to prevent tipping. Baste each oyster equally with butter mix. Top each with bacon-crumb mix. Bake 4 to 5 minutes in 425° oven. Good as an appetizer, luncheon dish, or entree.

## DELAWARE SEAFOOD CHOWDER

1/4 cup oil
1 cup chopped onions
1 cup chopped carrots
1 cup chopped celery
1 qt. clam broth
2 cups diced potato
1 cup chopped clams
1 cup chopped shrimp
1 cup crabmeat or whitefish

---

### BLUE COAT INN
### Dover

*Once a private home, the inn today offers diners a varied bill of fare in picturesque surroundings. The Blue Coat takes its name from the uniform worn by Col. John Haslet's Delaware Regiment of 1776. Delicious food amid historic surroundings.*

salt
pepper
3 tsp. sugar
1 cup sherry wine
1 large can evaporated milk

Sauté onions, carrots, and celery in oil. Add clam broth and bring to boil. Add potatoes, clams, shrimp, and crabmeat. Cook until vegetables are tender, then season to taste with pepper, salt, 3 teaspoons sugar and 1 cup sherry wine. Thicken with roux; add can evaporated milk.

## ROUX

1 cup melted margarine
1 1/2 cups flour

## DELAWARE PEACH CRISP À LA MODE

2 cups heavy peach syrup from canned
    peaches
2 tbsp. cornstarch
1/4 tsp. nutmeg
1/2 tsp. cinnamon
1 cup brown sugar
2 tbsp. honey
juice of 2 lemons
1/2 cup raisins
1/2 cup pecans
3 cups sliced cling peaches

Heat peach syrup until hot. Mix cornstarch, nutmeg, cinnamon, sugar, and honey and add to syrup. Then add lemon juice, raisins, pecans, and

---

peaches. Place all in baking pan, sprinkle with crumb topping, and bake for 90 minutes in 350° oven. Cool. Serve in bowls with scoop of vanilla ice cream on top of each. Serves six.

## CRUMB TOPPING

1 cup melted butter
2 cups flour
1 cup sugar

## VEAL CUTLET À LA BLUE COAT

4 veal cutlets
1/3 cup ketchup
1/2 cup mayonnaise
3 egg yolks
2 tbsp. Worcestershire
salt and pepper to taste
boiled ham, thinly chipped
bread crumbs

Combine ketchup, mayonnaise, egg yolks, Worcestershire, salt, and pepper. Dip cutlets in milk, then in crumbs, and fry in oil until golden. Place layer of thinly chipped ham on top of each cutlet and cover with sauce. Bake in 350° oven 5 to 7 minutes. Serves four.

## MUSHROOMS STUFFED WITH CRAB IMPERIAL

fresh whole mushrooms
1 lb. Maryland backfin crabmeat
2 tbsp. onions, finely diced
2 tbsp. sweet green pepper, finely
    diced
2 eggs
4 tbsp. mayonnaise
4 tbsp. butter
1 lb. bread crumbs or 1 lb. diced bread

Mix all together; add salt, pepper and Worcestershire sauce to taste. Stuff mushrooms with crab filling. Mix 1 egg with 4 teaspoons mayonnaise and pour over top of stuffed mushrooms. Bake in 350° oven for 20 minutes. Serves five.

## CRABMEAT AU GRATIN

6 oz. crabmeat
3 oz. Mornay sauce with paprika

Mornay sauce is a white creamy sauce, one-half milk and one-half fish bouillon. Let the sauce cook for 20 minutes. Add 2 oz. grated Swiss cheese and a dash of paprika plus an egg yolk. Then mix sauce and crabmeat together, put in casserole dish, and sprinkle top with Parmesan cheese. Cook in 375° oven for 10 minutes or until golden brown.

## AMELIA MUD PIE

SHELL:

Oreo cookies
2 tbsp. butter

Chop cookies very fine and mix with butter. Form the pie shell and place in freezer to thoroughly chill.

FILLING:

15 oz. chocolate ice cream
2 tbsp. ground coffee
2 tbsp. ground Sanka
2 tbsp. whipped cream
2 tbsp. brandy
4 tbsp. Kahlua

Whip ice cream with ground coffees, brandy, and Kahlua; then add whipped cream and place on the shell. Allow to get very hard, and cover with chocolate.

## SHRIMP JAMBALAYA

5 oz. deveined, peeled shrimp
1 oz. ham, diced to 1/2-inch pieces
1 oz. hot sausage
2 oz. onion
2 oz. celery
2 oz. sweet green pepper
white wine
2 oz. uncooked rice
1 bay leaf
touch of saffron
4 oz. peeled tomatoes
chicken and fish bouillon
Creole sauce (see recipe below)

## AMELIA ISLAND INN
## Amelia Island Plantation
## Amelia Island

*This great inn is at the world-famous Amelia Island Plantation. The very finest cuisine is served elegantly and graciously in a beautifully decorated dining room.*

Sauté shrimp, ham, sausage, onion, celery, and green peppers lightly. Then sprinkle mixture with white wine. Add rice, bay leaf, saffron, and tomatoes and cover up to 3/4 inch from the top of the pot with one-half chicken and one-half fish bouillon. Bake in oven for about 20 minutes. Serve with Creole sauce.

CREOLE SAUCE:

2 oz. onion, diced to 1/2-inch pieces
2 oz. celery
2 oz. sweet green pepper
2 oz. mushrooms

Sauté in oil, then add a little tomato sauce and bay leaves (as desired). Season well. Let cook slowly for 30 minutes.

## VEAL OSCAR

5 oz. veal scallopini
4 asparagus spears
1 oz. king crabmeat
Hollandaise sauce and horseradish

Pass veal through a flour and egg mixture and sauté in oil or margarine. Add asparagus and crabmeat and cover all with Hollandaise sauce containing a dash of horseradish. Glaze under broiler until golden.

## SOFT-SHELL CRAB

Dredge 3 medium soft-shell crabs in flour. Sauté until golden color. Add a sprinkle of chopped parsley and Meuniere sauce (see recipe).

## SHRIMP TASSERA

7 medium shrimp, peeled and deveined, leaving tail on
flour
1/2 tsp. finely chopped garlic and onion mixture
dash white wine
1 oz. fish bouillon
a little brown gravy
butter
1 tsp. chopped parsley

Dip shrimp in flour and sauté in a little oil until golden. Add other ingredients and simmer for 2 minutes; then add a little raw butter and the parsley.

## SHRIMP AND OYSTER CASSEROLE

4 oz. shrimp
4 oz. oysters
1 tsp. chopped onion
a little chopped garlic
dash white wine
4 oz. tomato sauce
dash oregano
1 tsp. chopped parsley

Sauté shrimp and oysters in oil. Add other ingredients and simmer for a few minutes. Serve immediately.

## SEA BASS AMELIA

8 oz. sea bass filets
flour
oil
1 oz. crabmeat
2 oz. Meuniere sauce (see recipe below)
finely chopped parsley

Dip filets in flour; sauté in oil. Cover with crabmeat and Meuniere sauce and top with parsley.

MEUNIERE SAUCE:

1 oz. melted butter
1/2 tsp. lemon juice
few drops Lea & Perrins
salt, pepper, and dash brown gravy

Mix together.

## ROAST DUCKLING WITH ORANGES
*(A Favorite at Cafe Chauveron)*

2 ducklings, each 4 to 5 lbs. (ready-to-cook weight)
3 medium oranges
2 tbsp. sugar
2 tsp. vinegar
2 cups thick veal stock or canned condensed beef broth
1 1/2 tbsp. lemon juice
3 tsp. arrowroot starch
1/2 cup sweet sherry
1/3 cup orange liqueur

Clean ducklings and pat dry. Rub inside of ducks with salt; skewer opening and lace shut. Prick skin well all over to allow fat to escape. Roast on a rack in shallow pan in hot oven (400°) about 1½ hours or until meaty part of leg feels tender when pressed (use paper towel). Spoon off fat occasionally. While ducks roast, shave peel from 2 of the oranges with vegetable peeler and cut into julienne strips. Squeeze juice from all 3 oranges. Set peel and juices aside. When ducks are done, place on heated platter. Keep hot while making Orange sauce: Remove drippings from roasting pan and skim off fat; set pan juices aside. Caramelize the sugar with vinegar in roasting pan. Add reserved pan juices, veal stock, orange juice and peel, and lemon juice. Cook sauce rapidly to reduce by one-half. Blend arrowroot and sherry; gradually stir into sauce. Cook, stirring, 6 to 8 minutes or until thick and clear. Do not let sauce bubble. Add orange liqueur just before serving. Trim ducks with orange sections; trim platter with orange "cups." Serves 8.

## QUENELLES DE BROCHET
*(Pike Dumplings)*

1 lb. pike filet
2 egg whites
2 cups light cream

Cut the pike, which should be completely free of skin and bones, into small pieces and pound it to a paste in a mortar. Force the fish through a fine sieve or put in an electric blender to make a smooth puree. Set bowl containing fish in a pan of ice. Slowly work in the egg whites with a wooden spoon. Gradually add about half the cream, stirring constantly. Season lightly with salt and white pepper, nutmeg, and cayenne and then stir in more of the cream. Test the mixture by poaching 1/2 tsp. in hot but not boiling salted water.

## CAFE CHAUVERON
## Bay Harbor Island

*In 1972 the internationally renowned Chauveron moved from New York City to Florida. The scene on a tributary of Biscayne Bay recalls Paris on the Seine. The elegant but subdued decor of the dining room provides the perfect background for the French haute cuisine.*

The quenelles should just hold their shape. The lighter the mixture, the better the quenelles, and frequent testing is the best way to determine how much cream may be added to the forcemeat. Heap a tablespoon with the forcemeat and with a second spoon shape an oval form. Dip the second spoon in hot water and scoop with quenelle onto buttered, flat pan. Shape all mixture in this fashion. Pour enough boiling water or fish stock into the pan to come halfway up the quenelles. Cover pan and simmer gently for 15 to 20 minutes. Drain quenelles on a napkin and serve immediately.

## BOUILLABAISSE À LA PARISIENNE
*(Parisian Fish Stew)*

3 lbs. sea bass
3 lbs. red snapper
4 lbs. lobster
24 Little Neck clams
24 moules (mussels)
2 onions, sliced
2 white leeks, sliced
4 cloves garlic
2 tsp. chopped parsley
2 tsp. powdered saffron
3/4 tsp. chopped fennel
1 lb. tomatoes (chopped or canned stewed tomatoes)
2 tbsp. olive oil
3/4 bay leaf
2 oz. Pernod
4 cups dry white wine

Cut fish and lobster into large pieces; crack claw of lobster. Place together with remaining ingredients in large bowl, add a little salt and pepper, and set bowl in refrigerator for 2 hours. Place mixture in a flat pan, add enough hot fish stock or boiling water to cover well, and bring to boil over high heat. Cover and cook for

30 minutes. Adjust seasoning with salt and pepper. Before serving, remove bone and skin of fish and shell of lobster, clams, and mussels. Serve very hot. Serves 6.

## CHICKEN IN CHAMPAGNE SAUCE

2 3-lb. chickens, cut up
1/3 cup white port wine
4 oz. dry champagne or dry white wine
1/2 lb. butter
2 oz. brandy
3 cups light cream
1 cup thick cream sauce
shallots*

Sauté chicken in butter. When lightly browned, season with salt and pepper and cover. Cook slowly for 25 minutes. Remove the pieces of chicken and pour off the cooked butter. Bring to boil the brandy, port wine, and champagne; simmer for 5 minutes. This will make a sauce. Then add the thick cream sauce and the fresh light cream. Cook over a hot fire for 6 minutes, stirring constantly. Do not boil anymore. Put the chicken back in sauce and simmer for 5 minutes. Serve with boiled white or wild rice.

*If you wish to use shallots, add one small head (finely chopped) for each serving when you begin to sauté the chicken. Serves 4.

## SOUFFLE VANILLE
*(Vanilla Soufflé)*

1/2 cup sugar
5 egg yolks
1/2 cup flour
2 cups milk
1 tsp. butter
5 egg whites
vanilla bean

Beat the egg yolks with the sugar until the mixture is light and fluffy; then beat in the flour. Scald the milk with a piece of vanilla bean and remove the bean. Pour the milk gradually into the egg mixture and cook, stirring constantly, for a minute or two or until mixture is smooth. Fold in egg whites, beaten stiff, and turn the batter into a buttered and sugared souffle dish. Bake in a moderate oven (350°) for from 30 to 40 minutes, until well puffed and browned. Sprinkle with confectioners' sugar and serve at once. Makes about 1 quart. Serves 2 or 3.

## SAUCE RAIFORT

This sauce is used on beef, shrimp, crabmeat, sausage, veal—in fact, almost the only thing it hasn't been tried on is ice cream!

1 cup milk
flour to thicken
salt and pepper
1 cup sour cream
2 tbsp. olive oil
2 tbsp. minced onion
2 tbsp. chopped parsley
1 tbsp. freshly grated horseradish

Heat milk, add flour to thicken, and cook until smooth and fairly thick. Adjust seasonings. Now add sour cream and blend. Sauté onion and parsley in olive oil until soft and add to sauce. Add horseradish and blend well and taste again. You may want more or less horseradish depending on how sharp you like the flavor. This sauce is very good as a cold dip, although it probably will need some thinning to use cold. Use a dry white wine for this purpose.

## CRABMEAT SAUTÉ WITH SOUR CREAM

1 1/2 lbs. thawed and drained Alaskan king crabmeat (Allow 5 to 6 oz. crabmeat per serving.)
4 oz. butter
2 tbsp. olive oil
1/2 tsp. salt
black pepper
4 tbsp. minced onion
2 tbsp. chopped parsley
2 tbsp. lemon juice
1/4 cup dry white wine
3/4 cup sour cream

Melt butter in saucepan. Add olive oil, salt, and black pepper. When butter and oil are hot, sauté onion and parsley. Cook, stirring constantly, until onion is softened. Now add lemon juice and wine. When well heated, thicken with 1 tbsp. of flour. Cook until sauce is thickened; then add sour cream. Mix well. When bubbling, add crabmeat. Allow to simmer for a few minutes, then serve on steamed rice. Shrimp may be prepared the same way, allowing 7 or 8 whole shrimp per person. Serves 4.

## CHICKEN BREAST GORGONZOLA

4 8-oz. chicken breasts, boned and skinned
butter to sauté breasts
salt and pepper
1 1/2 cups milk
flour to thicken

## SIPLE'S GARDEN SEAT
## Clearwater

*Over sixty years ago, Mary Boardman forsook the cold of New England for the warmth of Florida and established this great restaurant. She welcomed people warmly and delighted them with expertly prepared food served in a pleasing atmosphere. The same is true today as Dick Siple carries on his grandmother's traditions.*

8 oz. Gorgonzola cheese
2 tbsp. lemon juice
2 tbsp. vinegar

Season breasts with salt and pepper and sauté in hot butter until just lightly browned. Make a heavy cream sauce with the milk, thickened with flour. Cook until smooth, seasoning to taste. Puree the cheese, lemon juice, and vinegar in blender until smooth. Add to the cream sauce and blend well. Place breasts in pan just large enough to hold them and pour the sauce over. Cover with foil and bake in 350° oven for 15 to 20 minutes or until tender. Serve on steamed rice. Serves 4.

## AVOCADO PEAR SOUP

4 avocado pears, peeled
6 or 7 cups good chicken stock
6 tbsp. flour
a little sweet cream
salt, cayenne pepper, and chili pepper
crushed coriander seeds
red caviar or paprika for garnish

Moisten flour with cream and mix with chicken stock. The consistency should be a thin paste. Add a dash of salt, cayenne pepper, chili pepper, and crushed coriander seed. Stir over low heat until boiling, mixing in flour, and cooking until smooth. Put avocado pears through strainer; add to soup and blend well. Put through strainer again, then stir over ice until chilled. Garnish each cup with a bit of red caviar or paprika.

## CRABMEAT WITH LIME BUTTER SAUCE

2 lbs. Alaskan king crabmeat, thawed if frozen
3/4 lb. butter
juice of 2 limes

Melt butter and retain only the clear portion. Squeeze into the heated clarified butter the juice of 2 limes. Now grate the rind into the pan. Then drop in the remaining pulp of the lime and allow to simmer but not boil for 8 to 10 minutes. Strain the butter. Sauté crabmeat, after draining it well, in the lime butter sauce and serve with steamed rice or boiled noodles. Serves 6.

## STRAWBERRY OR PEACH DAIQUIRI

1 1/2 oz. light rum
1 1/2 oz. freshly squeezed lime juice
2 tbsp. sliced strawberries or sliced peaches, sweetened slightly
1 heaping tbsp. crushed ice

Place all ingredients in a blender and whir until the ice and fruit are slushy. Serve frothy and icy cold in 6-oz. prechilled cocktail glass. A garnish of fresh mint leaf helps.

## CREAM CHEESE MOLDED SALAD

9 oz. softened cream cheese
1 tbsp. sweet cream
1/2 tsp. dry mustard
1 #1 can crushed pineapple, drained (save juice)
1 small can pimento, cut small
1/2 cup heavy sweet cream, whipped stiff
2 packages lemon gelatin
2 cups boiling water

Mix together cream cheese, sweet cream, dry mustard, crushed pineapple, and pimento. When well mixed, add whipped cream. Prepare the lemon gelatin by mixing with the boiling water and juice of the pineapple. When gelatin begins to set, blend in other ingredients and put in salad molds.

## TOURNEDOS À LA GARDEN SEAT

1 1/2 lbs. peeled beef tenderloin, cut into 3-oz. tournedos
8 large fresh mushroom caps, peeled and lightly poached
4 oz. softened butter
2 tsp. garlic powder
2 tbsp. bread crumbs
freshly ground pepper
dash salt

Combine garlic powder, bread crumbs, salt, and pepper; then fill each mushroom cap with this mixture. Season tournedos and broil with the mushroom caps on top. Serve on toast cut round to fit tournedo. Sprinkle with chopped parsley. Serves 4.

## SWEETBREADS IN CREAM

3 pairs sweetbreads
4 cups water
1 tbsp. lemon juice
1 tsp. salt
1 medium onion, chopped
1/2 cup butter
1/2 cup dry white wine
1 cup heavy cream
salt and pepper
chopped parsley

Soak sweetbreads in enough cold water to cover for at least 1 hour. Put drained sweetbreads in saucepan with 4 cups water, lemon juice, and salt and cook over low heat for 12 to 15 minutes. Drain, cover with cold water, and let cool. Cut each pair in half and trim off all the tubes and membranes. Put sweetbreads on flat surface, cover with a tray or baking sheet and top sheet with a weight. Let stand for about 1 hour or until they are relatively firm. Dust lightly with flour. In heavy skillet, sauté 1 medium onion in 1/2 cup butter until tender but not brown. Push onion to one side of skillet, add sweetbreads, and sauté for about 3 minutes on each side or until golden brown. Remove sweetbreads and onion to a plate and deglaze skillet with 1/2 cup dry white wine. Pour in cream, return sweetbreads and onion to the sauce, and cook over very low heat for about 15 minutes. Season the dish with salt and pepper to taste. Serve the sweetbreads on a warm platter with the sauce spooned over them. Garnish dish with a sprinkling of chopped parsley.

## CRABMEAT BALLS WITH MUSTARD SAUCE

1 lb. flaked crabmeat
1/4 cup melted butter
1 tsp. salt
1 tsp. prepared mustard
1/8 tsp. nutmeg
1/8 tsp. cayenne pepper
1/2 cup soft bread crumbs
2 egg yolks, beaten

Mix together well the crabmeat, butter, salt, mustard, nutmeg, cayenne, and soft bread crumbs. Stir in egg yolks and chill mixture until firm enough to hold a shape. Form into small balls and dust with flour. Fry in hot deep fat until well browned. Drain. Serve hot with mustard sauce.

### MUSTARD SAUCE:

2 tbsp. flour
2 tsp. prepared mustard
1 tsp. sugar

## CREIGHTON'S RESTAURANT
### Fort Lauderdale

*At this restaurant you will find expertly prepared American cuisine, as well as gardens, a gilded harpsichord, the world's largest Baccarat chandelier, a million-dollar array of antiques—and the world's best apple pie.*

pinch salt
3/4 cup wine vinegar
2 egg yolks

In top of double boiler blend together the flour, mustard, sugar, and salt. Add the vinegar and cook over hot water, stirring constantly, until smooth and mixture begins to thicken. Remove pan from hot water; stir in 2 lightly beaten egg yolks. Return to heat (not in double boiler); stir constantly from bottom of pan until mixture has thickened. Serve hot or cold.

## FRESH CORN SPOONBREAD

1 1/2 cups corn cut from cob (about 3 ears)
1/3 cup yellow cornmeal
1/4 cup butter or margarine
1 1/2 tsp. salt
1 tbsp. minced onion
2 cups hot milk
2 tsp. sugar
white pepper to taste
2 eggs, separated

Mix corn with cornmeal and stir in milk. Cook and stir over moderate heat until thickened, 5 minutes or longer. Remove from heat; stir in butter, sugar, salt, pepper, and onion. Beat a little of hot mixture into 2 slightly beaten egg yolks; stir back into remaining hot mixture. Fold in 2 stiffly beaten egg whites. Turn into a buttered 1 1/2-quart casserole. Place in pan of hot water and bake in 325° oven until knife inserted in center comes out clean—about 1 hour. Serves 6 to 8.

## DINNER BISCUITS

2 cups flour
4 tsp. baking powder
1 tsp. salt
1 tsp. sugar
1/4 cup shortening
3/4 cup milk

In large bowl, combine flour with baking powder, salt, and sugar. Work flour between fingertips until it feels soft and silky; then add shortening and work into the flour again with fingertips until well blended. Stir in milk with a fork, stirring only until a soft dough is formed. Knead dough on floured board for 10 seconds and roll to 1/4-inch to 1/2-inch thickness, depending upon whether thin crusty biscuits or thick soft biscuits are desired. Trim the dough into a square with a long sharp knife and cut into 1 1/2-inch squares. Put biscuits on well-greased baking sheet, brush with cream or milk, and bake in very hot 450° oven for 12 to 15 minutes or until golden brown.

## APRICOT BRANDY POUND CAKE

2 sticks butter
3 cups sugar
6 eggs
3 cups flour
1/4 tsp. soda
1 cup sour cream
1/2 tsp. lemon extract
1 tsp. orange extract
1/4 tsp. almond extract
1/2 tsp. rum extract
1 tsp. vanilla extract
1/2 cup apricot brandy

Cream butter and sugar until light and fluffy; then add eggs, one at a time, beating well after each addition. Sift dry ingredients and add to creamed mixture. Combine sour cream with extracts and brandy and add to cake batter. Mix well. Bake in large well-greased and floured tube pan at 325° for 70 minutes. Let cool in pan before removing.

## BRUNSWICK STEW

2 squirrels or 3-lb. chicken, cut up
3 qts. water
1 large onion, sliced
1/2 lb. lean ham, cut into small pieces

Put in pan and simmer gently for 2 hours. Add:

3 pts. cut up tomatoes
1 pt. uncooked lima beans
4 large potatoes, diced
1 pt. fresh or canned corn, grated
1 tbsp. salt
1/4 tsp. pepper
1 small red pepper pod

Cover and simmer gently another hour, stirring frequently to prevent scorching. Just before serving, add 3 oz. butter. Serve hot.

## OMELETTE AU RHUM

4 eggs
1/2 cup milk
1/2 oz. butter
pinch salt
rum
confectioners' sugar

Beat the eggs with the milk; then add the salt. Heat butter in frying pan until it gives off the characteristic nutty smell. This will lend an exquisite taste to the omelette. Pour in the beaten eggs and stir briskly with a fork to heat the whole mass evenly. When well set, roll up the omelette. Transfer to a hot dish. Draw a piece of butter quickly across its surface to make it glossy. Sprinkle with confectioners' sugar and heated rum. Ignite the rum and bring omelette to table while flaming. Serves 2. For 8 servings, increase to 16 eggs and slightly increase amount of other ingredients.

## ICE CREAM PRALINE

1 1/2 pts. heavy cream
8 oz. granulated sugar
10 egg yolks
10 oz. praline paste
1 1/2 pts. whipped cream
1 pt. fresh strawberries

Mix cream, sugar, and egg yolks. Stir while cooking. Remove from fire before mixture boils. Cool. Add praline paste (previously prepared by cooking together equal quantities of almond nuts and sugar to the point of caramelization, then cooling and reducing to paste). Strain the mixture. Add whipped cream. Set aside in a paper-collared mould. Freeze for 1 1/2 hours. Remove paper and serve on ice form or block. Have very ripe fresh strawberries already macerated in Cordial Medoc liqueur or orange liqueur to serve as garnish. Serves 8.

## CERVELLES AU BEURRE NOIR
### (Calves' Brains in Black Butter)

2 lbs. calves' brains
water
1 oz. vinegar
1 tsp. salt per qt.
juice of 1/2 lemon
1/2 lb. butter
2 tbsp. capers
1 tbsp. chopped parsley
freshly ground black pepper

## LE DOME OF THE FOUR SEASONS
## Fort Lauderdale

*This national award-winning penthouse high above the Lauderdale scene is noted for its French cuisine and excellent wine cellar. It is a constant Holiday Award winner and one of six restaurants in the country to receive Mobil's coveted Five Star award. Walter Meyer, chef des cuisines, is the main attraction. All of the recipes here were prepared especially for this book; none has been published before.*

Soak the calves' brains in several changes of cold water for 2 hours. Carefully pull off as much of the outside membrane as possible without tearing the brains. Trim by cutting off the white opaque bits at the base. Simmer, uncovered, for 15 minutes in salted water with vinegar. Spread brains on napkin to dry. Bring butter to foam in heavy skillet. Just before foam subsides, add capers and chopped parsley. Arrange brains in serving skillet, sprinkle with pepper and lemon juice and pour on butter. Serve at once very hot. Serves 8.

## COQUILLE JACQUELINE

24 oz. bay scallops
8 tbsp. dry white wine
8 tbsp. clam juice
2 tsp. lemon juice
pinch salt
8 scallop shells
1 heaping tsp. arrowroot dissolved in 2 tbsp. water
1/2 cup heavy cream
2 tbsp. butter
1/2 avocado, diced

Preheat oven to 450°. Wash scallops under running water to remove any sand. In saucepan, combine wine, clam juice, lemon juice, and salt. Bring to boil. Add scallops. Reduce heat and simmer for 5 minutes. With slotted spoon, remove scallops and divide into the 8 shells. Add the dissolved arrowroot to the wine mixture. Remove from heat and fold in the cream. Melt butter in small pan and sauté half the avocado until soft, setting aside the remaining half. Combine wine mixture and sautéed avocado to make the sauce. Divide the raw avocado equally among the shells, mixing with the scallops. Pour the sauce over the scallops and transfer shells to baking sheet. Bake for about 8 minutes or until top is lightly browned. Serves 8.

## SAUTÉ DE VEAU MARENGO
### (Veal Sauté Marengo)

5 lbs. veal shank meat
4 tbsp. olive oil
1 cup Chablis wine
4 fresh tomatoes, peeled and quartered
1 clove garlic, crushed
2 cups tiny fresh mushrooms
1 truffle, cut in thin strips
18 pearl onions
salt and pepper
1 small bay leaf

Cut meat in medium cubes; brown in hot olive oil. Cover and cook slowly about 10 minutes. Remove meat. Add wine, tomatoes, garlic, mushrooms, truffle, and onions to oil. Simmer until mushrooms are tender. Season with salt and pepper. Add meat, cover, and simmer for about 1 hour or until tender. Serve in the sauce. Serves 8.

## FILET BEEFSTEAK TARTARE

1 egg, separated
8 oz. tenderloin, ground once
1 tsp. chopped capers
4 anchovy filets, chopped
1/4 medium onion, minced
1/8 tsp. pepper
1/2 tsp. salt
dash Worcestershire sauce
6 tbsp. dry red wine
pinch dry English mustard
1/2 tsp. brandy

Mix egg white with ground meat. Grind once again. Mix in remaining ingredients except the egg yolk. Form into a patty, making a well in the center and placing the egg yolk there. Serve at room temperature. Before eating, break the egg yolk with a fork and mix into the meat. Serves 1. For 8 servings, increase to 8 eggs, 64 oz. tenderloin, and slightly increase the quantities of the other ingredients.

## BRUTUS SALAD

4 heads Bibb lettuce
2 tomatoes, peeled
1/4 cup chopped green onion
1/2 cup crumbled, cooked bacon
1 cup croutons
1 clove garlic
1/2 cup freshly grated Romano or
    Parmesan cheese
1 cup olive oil
juice of 2 1/2 lemons
1/4 tsp. oregano
1/2 tsp. ground pepper
1 egg, coddled
1/4 tsp. chopped fresh mint

Pour 2 tbsp. of imported olive oil into a large wooden bowl. Sprinkle with salt and rub firmly with garlic. Place tomatoes cut in eighths in the bottom, then put the lettuce leaves on top. Add green onion, cheese, bacon, and dressing, and toss. Top with croutons.

**DRESSING:**

Put olive oil, lemon juice, pepper, mint, and oregano into a mixing bowl. Add the coddled egg and mix vigorously. Serves 4 to 6.

## LOBSTER THERMIDOR

6 1-lb. live rock lobsters
8 shallots
1/2 lb. fresh mushrooms
2 tbsp. English mustard
1/4 lb. grated Swiss cheese
2 qts. fish stock
1 cup butter
2 cups flour
1 pt. heavy cream
1/2 qt. dry white wine
1 large onion, sliced
1 tsp. thyme
3 bay leaves
1 tbsp. salt
1 cup vinegar

Boil enough water in a large pot to cover the lobsters. Add onion, thyme,

---

## THE DOWN UNDER
## Fort Lauderdale

*This restaurant, located on the Intracoastal Waterway under the Oakland Park Boulevard Bridge, houses romantic Victorian decor, authentic paintings, and antiques. It is a place of many treasures—including the delicious seafood and classics of French cuisine that abound here.*

bay leaves, salt, and vinegar and boil for 5 minutes. Cut the antennae and legs off the lobsters and put them in the boiling seasoned water for 8 minutes. Remove and let cool. Sauté the chopped shallots lightly, add the mustard and sliced mushrooms, stir for a few minutes, add the white wine, and let reduce until almost dry. Add fish stock and cook for 5 minutes. Cook butter and flour slowly, stirring for 10 minutes. Mix enough roux into the stock and ingredients to create a smooth sauce, not too thin. Cook for 5 minutes. Add cream and bring to boil once more, then remove from heat. Split lobsters lengthwise, remove meat, and cut into small pieces. Pour just enough sauce to cover bottom of shells and replace the pieces of meat. Cover with sauce and sprinkle with grated cheese. Bake in oven 15 to 20 minutes. Serves 6.

## OYSTERS KIRKPATRICK

36 large or 48 small oysters
1 qt. chili sauce
1/4 lb. diced, cooked crisp bacon
1/4 lb. Parmesan cheese
1/4 cup lemon juice
two dashes Worcestershire sauce
small dash Tabasco sauce, salt, and
    pepper

Mix ingredients. If too thick, add a little white wine. Spoon sauce over oys-

---

ters and place under broiler until sizzling. Serve immediately.

## OYSTERS SAVANNAH

36 large or 48 small oysters
1 lb. lean raw bacon
2 green peppers
2 slices pimento
1 tsp. salt
1 tsp. monosodium glutamate
1/2 tsp. paprika
1/2 tsp. pepper

Chop bacon finely and mix with green peppers that have been trimmed, seeded, and chopped. Add finely chopped pimento and the rest of the ingredients. Place oysters in the half shell on a bed of rock salt and cover each one completely with some of the bacon mixture. Broil oysters until sizzling. Serve immediately.

## COLD BUTTERED RUM DESSERT

For each serving, put 2 scoops butter pecan ice cream and 1 oz. light Jamaican or dark Puerto Rican rum into a blender. Blend until smooth. It can be sipped, milkshake style, or eaten with a spoon.

## QUICHE MICHELE

1 10-inch pastry shell, 3/4 cooked
2 eggs
1 cup cream
2 oz. ham
2 oz. grated Cheddar cheese
2 oz. thinly sliced fresh mushrooms
salt and pepper to taste
1/2 tsp. nutmeg

In a mixing bowl beat the eggs, salt, pepper, and nutmeg. Sauté mushrooms and ham until mushrooms are cooked. Add these and the cheese to the beaten eggs and pour into the partially baked pie shell. Pour cream over and bake in 350° oven for 25 minutes. Serve hot.

## ORANGE BOWL MOLD WITH CHICKEN SALAD

2 envelopes (2 tbsp.) unflavored gelatin
1 cup sugar
3 1/2 cups orange juice
1/2 cup lemon juice
few drops orange food coloring, if desired
2 large oranges, sectioned, white membrane removed
1 cup chicken salad

Combine gelatin and sugar; add 1 cup orange juice. Heat and stir over medium heat until gelatin and sugar dissolve. Remove from heat; add remaining orange juice and lemon juice. Tint with orange food coloring. Chill until partially set. Pour into lightly oiled, shallow 1-cup bowls; insert orange sections, spoke-fashion, around sides of bowls. Chill overnight or until very firm. With tablespoon, carefully scoop out 1/4 cup gelatin from center of each and fill with chicken salad, making top level with gelatin. To loosen from bowls, run knife around edge, invert, and cover with towel previously dipped in warm water and wrung out. Serves 4.

## BROILED GRAPEFRUIT

Count on half a large grapefruit for each serving. Have fruit at room temperature so it will be warm throughout when top is browned. Cut around every section of grapefruit half, close to membrane—fruit should be completely loosened from shell. Cut a hole in center of grapefruit half and fill with 1 to 1 1/2 tbsp. butter. Sprinkle 1/2 tsp. sugar over each half; then sprinkle each with 2 tbsp. cinnamon-sugar mixture (1 part cinnamon to 4 parts sugar). Broil grapefruit on shallow baking pan 4 inches from heat about 8 to 10 minutes or just long enough to brown tops and heat bubbling hot. At end of broiling time, place a cooked chicken liver in center of each grapefruit half and sprinkle lightly with sugar. Broil about 2 minutes longer.

## ORANGE RICE

The delicate fruit flavor is perfect with curried shrimp.

2 cups water
1 tbsp. grated orange peel
1/2 cup orange juice
1 tsp. salt
1 cup uncooked long-grain rice

---

| CHALET SUZANNE |
| Lake Wales |

*This inn and restaurant near the geographical center of Florida is world famous for its gourmet soups and sauces. A visitor feels he has stumbled into a fairy-tale land. The property consists of fifty acres of gorgeous grounds. Five dining rooms, each a different shape, serve unexcelled delicacies.*

Combine water, orange peel, orange juice, and salt; bring to boil. Stir in rice, return to boiling, and then lower heat. Cover and cook over low heat until tender and liquid is absorbed, about 25 minutes. Serve hot. Makes 3 1/2 cups.

## ANGEL COCONUT BALLS

1 10-oz. loaf angel cake
2 cups sugar
1/4 tsp. cream of tartar
1 cup hot water
1/2 tsp. vanilla
sifted confectioners' sugar
2 3 1/2-oz. cans (about 2 2/3 cups) flaked coconut

Trim crusts from cake; cut cake in 1 1/2-inch cubes. Cook sugar, cream of tartar, and water to thread stage (230°). Cool to lukewarm (110°). Add vanilla. Stir in sugar (about 1 1/4 cups) till frosting is of pouring consistency. Line up cake cubes on rack; pour frosting over and let drain. Roll in coconut. Serves 15 to 18.

## CURRANT CHUTNEY

Try with baked ham as well as curry.

1/2 cup chutney, cut in small pieces
1/2 cup red currant jelly
3 tbsp. dried currants
2 tbsp. cooking sherry

Combine all ingredients. Serve with curry of shrimp.

## FLORIDA ORANGE PUNCH

2 cups double strength tea
1 1/2 cups sugar
4 cups orange juice
2 1/2 cups unsweetened grapefruit juice
aromatic bitters
orange slices

---

To freshly brewed hot tea, add sugar and stir until dissolved. Let cool. Add fruit juices. Dash in bitters to taste. Chill. Pour over ice cubes or block of ice in punch bowl. Garnish with orange slices. Makes about 2 quarts.

## CURRY OF SHRIMP SUZANNE

1/3 cup butter or margarine
3 tbsp. enriched flour
1 to 2 tbsp. curry powder
1/2 tsp. salt
1/4 tsp. paprika
dash nutmeg
2 cups light cream
3 cups cleaned, cooked shrimp
1 tbsp. finely chopped candied ginger
1 tbsp. lemon juice
1 tsp. cooking sherry
1 tsp. onion juice
dash Worcestershire sauce
salt to taste

Melt butter and blend in flour, curry powder, salt, paprika, and nutmeg. Gradually stir in cream; cook until mixture thickens, stirring constantly. Add remaining ingredients; heat through. Pour into individual casseroles and bake in hot 400° oven about 10 minutes or until top is lightly browned. Serve with Orange Rice and curry condiments—currant chutney, finely shredded orange peel, flaked coconut, chopped roasted peanuts, and watermelon pickles. Serves 4.

## ORANGE WHIP

2 envelopes (2 tbsp.) unflavored gelatin
2 cups sugar
dash salt
4 egg yolks
2 1/2 cups orange juice
1 tbsp. shredded orange peel
2 tsp. shredded lemon peel
3 tbsp. lemon juice
1 cup orange sections (white membrane removed), cut in half
2 cups heavy cream, whipped

Thoroughly mix gelatin, sugar, and salt in saucepan. Beat together egg yolks and 1 cup of the orange juice; stir into gelatin mixture. Cook over medium heat, stirring constantly, just until mixture comes to a boil. Remove from heat; stir in peels and remaining juices. Chill, stirring occasionally, until mixture forms mounds when dropped from spoon. Stir in orange sections. Fold in whipped cream. Pour into a 2-quart mold. Chill until set. Unmold. Serves 10 to 12.

## QUICHE LORRAINE

1 cup half milk, half cream
4 eggs
salt and pepper
nutmeg
paprika
5 strips bacon, diced
1 medium onion, diced
chopped fresh parsley and chives

Smother onions and bacon in skillet until done. Add parsley and chives at the end. Place in a strainer and let drain. Use a bowl and stir milk and cream, eggs, seasonings, and the smothered ingredients together. Butter a pie pan and place rolled pie dough in pan. Bake 3/4 of the way through. Place mixture in pan and bake in 300° to 350° oven until golden brown and firm. Serve hot like a piece of pie. Also good with one-half broiled tomato or spiced peach on the side.

## DELICATE THIN PANCAKES

1/2 cup flour
3 whole eggs
1 pt. heavy cream
1 cup water
perhaps a little salt and sugar to taste

Mix together all ingredients and fill with maple butter. Roll and serve with strawberry sauce and crisp bacon.

## VACHERIN GLACE
### (Meringue Layer)

Whip 6 egg whites and 1 lb. sugar for about 10 to 15 minutes at medium speed until stiff. Add 1/2 tsp. cream of tartar. Use a pastry bag and pipe mixture on a sheet pan that has been lined with waxpaper. Make a round spiral 9 inches wide (will make 6 layers). Bake in a preheated oven, 250° to 275°, for approximately 1 1/2 to 2 hours. Leave oven door slightly open so steam can escape. Let cool. Cut 2 pieces of cardboard 9 inches round. Place 1 layer on cardboard and spread vanilla ice cream on top to 1/2-inch thickness. Do this gently, as the meringue layers are soft and too much pressure will cause breakage. Place next layer and spread raspberry sherbet to 1/2-inch thickness. Again, be gentle. Apply next layer. Finish with whipped cream all around sides and top. Garnish like a torte as desired and place in freezer until ready to serve. Good with blueberry sauce, strawberry sauce, peach sauce, or just plain.

---

### MARCO DINING ROOM
### Marco Beach Hotel
### Marco Island

*It is not hard to believe that many Miamians drive one hundred miles to dine at one of America's foremost resorts. The dining room at the Marco matches the luxury of the grand hotel, located on three miles of Gulf of Mexico beach among the Ten Thousand Islands. The decor is subdued, with polished woods, low lighting, and table settings of impeccable taste throughout the dining room.*

## BAKED STUFFED SHRIMP

24 large raw shrimp, peeled and deveined (leave tail on)

Split shrimp half through from inside. Wash and dry.

### FILLING:

1/2 lb. crabmeat (lump or Alaskan king)
4 shallots
1/2 cup sherry wine
3 tsp. flour
4 fresh mushrooms, diced
1/2 lemon
1 cup heavy cream
dash of Worcestershire sauce
salt and pepper to taste

In medium saucepan, melt butter and sauté onions and mushrooms. Add flour; stir thoroughly. Add sherry and heavy cream. Let come to boil, stirring constantly. Add Worcestershire, lemon juice, salt, and pepper. Cool. Place shrimp in a casserole and fill splits with mixture, tail up. Top with a white wine sauce or Hollandaise sauce. You may need a little water or white wine in casserole for moisture. Bake in 375° oven for 20 minutes or until done. Serves 6.

---

## BEAUTIFUL BALLOON

1 qt. heavy cream
1/2 bottle of Cherry Heering brandy
1 14-oz. can cherries, drained
2 oz. sugar
lemon wedge
raspberry sherbet

Wet rim of 8 brandy snifters or similar bulky glasses with lemon wedge; dip rims in sugar. Mix cream, Cherry Heering brandy, cherries, and rest of sugar. Stir thoroughly. Fill up glasses, being careful not to drop on rim. Place 1 scoop of sherbet in glass. Garnish as desired, using your imagination. Serve with wafer sticks. Serves 8.

## SPANISH COFFEE

1/2 oz. Kahlua
1/2 oz. Galliano
1 cup coffee
2 tbsp. whipping cream
dash grated lemon peel

Dip edge of long-stemmed glass in sugar after wetting with lemon juice. Heat glass, rotating over flame. Pour in Galliano and flame while adding the Kahlua. Fill with coffee. Top with cream. Grate lemon peel over top and serve at once. Sip hot through the cream.

## LOBSTER BISQUE

3 lbs. fresh lobster meat with shells
2 onions
2 carrots
1/2 stalk celery
5 tomatoes
1 pt. cognac
1/2 tsp. paprika
1 1/2 gal. clam juice
1 qt. dry white wine (not sweet)
1 qt. heavy cream
brandy

Cut lobster into pieces. Chop onions, carrots, celery, and tomatoes. Sauté lobster in pot for about 15 minutes. Add vegetables and continue to sauté for another 15 minutes. Flame with cognac. Dust with flour and paprika. Stir thoroughly. Add clam juice and white wine. Cook 40 minutes. Adjust flavor with seasoning and strain through a fine cheese cloth. Remove lobster meat from shell, dice, and put back into soup. Add heavy cream. If desired, add brandy to your liking. Makes 1 gallon.

## BREAST DE POULET BRAZILIAN COURT

1 3-lb. chicken
1 cup white grapes
1/2 cup white wine, dry Sauterne preferred

Bone breast, removing skin and second joint. Poach in wine for 10 minutes. Make a rich sauce from butter and chicken stock and pour over chicken in covered skillet. Simmer for 15 minutes or more if needed. Add 1 cup of white grapes and 1/2 cup of white wine. Serve on bed of fluffy rice.

## PALM BEACH SALAD

1 avocado, sliced
1 stalk Belgium endive, cut into 4 lengthwise pieces
4 sliced pineapple rings
watercress
lettuce

Arrange lettuce leaf cup. Put 1 piece of endive in center of pineapple ring. Arrange 2 slices of avocado beneath ring, all of this on the lettuce cup. Garnish with 2 sprigs of watercress. Serve with favorite dressing.

## STRAWBERRY PIE BRAZILIAN COURT

1 9-inch pie shell
1 qt. strawberries
1/2 cup flour
2/3 cup sugar
2 cups scalded milk
3 egg yolks, slightly beaten
2 tsp. butter
1 tsp. vanilla extract

## BRAZILIAN COURT HOTEL
## Palm Beach

*This hotel, a unique "corner of Old Spain," has two beautiful dining rooms. The south patio has a flower-banked fountain and gay umbrellas under which candlelight dinners are served beneath the twinkling stars. The main dining room re-creates the atmosphere of the haut monde in the Spanish manner with dramatic color and style. The service and cuisine are superb.*

Add flour, sugar, and butter to scalded milk. Bring to boil. Add egg yolks whipped together. Cool, then add vanilla. Pour into cold pie shell; arrange strawberries on top and garnish with whipped cream.

## SWEET POTATO PIE

1 cup mashed sweet potatoes
1/2 lb. butter
1/2 cup brown sugar
3 eggs, slightly beaten
1 cup dark Karo syrup
1 tbsp. vanilla extract
1/2 tsp. salt

Cream butter and brown sugar to a light fluff. Add sweet potato and mix well. Add eggs, syrup, salt, and vanilla. Blend well and pour into 8-inch pie shell. Bake for 30 to 35 minutes in 375° oven. Serves 8.

## POACHED BREAST DE POULET

4 young chicken breasts (about 3 lbs.)
1 1/2 cups Sauterne wine
1 cup white grapes
1/4 lb. butter
1/2 cup flour
4 cups chicken stock
1 cup heavy cream

Put wine in saucepan. Place chicken breasts in pan and cover. Simmer for 20 minutes. Take bones, legs, and second joints, an onion diced with 2 stalks of cut up celery, and boil for 30 minutes. Strain. Melt butter, add flour, and simmer slowly for 3 minutes. Then add chicken stock, beating rapidly to prevent lumping—about 3 minutes, stirring constantly. Then pour over chicken. Add grapes and let simmer for 15 minutes more. Then add heavy cream and simmer for 3 minutes. Serve on bed of rice.

## CITRUS SURPRISE STEAK

1/4 cup flour
1 tsp. pepper
2 lbs. round steak, 1/2 inch thick
3 tbsp. oil
1 cup ketchup
1/2 cup water or beef bouillon
1 medium onion, thinly sliced
1 orange, unpeeled, thinly sliced
1 lemon, unpeeled, thinly sliced
6 whole cloves

Heat oven to 350°. Mix flour, salt, and pepper and pound into steak. Cut steak into serving pieces and brown in oil. Mix ketchup with water or beef bouillon and pour over steak; place onion, oranges, lemon slices, and cloves over steak. Cover and bake 1 hour until meat is tender. Serves 6.

## CHEESE SOUFFLE

2 tbsp. butter
4 tbsp. flour
3 cups boiled milk
10 whole eggs
4 tbsp. grated Parmesan or Swiss cheese
salt and pepper

Use a large saucepan. Melt the butter and stir in the flour with a wire whisk on a slow fire. Add warm milk and cook about 3 minutes. Remove from fire. Add grated cheese. Separate the egg yolks and stir rapidly. Add salt and pepper. Beat the egg whites until they are very stiff. Fold whites of eggs gently into the other mixture. Put the souffle mixture into individual baking dishes, filling each 3/4 full because the mixture will rise. Preheat oven to 400°; put in souffle and turn the oven down to 375°. Cook for 30 minutes, and do not open the door during that time. When well browned, serve at once.

## EGGS FLORENTINE

1 lb. fresh or frozen spinach
12 eggs
1 tbsp. lemon juice or white vinegar
salt and pepper

Cook spinach, cool, and chop fine. Poach eggs, using lemon juice or white vinegar in the water in which they are poached. Sauté the chopped spinach very lightly with melted butter, and season with salt and pepper. Place the spinach in individual baking dishes that will hold 2 poached eggs and put the eggs, 2 to each dish, on top of the spinach. Salt and pepper the eggs. Glaze with Velouté de Volaille sauce.

## SPUMONE

In the galaxy of ice creams, spumone is a kind of imaginative and delicious Italian jigsaw puzzle. The slices of ice cream and sherbet are curled round an inner nest of fruits and nuts by a whimsical hand at desserts. Actually, the fashioning is quite simple.

4 egg yolks
1 cup candied mixed fruits
1/2 pt. white Karo syrup
1/2 cup chopped assorted nuts
6 wafers
2 oz. Grand Marnier liqueur
2 qts. vanilla ice cream
1 pt. raspberry sherbet
1 pt. lime sherbet
1 pt. heavy whipped cream

---

## PETITE MARMITE RESTAURANT
## Palm Beach

*This magnificent* Holiday *Award-winning restaurant is under the ownership and personal supervision of Costanzo Gus Pucillo. Patrons stand in line, waiting to be seated to partake of the many delicacies. Presidents and kings have dined in this truly great restaurant.*

Cook egg yolks in syrup in double boiler, beating until thick. Let cook a half hour, then crush the wafers (which in the case of this restaurant come from Holland in a tin and are thinner than those used for ice cream sandwiches; they are known as *gaufrettes* in France) and soak them in liqueur. Mix together the cream, syrup, eggs, nuts, candied fruits, and soaked wafer crumbs. Chill. Arrange the initial layer of ice cream around the sides and bottom of a long loaf pan, leaving space enough in the center for all other ingredients. Freeze. Do the same with a layer of sherbet, and freeze. Proceed in similar fashion with a third layer of sherbet, leaving enough space in the center to hold the fruit and nut mixture. Freeze again. Add the mixture of fruit and nuts in the center. Cover the top with remaining ice cream and freeze for 24 hours. Slice and serve. Serves 12.

## CHICKEN TETRAZZINI

The great diva, Luisa Tetrazzini, inspired this dish during an engagement in New York City more than 50 years ago, and fortified herself with it at the height of her glowing operatic career. (Orvieta, a straw-colored wine with very little sugar content from the picturesque hill town in Italy goes well with Chicken Tetrazzini.)

3 medium-size chickens
1 bunch celery
1 carrot
2 onions
3 tbsp. flour
1/4 pt. heavy cream
10 fresh mushrooms
1/2 lb. green noodles or spaghetti
1 tbsp. butter
1 glass sherry
1/4 lb. grated Parmesan cheese
4 egg yolks
salt and pepper

---

Boil chicken until tender in water that covers the chicken and to which has been added celery, carrots, and onions, all chopped. Strain. Put 2 tbsp. flour in a saucepan containing 1 tbsp. butter and stir the mixture until smooth. Add 1 pint of the hot chicken stock to 1/4 pint of heavy cream in another pan and heat, but do not heat to boiling. Stir the hot stock and cream mixture into the light brown butter and flour roux to make a cream chicken velouté base. Add 4 egg yolks, salt, and pepper. Put the sliced chicken, mushrooms, and sherry into a pan. Put the creamed base on this and stir constantly over a slow fire. Next use either individual crockery dishes or a large baking dish. Place boiled noodles or spaghetti in the bottom as a nest for the chicken mixture. Add the chicken and mushrooms. Sprinkle with Parmesan cheese. Bake in 350° oven for 15 minutes or under broiler until brown.

## FRENCH BREAD

2 1/4 lbs. bread flour
4 egg whites
2 oz. yeast
1 tbsp. salt
1 tbsp. sugar
1 tbsp. oil
1/2 qt. cold water

Dissolve yeast in cold water. Sift salt, sugar, and flour together into a mixing bowl. Add eggs and water and mix. Make a well in middle of mixture and add yeast dissolved in water. Knead well until a stiff dough results. Let the dough rise for 1 hour or two depending on temperature of room. Punch the dough down and knead again. Cover and let rise again for another 2 hours. Place in pans that have been sprinkled with cornmeal to prevent the bread from sticking. Bake in 400° oven for 40 minutes.

## TEA BISCUITS

1 lb. bread flour
1 tbsp. salt
4 tbsp. sugar
6 tbsp. butter
2 tbsp. baking powder
1/3 qt. milk

Sift the flour, baking powder, sugar, and salt together. Add butter. Add milk and mix well to make a soft dough. Cut in half-dollar sizes. Butter a baking sheet, using hot melted butter. Bake in 400° oven for 40 minutes. This makes 2 to 2 1/2 dozen cookies.

## HOLLANDAISE SAUCE

8 egg yolks
2 lbs. melted butter
2 tsp. fresh lemon juice
2 tsp. Worcestershire sauce
salt and pepper to taste

Whip eggs in bowl over low heat (200° to 250°). Add warm butter, lemon juice, Worcestershire, salt, and pepper. Mix well. Serves 8.

## MUSHROOMS CORDON BLEU

2 lbs. fresh mushrooms (washed and sliced)
2 cups sweet vermouth
8 slices white toast
32 slices bacon, cooked
8 slices Swiss cheese (2 oz. each)

Cook mushrooms in white vermouth until boiling and vermouth disappears. Divide into 8 equal portions and spread on top of toast. Place 4 slices of bacon on top of mushrooms on each piece of toast. Place a slice of cheese on top of each portion and melt in oven. Serve hot with oven-browned potatoes. Serves 8.

## CARROTS AND GRAPES

2 lbs. baby carrots
1 lb. seedless grapes (or 1 large can)
4 cups water
4 cloves
1 cup brown sugar
2 tsp. cinnamon
4 oz. cornstarch

Cook carrots and cloves in water until done. Add grapes, brown sugar, and cinnamon. Dissolve cornstarch in 2 oz. water and add to mixture. Serves 8.

## SCAMPI ROMANO

2 lbs. butter
1 lb. top quality margarine
2 oz. chopped garlic (about 30 medium cloves)
2 oz. chopped shallots (12 medium)
6 oz. Sauterne (12 tbsp.)
1 oz. Tabasco sauce (2 tbsp.)
12 tbsp. lemon juice
2 cups chopped chives
2 tbsp. dry mustard
5 lbs. shrimp (5 shrimp per serving)

---

## ROMANO'S 300
## Palm Beach

*One of Florida's and the nation's most famous restaurants, Romano's 300 is the winner of many coveted awards. Waitresses clad in authentic costumes of the 1600s contribute to the old-world atmosphere, as do the brick and plank floors and wood paneling.*

Melt butter and margarine (margarine gives the sauce lightness). Add other ingredients except shrimp and blend well. Split and devein shrimp but do not peel (split at the back). Pour 1 1/2 cups of scampi sauce over shrimp. Broil about 4 inches from heat for 6 to 8 minutes. Shrimp should be lightly browned, the shells pink and the meat white. Do not overcook. Serve with crusty bread for dipping into the sauce. Serves 8.

## CHICKEN ALASKA

4 whole chicken breasts, halved
1/2 lb. butter
4 oz. flour
1 qt. milk
salt and pepper
6 oz. white wine
1 lb. cooked lobster meat
Parmesan cheese

Sauté breasts in butter until done. To prepare white wine (béchamel) sauce, mix 1/2 lb. butter, flour, milk, salt and pepper to taste, then the white wine. Add lobster meat to one-third of sauce. Divide into 8 equal portions and place on top of each chicken breast. Use the remaining sauce for topping and pour over each chicken breast. Sprinkle with Parmesan cheese and brown under broiler. Serves 8.

## BAKED STUFFED SHRIMP

1 large or 2 small onions
1 lb. butter
2 sweet green peppers
16 slices bread, diced
1/2 lb. chopped lobster meat
1/2 lb. chopped king crab meat
1/2 lb. chopped broken shrimp

---

4 eggs
1/2 lb. mayonnaise
2 tsp. paprika
2 tsp. dry mustard
2 tsp. Tabasco sauce
2 tsp. Worcestershire sauce
salt and pepper
2 lbs. peeled, cleaned fresh shrimp (about 16)

Sauté onion and green pepper in butter. Lobster, crab, and shrimp should be chopped before measuring. Add all ingredients together plus salt and pepper to taste. Bake in 400° oven for 20 minutes or until brown. Serve with oven-browned potatoes. Serves 8.

## PORK WELLINGTON

1 whole boneless pork loin, about 8 to 10 lbs.

Roast until done, approximately 1 hour in 400° oven.

**WELLINGTON DOUGH:**

3 lbs. white bread flour
4 cups cold water
2 cups powdered sugar
2 tbsp. cinnamon
2 lbs. margarine

Prepare dough while pork is roasting. In large mixing bowl, measure the flour; add cold water, sugar, cinnamon, and mix together until pasty. Spread on table with rolling pin. Spread margarine over top and roll dough until margarine is thoroughly mixed. When pork is done, place on top of dough.

**APPLE PASTE:**

8 fresh apples, peeled
6 celery stalks
2 small onions
1 lb. butter
1 doz. eggs
1 loaf bread (14 to 16 slices)
4 oz. brown sugar
2 tsp. cinnamon powder

Cut apples, celery, and onions in small pieces and sauté in butter. Grind all ingredients together. Add raw eggs. Make crumbs from bread and add; then add brown sugar and cinnamon. Mix together to form a paste and cover entire pork roast. Cover entire loin with dough. Brush corners with whipped egg so that dough sticks together properly. Bake 30 minutes in 350° oven. Serve with carrots and grapes. Serves 8.

## VEAL SCALLOPPINE TESTA

2 lbs. thin veal cutlets
1 large onion, chopped very fine
2 cloves garlic, chopped fine
olive oil
3 tbsp. tomato paste
1 cup Marsala wine

Cook garlic in olive oil until brown; add onions and tomato paste. Season cutlets with salt and pepper and brown in olive oil in hot skillet. Add cooked garlic and onion mixture, then the wine. Simmer a few minutes and serve. Serve a side dish of green noodles with butter and garlic sauce and grated Romano cheese.

## SPAGHETTI SAUCE TESTA

3 medium onions, chopped
2 cloves garlic, diced
2 #2 1/2 cans peeled Italian-style tomatoes
2 small cans tomato paste
salt and pepper
dash crushed red pepper

Brown garlic in olive oil, add onions, and cook. Add tomatoes and tomato paste, then salt and pepper.

## MEATBALLS:

1 lb. ground beef
2 whole eggs
3 tbsp. chopped parsley
3 tbsp. grated cheese
salt and pepper
1/2 tsp. oregano
4 tbsp. bread crumbs
small amount of milk

Mix well. Shape into balls and cook in the sauce until done. Remove from sauce. Cook sauce for about 3 hours on low heat. Strain to remove seeds. This is a basic sauce and can be used to make meat, or meat and mushroom sauce.

---

## TESTA'S RESTAURANT
## Palm Beach (winter)
## Bar Harbor, Maine
## (summer)

*In Bar Harbor, Maine, Testa's Restaurant has three lovely dining rooms, one of which overlooks an old-fashioned herb garden. At the Florida location, there are four dining areas, one a sidewalk cafe overlooking beautiful Royal Poinciana Way in the heart of Palm Beach, another appointed with tropical decor.*

---

## BLUEBERRY PANCAKES TESTA

1 cup flour
2 tbsp. sugar
2 tsp. baking powder
1/2 tsp. salt
1 egg
1/2 cup milk
2 tbsp. melted butter
3/4 cup fresh blueberries

In bowl, sift together flour, sugar, baking powder, and salt. In another bowl, beat egg, milk, and butter. Add the liquid mixture to the dry ingredients, stirring only enough to dampen the flour. If batter seems too thick, thin it with a little more milk. Add blueberries and thoroughly drain before adding. Pour batter from a ladle onto a lightly buttered griddle. Cook pancakes until the underside of each begins to brown and bubbles appear on surface. Turn pancakes and brown on other side.

## FISH CHOWDER TESTA

4 lbs. skinned haddock (save head and backbone)
4 cups diced potatoes
1 onion, sliced

---

2 pieces salt pork, 1/4 inch thick and 4 inches long, or enough to make 2 heaping tbsp. finely diced
salt and white pepper to taste
4 tbsp. butter
1 qt. scalded milk

Cook head (eyes and gills removed) and backbone in 3 cups of water for 15 minutes. Fry salt pork and then pour into large pan. Add potatoes and cover with strained broth from fish head. Pick meat from backbone and from cheeks and add to cooking chowder along with fish cut into 1-inch pieces. Add salt and pepper. Cook for 10 minutes and add scalded milk. Serve right away. Makes 10 bowls.

## LOBSTER À LA NEWBURG

2 1 1/4-lb. cooked Maine lobsters
4 tbsp. butter
1/4 cup sherry
1 cup heavy cream
3 egg yolks, slightly beaten
salt and white pepper to taste

Remove cooked meat from lobster shell. Cut meat in good-sized pieces. Melt butter in heavy skillet. Add lobster and cook until lobster turns butter bright red. Combine cream and slightly beaten egg yolks. Cook in top of double boiler until thickened. Add lobster meat, sherry, and seasoning. Allow to stand over very low heat at least 5 minutes before serving to allow the lobster flavor to penetrate sauce. Serve on toast wedges.

## STRAWBERRY PIE TESTA

1 qt. fresh strawberries
1 cup sugar
3 tbsp. cornstarch
1 cup water
1/2 stick butter
1 drop red food color

Cook half the berries with the water for 5 minutes. Mix cornstarch and sugar together and add to boiled berries; then add butter and color. Cook 25 minutes more. Put berries from refrigerator into baked pie shell and pour the above mixture over the raw berries. Serve topped with whipped cream.

## KALBS SCHNITZEL HOLSTEIN

4 8-oz. veal cutlets
salt
ground white pepper
1 tbsp. flour
1 egg, beaten
1 tbsp. butter
4 eggs, fried

Flatten veal cutlets. Season with salt and pepper. Coat well with flour and dip in beaten egg. Heat butter in skillet and brown cutlets over low heat for 6 to 8 minutes, turning once. Place cutlets on preheated plate and top each with a fried egg. Serve with lemon wedges and add a colorful canape border of smoked salmon, anchovy filet, and caviar. Serves 4.

## COLD CREAM OF CUCUMBER SOUP

1 medium onion, chopped
5 cucumbers, peeled, seeded, and chopped
1/4 lb. butter
1/2 cup flour
1 1/2 qts. hot beef broth or chicken stock
2 cups hot milk
1 cup light cream
salt and ground white pepper
chopped chives

Sauté onion and cucumber in butter until clear but not brown. When soft, add flour to form a roux. Add hot stock and let simmer 15 minutes. Then add hot milk and let simmer 10 minutes longer. Remove from heat and rub through sieve. Add light cream and season with salt and ground white pepper. Chill. To each cup of soup add some chopped chives and serve in crushed ice. Serves 8.

## HERRING SALAD

4 salt herrings
6 potatoes, boiled
3 apples
4 dill pickles
1/2 onion
1 veal knuckle, boiled
pepper
1 tsp. sugar
dash dry mustard

# FAR HORIZONS' REEF RESTAURANT
## Sarasota

*One of Florida's and the nation's very best dining rooms, this restaurant is a* Holiday *Award winner. Sumptuous Continental cuisine, seafoods fresh from the Gulf, and the best of American specialties are superbly prepared by chef de cuisine Harold Wuelfrath. The main dining room of one of America's finest resorts is truly an oasis on the west coast of Florida.*

1/2 cup olive oil
1/2 cup tarragon vinegar
1 cup bouillon

Rinse herrings; drain. Cover with cold water and let stand 12 hours or overnight in refrigerator. Drain. Filet, remove skin, and dice. Peel and dice potatoes, apples, pickles, and onion. Dice veal. Combine all with fish. Mix rest of ingredients thoroughly and pour over fish mixture. Cover and let chill in refrigerator. Serve over lettuce and decorate with quartered hard-boiled eggs, sliced beets, capers, and anchovy filets. Serves 6.

## OYSTERS ROCKEFELLER

rock salt
6 bluepoint oysters
1 tbsp. butter, divided
3 oz. chopped spinach
1/2 cup light cream
salt and pepper
ground nutmeg
2 tsp. flour
1 egg yolk
1/4 cup heavy whipping cream

Place rock salt on small baking sheet. Open oysters into saucepan (with liquid). Keep deep part of shell and place firmly on rock salt. Put half of butter into shallow saucepan. Melt butter, add chopped spinach, and season to taste. Cook until done and fill oyster shells. Bring oysters and liquid to a simmer; remove oysters from liquid and place on top of spinach. Add light cream to oyster liquid. Season with salt, pepper, and nutmeg and bring to boiling point. Mix remaining butter and flour to form a paste; add to liquid, stirring constantly. Remove from heat. Stir in egg yolk. Fold in whipped cream and top oysters with this sauce. Place in oven at 450° until top shows light brown coloring. Serves 2.

## FROG LEGS À LA PROVENÇALE

Cut 1 1/2 lbs. frog legs at joints and remove spinal bone. Wash pieces and let stand in milk for 3 to 5 hours. Dry frog legs and season lightly with salt and pepper. Coat well with flour and dip in whipped egg. Preheat skillet with 3 to 4 tbsp. olive oil. Add frog legs and brown on both sides. Place skillet in preheated 375° oven for 8 to 10 minutes. Remove frog legs to preheated platter and discard the olive oil. Sauté 1/2 tsp. finely chopped garlic in 3 heaping tbsp. butter. Pour over frog legs and sprinkle with fresh chopped parsley. Serves 2.

## ASPARAGUS BELLE TERRASSE

Wrap blanched asparagus with thinly sliced smoked salmon (Nova Scotia with a fresh, light pink color preferred). Serve with a sour cream sauce made by blending sour cream with lumpfish caviar to taste.

## LUMP CRABMEAT MORNAY

1 lb. fresh lump crabmeat
1 1/2 pt. light cream
2 tbsp. sherry wine
1/2 tsp. salt
dash ground white pepper
2 tbsp. butter (salted)
2 tbsp. all-purpose flour
2 tbsp. Hollandaise sauce
3/4 cup grated Parmesan cheese

Mix butter and flour to form a paste. In a shallow saucepan heat light cream to boiling point. Add salt, white pepper, sherry wine, and 1/4 of the Parmesan cheese. Stir in flour and butter mixture gradually until sauce thickens. Add crabmeat and fold carefully into sauce. Pull saucepan onto slow fire to heat crabmeat thoroughly. Fold Hollandaise sauce into crabmeat. Fill into shallow fireproof dishes. Sprinkle lightly with remaining cheese and brown under broiler. Serve immediately. Serves 4.

## CHICKEN KIEV

Stuff 4 boneless breasts of chicken with 1 tbsp. butter, 1 tsp. chopped chives, and a pinch of garlic powder. Roll meat into a compact roll with edges tucked under. Place meat in pan and chill in refrigerator for at least 6 hours. Set out 4 suitable pans. In one pan, place all-purpose flour. In next, put 1 large egg and 1/4 cup milk plus 1 tsp. salt, beating thoroughly with a fork. In next pan, put bread crumbs. The fourth is to hold the chicken kievs. First place chicken in flour, coat thoroughly, and shake off excess. Next, place chicken in egg-milk mixture and coat; drain off excess. Next, place chicken in bread crumbs and coat thoroughly; shake off excess. Place chicken in fourth empty container. When ready to be cooked, coat kievs with 1 tbsp. melted butter. Bake in preheated 425° oven for about 25 minutes or until chicken is done. Place cooked chicken in suitable casserole or platter, coat with hot Poulette sauce, and garnish with peach slices. Serve at once. Serves 4.

## POULETTE SAUCE:

Place 1 1/2 cups chicken stock or broth and 1/2 cup milk in saucepan and heat to boiling point. Add 1 tbsp. sherry wine and a pinch of white pepper. In a skillet, place 1/4 cup unsifted flour and 1 1/4 cups butter. Mix and cook 5 minutes. Do not brown. Add hot liquid, whipping constantly with wire whip for smoothness. Pour sauce over chicken kievs. Garnish and serve.

## STUFFED BAKED MUSHROOMS

Sauté 1/4 cup finely minced onion in 1 tbsp. butter, using 9-inch skillet. Add 1 tbsp. sherry wine, 2/3 cups finely

---

## THE LIDO BILTMORE INN
## Lido Beach
## Sarasota

*Located on the snow white sands of Lido Beach, this fine year-round resort hotel offers many attractions to its visitors including sumptuous dinners served in the elegant informal dining room that has a grand ocean view. Fred Oplinger is the great master chef here.*

---

chopped king crab meat, 1/4 cup bread crumbs, 1 tbsp. parsley flakes, 1/2 tsp. nutmeg, 1/2 tsp. rubbed oregano, pinch of ground cloves, 2 tbsp. melted butter, 1/2 tsp. salt, 1/2 tsp. lemon juice, 1/4 cup mayonnaise or salad dressing, and 1 tbsp. grated Parmesan cheese. Blend all together thoroughly. Use this mixture to stuff 12 medium mushroom caps. Serve 3 mushrooms per person in a casserole with Mornay sauce atop. Serves 4.

## MORNAY SAUCE:

Put 1 cup milk in saucepan. Add 1 tsp. salt, 1/2 tsp. Worcestershire sauce, and a pinch of white pepper. Heat just to or a little less than boiling. In skillet, put 2 tbsp. butter and 2 tbsp. flour. Heat and mix and cook 5 minutes. Do not brown. Add the hot liquid, whipping constantly with a wire whip for smoothness. Add 2

---

tbsp. grated sharp cheese and 1 tbsp. grated Parmesan cheese. Separate 2 eggs. Place yolks in small bowl. Add 2 tbsp. cream and blend. Add to sauce and stir with wire whip, blending until sauce is smooth.

## CRAB IMPERIAL

Place 2 cups clam juice and 2 cups fresh half milk, half cream, in saucepan and heat to very warm. Do not boil. In large skillet, place 1/2 cup unsifted flour and 1/2 cup drawn butter. Make a roux, cooking for 5 minutes. Do not brown. Pour hot liquid into roux at a moderate rate, whipping constantly with wire whip to make a very smooth sauce. Add 1/4 cup sherry wine. Cut 1 large green pepper into thin strips and cook in another skillet with a little butter until just tender. Add 3 cups king crabmeat cut into 1-inch pieces. Heat a few minutes until warm. Add crabmeat and cooked pepper to sauce, stirring to coat the mixture. Season with 1 tsp. salt and 1/4 tsp. ground white pepper or to taste. To serve, place an 8-oz. portion in individual casseroles with toast points. Serves 6.

## SHERRY BAKED SCALLOPS

In clean scallop shells, place 18 fresh, unbreaded bay scallops. Sprinkle scallops with a pinch of salt. Add 1/2 tbsp. butter and 1 tbsp. sherry wine to each. Make a bread crumb mixture by combining in a mixing bowl 1 cup bread crumbs, 3 tbsp. parsley flakes, a pinch of white pepper, and 1/2 tsp. rubbed oregano. Sprinkle scallops evenly with 1 1/2 tbsp. of this mixture for each coquille. Bake in 425° oven on a metal pan for 20 minutes or until bread crumbs are brown and scallops are done.

## FILET STEAK COLUMBIA

1-inch filet steak
1/2 green pepper
1 oz. ham
1 oz. brown gravy
parsley
1/2 onion
1 oz. tomato sauce
1 oz. white or red wine
2 strips bacon

Wrap steak with 2 strips of bacon. In saucepan, cook tomato sauce, green pepper, chopped onion, salt, pepper, and wine for 10 minutes. Place filet in clay casserole dish; pour sauce over and bake until sauce permeates the meat. Garnish with parsley. Serves 1.

## BLACK BEAN SOUP

1 lb. black beans
2 green peppers, chopped
1 onion, chopped
1 pod garlic, finely chopped
1/2 lb. white bacon
3 oz. olive oil
2 bay leaves

Wash beans well and put in pot with 2 qts. water, green peppers, onion, and garlic. When boiling, lower heat. When beans thicken, fry olive oil, bacon, garlic, and bay leaves in a frying pan until done; then add to beans. Serve with white rice. For puree, strain the beans and add 1 oz. sherry wine. Serves 4.

## PAELLA VALENCIANA

1/4 lb. pork
1/2 fryer
1/2 lb. crawfish
1/2 lb. shrimp
4 oz. oysters
4 oz. scallops
1/2 red snapper
1 onion
2 bay leaves
1 green pepper
3 cloves garlic
4 oz. whole tomatoes
pinch saffron
pinch yellow coloring
6 oz. Spanish olive oil
2 1/2 cups rice
2 qts. seafood stock
1 tbsp. salt

Pour olive oil into casserole. When hot, add minced garlic. Braise the pork and chicken with the garlic. When tender, add onions, green peppers, and then the seafood. When seafood is almost done, add 2 qts. seafood stock and the rice. When boiling, add bay leaf, saffron, and coloring. Salt and pepper to

---

## COLUMBIA
## Tampa

*With eleven dining rooms seating 1,660 people, the Columbia is the world's largest Spanish restaurant. It has been the winner of a large number of culinary prizes for many consecutive years, including the coveted* Holiday *Award. Strolling violinists and singers help to create the exotic and unusual atmosphere, along with such dishes as Soup Tartara, Hearts of Artichoke Siboney, Paella Valenciana, Pompano Papillot, Lobster Criolla, and Chicken Cacerola.*

---

taste. When rice begins to thicken, cover and bake for 15 minutes in 350° oven. Garnish with petit pois and pimentos. Sprinkle with white wine.

## RED SNAPPER ALICANTE

1 lb. red snapper steak
1 onion
1/2 cup brown gravy
1/4 cup Spanish olive oil
1/2 tsp. salt
3 green peppers, cut into rings
pinch white pepper
1/2 cup white wine
12 almonds, grated
4 jumbo shrimp
4 rings breaded eggplant
parsley

Place red snapper steaks atop 3 slices of onion that have been spread over bottom of clay casserole. Over the fish, pour 1/4 cup olive oil, salt, white pepper, brown gravy, white wine, grated almonds, and green pepper rings. Bake in 350° oven for 25 minutes. Garnish with breaded eggplant rings and 4 shrimp supreme. Serves 2.

## CHICKEN AND YELLOW RICE, VALENCIA STYLE

2 1/2 lb. frying chicken
1 onion
2 cloves garlic
pinch Spanish saffron
pinch egg coloring
1/2 lb. Spanish Valencia rice
1/2 cup Spanish olive oil
1 bay leaf

---

1 green pepper
1 tbsp. salt
1/4 cup whole tomatoes
1 qt. water or broth
1/2 cup small green peas
parsley
Spanish pimento
4 asparagus tips

Cut chicken into quarters and simmer in olive oil until brown. Remove chicken and in the same oil, braise the onion, garlic, green pepper, and tomatoes. Place browned chicken in a casserole, and add chicken broth or water. When boiling, add salt, saffron, yellow coloring, and rice. After adding rice, when it begins to boil again, cover casserole and bake in 350° oven for 20 minutes. Garnish with small peas, pimento, chopped parsley, boiled egg, and asparagus tips. Serves 4.

## 1905 SALAD

1/2 head lettuce, chopped
1 tomato, cut into 6 or 8 pieces
2 slices onion
3 oz. olive oil
10 green olives
4 slices cucumber
6 slices green pepper
3 oz. Swiss cheese
10 ripe olives

Mix all ingredients with 3 oz. pure olive oil, a small amount of vinegar, and juice of 1 lemon. Lastly, add 1/4 cup Parmesan or Pecornino cheese. Serves 2.

## POMPANO PAPILLOT

4 pompano steaks
1/4 lb. butter
1 onion, chopped fine
1 cup flour
1 pt. boiled milk
2 eggs
dash nutmeg
dash Tabasco sauce
1 oz. Sauterne wine
1/2 lb. shrimp, chopped after boiling
1/2 lb. crawfish, chopped after boiling

Into 1/4 lb. of melted butter, drop an onion chopped fine. Cook for 5 minutes. Slowly add flour to form a paste. Cook until dry. Add boiled milk and cook to a thick cream sauce. Beat eggs with nutmeg, Tabasco sauce, Sauterne wine, and fold into cream sauce. Add shrimp and crawfish. On buttered paper, spread part of the paste; then place a slice of skinned pompano steak on top. Spread more paste, then another slice of pompano. Spread remaining sauce over top. Fold paper to form a bag with crimped edges. Brush melted butter over paper and bake 30 minutes at 350°. Serves 4.

## AVGOLEMONO SOUPA
*(Lemon and Egg Soup)*

3 lb. stewing chicken
3 qts. water
1 tbsp. salt
3/4 cup Manestra macaroni (or rice)

Wash and clean fowl, cover with water, add salt, and cook for about 2 hours or until meat is tender. When done, remove fowl and add enough water to make 3 qts. of liquid. Bring back to boil and add macaroni or rice. Boil gently for about 25 minutes. Giblets may be cut up and added to broth.

### SAUCE:

4 whole eggs
1 tbsp. water
1/2 cup strained lemon juice

Prepare sauce by beating the eggs and water until very light and then adding lemon juice, again beating to blend well. Slowly add 4 cups of the hot broth to the egg mixture and then combine with rest of the broth. Serve in small bowls or cups.

## BAKED FISH WITH VEGETABLE SAUCE

4 lbs. snapper, black grouper, or trout, cut into serving pieces
salt
2 tbsp. fresh lemon juice
1/4 cup olive oil
2 cups sliced onion
2 medium carrots, sliced
2 stalks celery, cut into pieces
1 small green pepper, sliced
3 sprigs parsley, chopped fine
2 cups canned tomatoes
2 tbsp. tomato paste
3 cloves garlic, chopped fine
2 tsp. salt
1 tsp. pepper
1 cup hot water

Wash fish, salt well, and put in strainer to drain for 10 minutes. Brush with lemon juice on both sides. Heat oil in skillet and when hot, sauté sliced onions and chopped garlic for 5 minutes. Add carrots, green pepper, celery, parsley, tomatoes, tomato paste, salt, and pepper. Cover and cook gently for 15 minutes. Place fish in a baking dish and bake in 350° oven for 10 minutes to dry slightly. Pour vegetable sauce over fish and continue baking another 45 minutes. More water may be added if necessary. Serve with hot rice, spooning gravy over all.

---

## LOUIS PAPPAS' RIVERSIDE RESTAURANT
## Tarpon Springs

*In 1925, after returning from World War I during which he was a cook for General Pershing, Louis Pappas opened this famous restaurant with his wife, who is affectionately known as "Mama." It specializes in Greek-American foods. The salad Louis Pappas created has become internationally known.*

### MELITZANOSALATA
*(Eggplant Salad)*

1 large eggplant
1/4 cup olive oil
salt and pepper
1 clove garlic
1 tomato, diced
2 tbsp. minced parsley
1 tbsp. grated onion
1 tsp. oregano
2 tbsp. white wine vinegar

Bake eggplant in 350° oven for 1 hour. Cool, peel, and dice. Put olive oil, salt, and pepper in bowl and rub with cut clove of garlic. Discard garlic. Combine eggplant, tomato, parsley, onion, and oregano in the bowl. Pour vinegar over and mix well. Chill. Serves 4.

### FAKI
*(Lentil Soup)*

1/2 lb. well-washed lentils
1/2 cup olive oil
2 medium onions, chopped fine
2 celery stalks, cut fine
1 clove garlic, minced
1 carrot, sliced
1 parsley sprig, chopped fine
1 tbsp. salt
dash pepper
1 tbsp. lemon juice
6 cups water
2 beef bouillon cubes

Wash the lentils and cover with water. Bring to boil and cook gently for 10 minutes. Drain off water. Heat the oil in skillet and sauté the onions and garlic for 5 minutes. Add the chopped vegetables and cook slowly for 15 minutes. Add the drained lentils, 6 cups of hot water, salt, and pepper. Bring to boil and cook for

---

30 minutes at reduced heat. Add 2 bouillon cubes and stir until dissolved. Before serving, add 1 tbsp. lemon juice for better flavor.

## MOUSSAKA
*(Ground Beef with Eggplant)*

3 medium eggplants
salt
2 lbs. ground lean beef
6 tbsp. butter
1 1/2 cups chopped onion
2 cloves garlic
1 tbsp. salt
1 tsp. pepper
1 cup salad oil
6 medium potatoes
2 tbsp. chopped fresh parsley
1 tbsp. dried mint
1/2 tsp. cinnamon
4 tbsp. tomato paste

Leaving the skin on, slice eggplant into 1/2-inch slices. Sprinkle well with salt and allow to drain for about 20 minutes. Wash salt off and dry eggplant on a towel. Heat the 1 cup of salad oil and fry the slices a few at a time until golden brown on both sides. Slice peeled and washed potatoes into 1/4-inch slices and fry in the same manner, adding more oil if necessary. Sauté chopped onion and garlic in 6 tbsp. of butter and add ground beef. Brown 10 minutes. Add salt, pepper, mint, parsley, cinnamon, and tomato paste. Remove cover and cook another 10 minutes to reduce liquid. Arrange 1/2 of eggplant in a 9 x 12-inch baking dish about 4 inches deep. Top with half of potatoes and half of meat. Repeat this process with remaining eggplant, potatoes, and meat. Cover evenly with the following cream sauce.

### CREAM SAUCE:

1/4 lb. butter
3/4 cup flour
1 qt. warm milk
4 eggs, slightly beaten
1/2 tsp. salt

Melt butter in saucepan, remove from heat, and stir in flour, blending until smooth. Slowly add warm milk, stirring all the time. Add this mixture to slightly beaten eggs. Cook over a low heat until thick, being careful not to scorch. Pour over Moussaka and bake in 375° oven for 30 minutes or until custard is set. If not brown enough, place under broiler for a few minutes, watching carefully so as not to burn.

## CHICKEN COUNTRY CAPTAIN

The story goes that this dish was shared with a Savannah friend by a seafaring captain. It spread all over the South and quickly became a favorite.

1 chicken
2 onions, chopped
1 clove garlic
1 bell pepper, chopped
2 #303 cans tomatoes
2 tsp. curry powder
1 tsp. thyme
1 tsp. salt
1 tsp. sugar
1 banana, sliced
dash red pepper
1/2 cup currants
1/2 cup blanched almonds
2 cups rice
shredded coconut
chopped peanuts
chutney (optional)

Cook chicken in white wine, salted water, and chopped celery. Cool, disjoint, and remove breast bones. Sauté onion, garlic, bell pepper, and tomatoes for 5 minutes. Add curry, banana, thyme, salt, pepper, sugar, red pepper, and cook 10 minutes more. Add chicken with drippings, currants which were soaked in chicken stock, then blanched almonds. Serve on plate, ladle sauce over top, cover with peanuts and coconut. Serve with wild rice.

## CRABMEAT RAVIGOTE, SAVANNAH

1 lb. lump crabmeat
1/4 lb. fresh mushrooms
4 tbsp. butter
2 tbsp. flour
1/2 cup milk
1/2 cup white wine
1/2 tsp. dry mustard
1/4 tsp. dry tarragon
salt, pepper, and hot sauce to taste
3/4 cup fine bread crumbs

Sauté mushrooms in butter. Make creamy sauce by blending in the flour, milk, wine, mustard, tarragon, salt, pepper, and hot sauce. Cook 3 minutes. Cool. Add crabmeat and mushrooms. Shape into balls and roll in the bread crumbs. Place atop giant mushroom buttons and bake for 20 minutes. Before serving, cover with Sauce Ravigote.

### SAUCE RAVIGOTE:

1/2 cup melted butter
1 cup milk

## ANTHONY'S
## Atlanta

*This is the only preserved authentic plantation manor in Atlanta. It was originally built in 1797 and restored between 1964 and 1967. All decor and appointments are those of the plantation period of the South. The cuisine duplicates the rich fare of this period, served from the coastal area of Charleston to Savannah.*

2 tbsp. vinegar
1/2 tbsp. dry mustard
4 egg yolks
2 tbsp. lemon juice
2 tbsp. green part of spring onions (chopped)
1 clove garlic
white wine

Using blender, blend together melted butter, mustard, milk, vinegar, lemon juice, and egg yolks. In saucepan, combine 2 tbsp. green part of spring onions (chopped), wine, garlic, and bring to boil. Simmer 15 minutes. Combine with blended white sauce.

### PLANTATION OYSTERS

1/4 lb. butter
1/2 cup flour
1/2 cup chopped green onions
2 cloves garlic
1 1/2 cups sherry wine
4 cups chicken stock
3/4 cup chopped mushrooms
2 tbsp. chopped parsley
1 tbsp. Lea & Perrins
2 cups artichoke bottoms
few drops lemon juice
1/2 tsp. black pepper

Bring all ingredients to boil, then simmer. Sauté oysters in butter, then stuff oysters into artichokes and pour 1 tbsp. sauce over oysters.

### POMPANO CHARLESTON

4 pompano filets
1 stick butter

#### STUFFING:

1 cup crabmeat
2 tbsp. bacon drippings
1 medium-size onion, finely chopped

1 shallot, chopped
2 cloves garlic, chopped
2 tbsp. chopped celery
1 tsp. salt
1/2 tsp. pepper
1/2 tsp. thyme
1 tbsp. parsley
1 egg
1/2 cup fine bread crumbs

Sauté vegetables in drippings, then mix in rest of ingredients. Put pompano filets on a flat surface, skin side down, and place stuffing on one-half of filet; then flip other half over. Put in pan with white wine mixed with lemon juice and butter. Bake 20 minutes. Before serving, cover with Hollandaise sauce.

## ROAST DUCK, OLD SOUTH STYLE

2 cups chopped onion
2 cups diced celery
1/3 cup butter
4 cups toasted bread cubes
1 egg, well beaten
1/3 cup hot water
1/2 tsp. poultry seasoning
salt and pepper
caraway seeds

Wash, drain, and dry duck. Sprinkle with salt and pepper outside and in cavity. Cook onion and celery slowly until tender. Do not brown. Pour this mixture over bread cubes. Add eggs, hot water, salt, pepper, and poultry seasoning. Mix. Fill body cavity with stuffing. Cover opening with foil. Place on rack in shallow roasting pan. Sprinkle with caraway seeds. Bake in 325° oven 2 1/2 to 3 hours or until drumsticks are tender. Serve with spicy sauce.

### SAUCE:

1 can fruit cocktail or 1 pkg. frozen fruit
2 tbsp. sugar
a little cornstarch
1 tbsp. mustard
1/2 tsp. cinnamon
1/8 tsp. cloves
1 tbsp. lemon juice
2 tsp. grated orange rind
1 oz. Grand Marnier (optional)

Drain fruit, save syrup. Combine sugar, cornstarch, and cloves, then add syrup. Cook, stirring constantly until thick and clear. Add drained fruit, lemon juice, orange rind, and 1 oz. Grand Marnier (optional). Heat. Serve with or over the duck.

## BEEF KIDNEY STEW

4 beef kidneys
beef stock
4 tbsp. wine vinegar
salt
fresh ground pepper
flour for dredging
1/2 cup butter
6 tbsp. oil
2 cloves garlic, chopped
1 cup chopped onion
1 tbsp. rosemary
1 tbsp. thyme
2 bay leaves
1 cup red wine
1 cup stock

Soak the cleaned kidneys in beef stock and vinegar for 2 hours. Drain and wipe dry. Cut into thin slices; sprinkle with salt and pepper. Dredge lightly in flour and brown quickly in hot oil. Add garlic, onion, and herbs and cook 5 minutes. Add wine and stock and simmer 15 minutes. Serve with rice or boiled potatoes. Serves 8.

## CHICKEN ALFARO

16 small lobster tails, unshelled
16 halves boneless chicken breast
15 shallots, chopped
4 oz. roasted, blanched almonds
1 cup sherry wine
4 cups Bordelaise sauce
flour for dredging

Dredge chicken and unshelled lobster tails in flour and sauté in half butter and half oil. When halfway done, remove excess oil and add shallots. Sauté until light golden brown, then add sherry and let cook for about 4 minutes. Add crushed almonds, then Bordelaise sauce. Simmer another 5 minutes, then serve with buttered broccoli or rice. Serves 8.

## SHRIMP OR CHICKEN CURRY

1 medium apple, finely diced
2 stalks celery, finely diced
1 medium onion, finely diced
1 tbsp. chutney
1 pinch rosemary leaf
1/2 cup melted butter
1/3 cup flour
1 qt. chicken stock
1 tbsp. curry powder
1 qt. milk

---

# THE COACH AND SIX
## Atlanta

*This is a great restaurant in a great city. Its motif is Country English with wood paneling and brick walls, as well as French Impressionist paintings. The food is excellent and is served in a quiet, luxurious atmosphere.*

Sauté apple, celery, and onion in butter for 4 minutes. Add chutney and rosemary. Let cook for another 2 minutes, then add flour and curry powder. Mix well, then add milk and chicken stock. Keep stirring while cooking over slow heat until sauce is nice and smooth. Season with salt, Accent, and a little sugar to taste. Strain through a fine sieve. Mix with chicken or shrimp previously cooked. Serve with rice. Serves 8.

## CHICKEN À LA SOLOFF

24 chicken pieces
olive oil
melted butter
6 shallots, chopped
1/2 cup sliced fresh mushrooms
1 cup Sauterne wine
3 cups Bordelaise sauce
pinch cayenne pepper
pinch Accent
few drops lemon juice

Wash chicken pieces well (do not use the backbones). Sauté chicken in olive oil and butter. When half done, remove excess oil and add shallots and mushrooms. Allow to cook for about 4 minutes, then add wine. Boil until reduced to one-third, then add Bordelaise sauce. Season with cayenne, Accent, salt, and lemon juice. Continue to cook over very slow heat for about 15 minutes. Serve in very hot plate with rice sprinkled with chopped parsley.

## PAELLA À LA VALENCIANA

1/2 cup olive oil
1 medium onion, minced
4 cloves garlic, finely chopped
1 cup fresh sliced mushrooms

---

1 large green pepper, chopped
3 medium fresh tomatoes, chopped
2 bay leaves
1 tbsp. capers
16 clean, peeled shrimp
16 lobster tails (4 to 5 oz. each)
4 clams
16 chicken pieces, half-fried
a little diced red pimento
saffron leaf
4 cups rice
4 cups clam juice
1 1/2 cups Sauterne wine
salt to taste
white pepper to taste
Accent to taste

Sauté onion in olive oil until golden brown. Add garlic, mushrooms, green pepper, tomatoes, bay leaves, and capers. Then add shrimp, lobster tails, and chicken pieces (chicken pieces should be half-fried). Mix all together, then add saffron leaf (to taste). Sauté for 5 minutes, then add rice, clam juice, wine, salt, white pepper, and Accent. Mix well. Add 4 clams and pimento and cook about 10 minutes. Then put in 350° oven for 20 minutes. Serves 8.

## OUR FAMOUS COACH AND SIX BLACK BEAN SOUP

3 lbs. black turtle beans
2 medium onions, divided and minced
2 whole carrots, divided
2 stalks celery, divided
1 lb. ham bones
1 tbsp. ham base
1/2 lb. bacon fat
1/2 tsp. salt
1/2 tsp. Accent

Wash beans well and put in water to cook with 1 stalk of celery. Add 1 carrot, ham bones, and 1 onion cut into 4 pieces. Use 3 times as much water as beans. Place pot in steam cooker for 4 hours. After cooked, allow to cool for 1 hour, then grind through a grinder into heavy pot. Add chicken stock and bring to boil, stirring constantly. At midpoint, sauté the second onion in bacon fat, also adding second celery stalk and second carrot. Add bay leaves, then add all this to bean soup and season with very little salt, Accent, and ham base. Strain through very fine sieve. At the last minute, add some finely chopped hard-boiled egg. Serve very hot with 1 lemon slice dipped in chopped parsley floating atop. If desired, 1 tbsp. sherry may be added per serving. Serves 8.

## BASIC TOMATO SAUCE

1/2 cup chopped onion
1 clove garlic, minced
3 tbsp. oil
2 cans (1 lb. 4 oz. each) whole peeled
    tomatoes
1 can (8 oz.) tomato sauce
1 can (6 oz.) tomato paste
1 cup water (to rinse cans)
2 tbsp. chopped celery
2 tsp. salt
1/2 tsp. sweet basil
1/4 tsp. black pepper
1/4 tsp. oregano
1 bay leaf

Sauté onions and garlic in oil. Mash whole tomatoes thoroughly and place in large saucepan. Add all other ingredients and simmer over low heat for 1 hour. Partially cover saucepan with lid to allow steam to escape.

## BRACIOLE

3/4-lb. top or bottom round steak cut
    about 1/4 inch thick
salt to taste
pepper to taste
1 clove garlic, finely chopped (garlic
    powder may be substituted)
1 tbsp. raisins
3 slices prosciutto (Italian ham) (bacon
    with streak of lean may be used)
1 hard-boiled egg, chopped
1 tbsp. Romano or Parmesan cheese
1 tbsp. ground bread crumbs
1 tsp. parsley

Pound and flatten meat with mallet or other device so that it is less than 1/4 inch thick. Cover the meat with the above-mentioned ingredients and condiments; then roll firmly in jelly-roll fashion starting with the shortest width of the meat and tie crosswise with string. Brown meat-roll on all sides in skillet using enough olive or salad oil. Do not cook all the way through. Brown the outside portion of meat only. Simmer meat in Basic Tomato Sauce for about 2 hours.

---

## VITTORIO'S RESTAURANT
## Atlanta

*This is one of the South's best restaurants. It is owned and operated by a master, Victor J. Impeciato. He serves the best Italian food available anywhere.*

### STUFFED PEPPERS

4 large green peppers
1 lb. ground beef
1/2 tsp. salt
1/4 tsp. black pepper
1/2 cup grated Parmesan cheese
1/2 cup dried bread crumbs
1 tsp. parsley
2 eggs
1 clove garlic, chopped
1 can (16 oz.) peeled tomatoes
1/4 tsp. sweet basil

Combine beef, salt, pepper, grated cheese, bread crumbs, parsley, eggs, and garlic. Mix well. Stuff hulled green peppers with meat mixture and place in saucepan open end up. Add the canned tomatoes (preferably ground) and rinse can with water to cover peppers. Add salt, pepper, and sweet basil. Simmer slowly for about 1 hour and 15 minutes. Serve in soup bowls with the sauce and Italian or French bread.

### RAW MUSHROOM SALAD

1/2 lb. halved fresh mushrooms
1 tbsp. lemon juice
3 tbsp. olive or vegetable oil
1/2 tsp. salt
2 tbsp. sliced sweet or Spanish onion
1/4 tsp. pepper, preferably white
1/4 tsp. oregano

In a salad or serving bowl, toss the mushrooms with the lemon juice until moistened. Add the remaining ingredients and chill before serving. Toss lightly.

---

## BAKED OR GRILLED SHRIMP

12 large shrimp, 10 to 15 count,
    shelled, deveined, and washed
1/2 cup olive or vegetable oil
1/2 tsp. salt
1/4 tsp. pepper
1/4 tsp. garlic powder
2 tbsp. minced parsley
paprika
2 lemons

Mix together the oil, salt, pepper, juice of 1 lemon, garlic powder, and parsley. Marinate shrimp in mixture for about 30 minutes, basting and turning frequently. Arrange shrimp in a baking pan, pour marinade over shrimp and sprinkle with paprika. Bake in 400° oven for about 10 minutes or until meat is all white. Squeeze extra lemon juice if desired. May be served with fruit or vegetables.

## PASTA I FAGIOLI
*(Bean and Macaroni Soup)*

2 cans red kidney (or white) beans
    (other type beans may also be used;
    dried beans soaked and cooked in
    the traditional manner may also be
    substituted)
1 cup macaroni such as small elbow or
    spaghetti cut into 1-inch pieces
1/2 cup finely chopped onions
1 clove garlic, finely chopped
1/2 tsp. salt
1/4 tsp. pepper
1/2 tsp. parsley
3 tbsp. olive oil
1 small can tomato sauce or its equiva-
    lent in chopped tomatoes

In a saucepan, lightly brown the onions about 6 minutes. Add garlic and continue to simmer about 2 minutes. Add tomato sauce, parsley, salt, pepper, and about 2 cups water. Simmer about 10 minutes. Add cooked beans. In a separate pot, cook macaroni in 2 to 2 1/2 quarts salted water about 9 minutes. Drain macaroni and add to the beans. Serve in soup bowls and sprinkle with grated cheese.

## CELERY SEED DRESSING
*(Good over fruit salad)*

1/2 cup sugar
1 tsp. mustard
1 tsp. salt
1 tsp. paprika
1 tsp. onion juice
1 tbsp. celery seed
3 tbsp. vinegar
1 cup Wesson oil

Mix ingredients except oil in blender. Add oil very slowly. Beat until smooth.

## SUNSHINE SAUCE
*(Good on ham)*

1 cup raisins
1 cup water
1 cup orange juice
1/2 cup orange marmalade
2 tbsp. flour
2 tbsp. cornstarch
4 tbsp. flour
1/4 tsp. salt
dash cloves

Mix first 5 ingredients and bring to boil. Mix last 4 ingredients and add to sauce, stirring well. Cook and stir until thick. Makes 3 cups.

## CORN PUDDING

1 large can creamed corn
1/2 cup milk

---

# OLD MILL RESTAURANT
## Cedartown

*The Old Mill is certainly one of the Southeast's most delightful restaurants. Delicious food is prepared by those who continue to uphold the ideal of Southern hospitality.*

1 egg, beaten
2 tbsp. flour
3 tbsp. melted butter
3 tbsp. sugar

Mix all ingredients and pour into baking dish. Bake 1 hour at 350° or until silver knife inserted comes out clean. Serves 6.

## CORNBREAD

2 1/2 cups self-rising meal
1/2 cup self-rising flour
1/4 tsp. baking soda
1 tbsp. sugar
1 egg, slightly beaten
1 1/4 cup buttermilk

Mix ingredients, adding egg last. Heat 3 tbsp. bacon drippings in 9-inch iron skillet. Pour hot drippings into mixture and return to skillet. Bake in 250° oven 20 to 25 minutes or until golden brown. Cut into 6 to 8 wedges. Serve hot.

## APPLE DUMPLINGS

1 1/2 cups sugar
3/4 tsp. cinnamon
1/2 cups butter or margarine
water
2 cups sifted flour
1 tsp. salt
2/3 cup shortening
6 small apples, peeled and cored
heavy cream, whipped

Combine 1 cup sugar, 1/2 tsp. cinnamon, 1/4 cup butter, and 1 cup water in saucepan; bring to boil. Remove from heat. Sift flour with salt. Cut in shortening until size of peas. Sprinkle in 5 to 7 tbsp. cold water. Mix well. Roll dough on lightly floured surface to 24 X 16-inch rectangle. Cut into six 6 X 8-inch pieces. Place whole apple on each piece of dough; put 2 tbsp. butter into each apple cavity. Combine remaining sugar and cinnamon. Reserve 2 tbsp. of the sugar and cinnamon. Sprinkle sugar mixture into apples. Bring corners of dough up over apples and pinch together. Place in pan and pour cooked syrup over apples. Sprinkle with reserved sugar mixture. Bake in 400° oven for 35 to 40 minutes. Serve topped with whipped cream. Serves 6.

## JOHNNY CAKE

1 cup cornmeal
1/2 cup sugar
1/2 tsp. soda
1 tsp. cream of tartar
1/8 tsp. salt
1 cup milk
1 egg, beaten
1 tbsp. molasses
1 tbsp. melted butter

Sift dry ingredients together. Add other ingredients, beating thoroughly. Pour into shallow greased pan. Bake at 375° for 30 minutes.

## SWEET POTATO BISCUITS

2 cups sifted flour
3 tsp. baking powder
1 tsp. salt
2 tbsp. light brown sugar
1/2 cup butter or margarine
3/4 cups mashed sweet potatoes
1/2 tsp. baking soda
3/4 cup buttermilk

Sift flour, baking powder, and salt in medium bowl. In a small bowl combine brown sugar and melted butter with sweet potatoes. Beat until fluffy. Stir soda into buttermilk and pour into dry ingredients together with sweet potato mixture. Stir only until moist. Roll out on floured board. Bake on ungreased sheet for 20 minutes in oven preheated to 400°.

## HUSHPUPPIES

1 1/4 lbs. cornmeal
1/2 cup flour
1/4 cup sugar
2 1/4 tsp. baking powder
1/4 tsp. salt
1/4 cup chopped onion
1 egg
1 1/2 cups milk

Mix all dry ingredients thoroughly. Add onion. Stir in egg. Add milk. Mixture should be stiff enough to drop from tablespoon in a solid mass. Chill. Mold dough in tablespoon and drop from spoon into moderately hot cooking oil, 3 to 4 inches deep. When nut brown, remove from oil and drain.

---

## THE PIRATES' HOUSE
## Savannah

*This old inn was built in 1754. It is composed of seventeen dining rooms and also houses a museum. The menu is extensive. The food is excellent and many regional specialties are featured.*

## OLD-FASHIONED CRACKLING BREAD

1 1/2 cups cracklings or chopped crisp bacon
1 1/2 cups white cornmeal
3 tbsp. flour
1 tsp. salt
1 tsp. soda
2 cups buttermilk
1 egg, beaten

Mix cracklings with dry ingredients. Add buttermilk and egg. Pour mixture into a hot greased skillet. Bake at 450° for about 25 minutes or until light brown.

## BANANA BREAD

1/2 cup butter
1/2 cup sugar
4 medium-sized bananas
1 tbsp. lemon juice
3 eggs
3 1/4 cups flour
3 tsp. baking powder
1/4 tsp. salt
1 cup chopped nuts (optional)

Cream butter and sugar. Mash bananas well and sprinkle with lemon juice. Beat eggs. Add mashed bananas. Add to first mixture. Add flour sifted with baking powder and salt. Blend with banana and egg mixture. Add nuts. Pour into greased loaf pan. Bake at 350° for about 1 hour.

## SPOON BREAD

1/2 tsp. salt
1 cup cornmeal

---

1 cup boiling water
2 tbsp. bacon drippings
2 eggs, separated
1 cup milk

Add salt to cornmeal and add this mixture to boiling water. Add bacon drippings. Beat egg yolks and add to milk. Stir into cornmeal mixture. Beat egg whites. Fold into mixture. Pour into greased casserole. Bake at 350° for 40 minutes.

## HOPPING JOHN
*(A Must for New Year's)*

2 cups cow peas
1 cup raw rice
3 tbsp. bacon drippings
2 cups water

Boil peas until tender. Add well-washed rice and bacon drippings. Add 2 cups water. Bake in oven at 350° for about 45 minutes, or cook in double boiler over low heat for 1 hour. Serves 6 to 8.

## HARVARD CARROTS

1/4 cup sugar
2 heaping tsp. cornstarch
1 tbsp. vinegar
3 tbsp. water from cooked carrots
2 cups sliced, cooked carrots
2 tbsp. butter

Mix sugar and cornstarch. Add vinegar and water. Cook until thick and transparent, stirring constantly. Add a little yellow coloring. Add carrots and butter. Serves 4.

## BISCUITS

2 cups flour
1 tsp. salt
3 tsp. baking powder
3/4 cup milk
1/3 cup liquid shortening

Sift flour, salt, and baking powder. Add milk and melted shortening, stirring just enough to blend. Roll out on floured board. Cut and bake at 450° for about 15 minutes.

## SALADE NICOISE

2 tomatoes, quartered
1 cup cooked string beans
2 medium-size potatoes, sliced and cooked
8 filets anchovies, cut in half
1 small onion, sliced thin
2 hard-boiled eggs, quartered
8 or 10 black Greek olives

Mix the ingredients in a salad bowl and marinate with a French dressing. Serve on a bed of iceberg lettuce.

## LEMON CHIFFON PIE

1 envelope unflavored gelatin
1 cup sugar, divided
1/8 tsp. salt
5 eggs, separated
1/2 cup water
1/2 cup lemon juice
1 tsp. grated lemon rind
1 9-inch baked pie shell

Mix together the gelatin and 1/2 cup sugar and salt on top of a double boiler. Beat the egg yolks slightly; stir in water and lemon juice. Add to gelatin mixture. Place over boiling water and cook, stirring constantly, until the gelatin is dissolved and the mixture is slightly thickened. Add the lemon rind. Chill until the mixture is slightly thicker than the consistency of an unbeaten egg white. Beat egg whites until stiff, but not dry. Gradually add the remaining 1/2 cup sugar and beat until very stiff. Fold egg yolk mixture into prepared pie shell. Chill until firm.

## CREPES OF CHICKEN À LA REINE

2 cups diced turkey or chicken
1/2 cup sliced sautéed mushrooms
1/4 cup cream sherry
salt and white pepper to taste
1 cup medium cream sauce
1/2 cup grated Romano cheese
paprika
8 French crepes
3 cups medium cream sauce

Place first 5 ingredients in a mixing bowl and blend well. Divide this mixture over 8 French crepes and roll. Place 2 rolls in individual casserole dishes. Cover with the remaining 3 cups cream sauce. Sprinkle with grated Romano cheese and dust with paprika. Place casseroles in a preheated 375° oven for 15 minutes or until crepes are hot and bubbly.

---

# THE COACH HOUSE
# Lexington

*Kentucky's only* Holiday *Award-winning restaurant, the Coach House has superb food and wines, and the service is impeccable. Owner/chef Stanley Demos's culinary abilities are legendary.*

## CHEESE SOUP

3 tbsp. grated onion
3 tbsp. grated carrots
1/2 stick butter
2 13-oz. cans chicken broth
1/2 tsp. dry mustard
1/4 cup milk
4 tbsp. cornstarch
1 cup grated sharp Cheddar cheese

Put butter, onions, and carrots in a saucepan and sauté for 3 minutes. Add broth and dry mustard and simmer for 5 minutes. Mix cornstarch with milk and pour into the boiling broth, beating with a wire whisk. Simmer soup until it thickens. Add grated cheese and continue to simmer until the cheese melts. Serve in cups and top with garlic croutons.

## QUICHE LORRAINE

1 9-inch pie shell, half baked
5 strips bacon, cooked crisp
3 slices Swiss cheese, cut julienne
1 medium onion, sliced and sautéed in butter
2 whole eggs plus 2 egg yolks
1 1/2 cups Half & Half
pinch nutmeg
salt and white pepper to taste

Arrange bacon and Swiss cheese in bottom of pie shell. Sprinkle onions over bacon and cheese. Put the eggs in a blender and beat until frothy. Season with salt, pepper, and nutmeg. Add the cream and blend well. Preheat oven to 375°. Place the pie shell in center of rack and pour in egg mixture over other ingredients gently so as not to spill over pan. Bake the quiche until the custard sets and the top is golden brown. Serve as an appetizer or as a luncheon entree.

---

## SWEETBREADS SAUTÉ AU BEURRE NOISETTE

2 lbs. fresh veal sweetbreads
3 cups water
1 small onion, sliced
2 tbsp. vinegar
12 peppercorns
2 bay leaves
vegetable shortening
4 slices bread, toasted
1 1/2 stick butter
2 tbsp. chopped parsley

Rinse the sweetbreads under some cold running water for 10 minutes. Place them in a saucepan along with the water, onions, vinegar, peppercorns, and bay leaves. Bring to a boil, lower the heat, and simmer for 20 minutes. Turn off heat and let sweetbreads cool in the broth. When cool, remove from broth and with a paring knife, remove the outer fatty membranes, being careful not to puncture the inner membrane. Slice each sweetbread into 3 pieces. Dust with seasoned flour and sauté in some vegetable shortening. When golden in color, remove from skillet and divide on 4 dinner plates over a slice of toast. Discard fat from skillet and into the drippings add butter and melt until it foams. When it takes on a brown nutty color, add the parsley and divide over the sweetbreads. Serves 4.

## DOVER SOLE MY WAY

12 filets Dover sole
1/3 stick butter
1 medium onion, diced
2 cloves garlic, finely chopped
1 cup drained, diced tomatoes
2 tbsp. chopped parsley
salt and pepper to taste
1 cup medium Mornay sauce
2 tbsp. grated Romano cheese
paprika

Dust filets of Dover sole in some flour. Sauté in some vegetable shortening until golden in color. When done, remove into a flat baking dish, placing filets side by side. To prepare the tomato sauce, melt butter in a heavy skillet. Add the onions and cook until transparent. Add the garlic and sauté 10 seconds longer. Add tomatoes, parsley, and seasoning. To assemble dish, take a teaspoon and divide the tomato sauce over each filet. Over tomato sauce, spoon over the Mornay sauce. Sprinkle with Romano cheese and dust with some paprika. Set dish under the broiler and cook until the sauce is bubbly. Serves 4.

## ZUPPA INGLESE
*(English Soup)*

The name comes from teasing the English about their love of rum; the first Zuppa was so rum-soaked that it had to be eaten with a soup spoon. Some stories say that this Zuppa was first served to Lord Nelson and Lady Hamilton in the eighteenth century.

### SPONGE CAKE:

**6 egg yolks**
**1 1/2 cups sugar**
**1 1/2 cups all-purpose, sifted flour**
**1 tsp. baking powder**
**1/2 tsp. salt**
**6 tbsp. water**
**1 tsp. vanilla flavoring**
**6 egg whites, stiffly beaten**
**1/2 tsp. cream of tartar, added to eggs before beating**

Mix yolks and sugar together until spongy. Add flour into which has been mixed the baking powder and salt and mix well. Add water and flavoring and mix again. Fold in beaten egg whites and tartar mixture and bake in 3 9-inch round cake pans at 325° for 35 to 40 minutes.

### CUSTARD FILLING:

**6 eggs**
**3/4 cup sugar**
**4 cups hot milk**

Mix together and cook over hot water until thick. Cool over cold water.

### PRESERVES FILLING:

**2 cups strawberry preserves**
**1/2 cup rum**

Mix together. Pour half of this filling over 1 cake layer, then pour 2 cups of custard over this. Place on another cake layer and pour on remainder of filling, then 2 more cups of custard. Top with remaining layer and pour 1/3 cup of rum over top. Then top cake with whipped cream. Keep refrigerated until ready to serve.

## VEAL SALTIMBOCCA

**1/2 cup clarified butter**
**1 cup cake flour**
**8 sage leaves**
**4 paper-thin slices prosciutto ham**
**4 6-oz. veal cutlets, beaten thin**
**4 cups chicken stock**
**1 cup white wine**

Place the ham and sage leaves on the veal cutlet, then fold in half and fasten with toothpicks. Lightly flour the veal and sauté in clarified butter until light brown. Drain butter from pan and add wine and chicken stock. Simmer for about 5 minutes while deglazing the pan with a wooden spoon. Serves 4.

## GREEN FETTUCINE WITH WHITE CLAM SAUCE

**1/2 cup pure olive oil**
**2 large cloves garlic, minced**
**1/4 cup finely chopped parsley**
**1/2 tsp. salt**
**1/2 tsp. pepper**
**1 lb. cooked spinach fettucine**
**2 7 1/2-oz. cans minced clams and juice**

Brown garlic lightly in oil over low heat. Add clam juice (but not clams) and remaining ingredients except fettucine, and cook over higher heat while stirring constantly. Add clams, bring to boil, and serve over hot fettucine. Serves 4.

## MINESTRONE SOUP

**1/2 oz. finely chopped garlic**
**1/3 lb. diced beef brisket**
**2 qts. beef stock**
**3 1/2 oz. pinto beans**
**3 1/2 oz. chopped leeks**
**3 oz. diced cabbage**
**7 oz. diced potatoes**
**7 1/2 oz. diced Bermuda onion**
**3 1/2 oz. diced celery**
**7 oz. diced carrots**
**7 1/2 oz. zucchini cut into 1/2-inch pieces**
**1 bay leaf**
**3 whole tomatoes, skinned**
**3 1/2 oz. chick peas**
**1 cup tubetti noodles**
**salt and pepper to taste**

Using a small amount of olive oil, sauté garlic and beef brisket until brown. Then boil the pinto beans in water until done. Into the simmering stock add all ingredients except pinto beans, chick peas, and tubetti and simmer for 30 minutes. Then add beans, peas, and tubetti and simmer an additional 15 minutes. Serves 8.

## OYSTERS VENETIAN

**16 oysters in shell**
**8 tbsp. caviar**
**juice of 4 lemons**
**dash cayenne pepper**

Open oysters, cover with caviar, and season with lemon juice and cayenne. Put shell back on and chill for several hours. Serve on crushed ice. Serves 4.

---

# CASA GRISANTI
## Louisville

*In 1908, Pacifico and Zefrio Grisanti moved to Louisville. They were ornamental plasterers. However, Pacifico Grisanti's two grandsons, who now operate this delightful restaurant, feel that the family talent most resembles that of the Italian cooks whom Catherine de Medici took with her to Paris in 1553. Casa Grisanti is an elegant restaurant where great food is graciously served.*

## BREASTS OF CHICKEN WITH HAM AND APRICOTS

Season 6 boned chicken breasts with salt and pepper and dredge them lightly with flour. Melt 6 tbsp. butter in a heavy skillet and sauté the breasts about 20 minutes, turning them until they are browned and cooked through. Remove breasts and keep hot. Put 2 tbsp. of butter in skillet and sauté 6 slices of cooked ham. Remove ham and keep hot with chicken breasts. In the same skillet heat 12 whole pitted apricots. Add 1/2 cup apricot juice and 2 jiggers of Courvoisier. Thicken sauce with 1 tbsp. butter kneaded with 1 tbsp. cornstarch. Arrange breasts on ham slices and pour apricot sauce over them.

## OLD HOUSE CREPE POULET

Sauté 2 cups cubed cooked chicken or any fowl with 1 large sliced onion until golden and 1/2 cup diced celery. Add 1/2 cup sliced mushrooms, 1 tsp. chopped parsley, 1 tsp. salt, 1/4 tsp. pepper, and 1 tsp. thyme. When onions and celery are soft, remove from skillet and combine all ingredients with 1 cup of thick white sauce. Add 1/2 cup Garvey Amontilado sherry and mix well.

Make very thin pancakes by barely coating a small greased skillet with batter. Cook crepes on both sides. Place desired amount of chicken mixture in the center of each crepe. Fold pancake over. Sprinkle with a little nutmeg and serve piping hot.

---

### THE OLD HOUSE RESTAURANT
### Louisville

*Southern hospitality and delicious cuisine await visitors of this great restaurant. You will enjoy the benefits of expert management as well as an atmosphere created by delightful surroundings.*

---

## OLD HOUSE COQ AU VIN
*(Chicken Stewed in Red Wine)*

Cut a 2-lb. chicken into serving pieces or quarters. Flour them and brown lightly in butter. Add 1/4 lb. of chopped bacon and 2 large sliced onions. When all is nicely browned, sprinkle with 1 tbsp. flour. Let this brown also, then add a half bottle of Cruse Beaujolais Burgundy. Add 1/2 tsp. salt, 1/4 tsp. coarsely ground black pepper, and 1/4 tsp. thyme. Add 1 tsp. chopped parsley. Cover and cook until chicken is done. Thicken at the last minute with a piece of butter the size of a walnut kneaded with 1 tbsp. of flour.

## SPRING CHICKEN WITH ROQUEFORT

Disjoint a 2-lb. chicken. Season lightly with salt, pepper, and flour. Sauté in 4 tbsp. of butter until browned on all sides. Cover and simmer until chicken is tender, about 30 minutes. Remove chicken from skillet and keep hot. To juices in pan add: 1/2 lb. sliced mushrooms, 1 tsp. chopped onions, 1/2 cup chopped tomatoes, fresh or canned, 1/2 cup Cruse Chablis or dry white wine, and cook briskly until most of the liquid is cooked away. Add 1 cup sweet cream, 1 cup crumbled Roquefort cheese, and cook until cheese is melted. Correct seasoning. Pour sauce over chicken and sprinkle with chopped parsley.

## CHICKEN LIVERS WITH MUSHROOMS AND MADEIRA

Dredge 1 lb. of chicken livers with flour, salt, and pepper. Sauté in hot fat until crisp on all sides. Remove the livers and keep hot. Into the pan juices, stir 2 tbsp. of flour, stirring constantly. Add gradually 1/2 cup Sandeman's Madeira and 1 cup chicken stock. Cook, stirring until sauce is thick and smooth. Season with salt and pepper to taste. Return chicken livers to sauce, add 1/2 cup cooked or canned mushrooms, and heat thoroughly.

## CHICKEN LIVERS WITH APPLES

Wash and dry 1 lb. of chicken livers. Dredge lightly with flour, salt, pepper, and paprika. Brown livers in 2 tbsp. of butter, turning frequently until crisp on all sides. Remove from skillet and keep hot. In another pan sauté 3 large onions sliced with 3 large tart apples, peeled and sliced in rings. Cook only until onions are soft and apples are still firm but softened. Sprinkle onions and apples with salt and pepper and serve on top of livers.

## MOROCCAN SALAD

2 oz. leaf lettuce
2 oz. curly endive
2 oz. escarole
2 oz. watercress
2 oz. parsley
1 banana
1 tbsp. shallots
3 oz. almond slivers
3 oz. currants
1 cup olive oil
1/3 cup red wine vinegar
salt to taste
pepper
1 tsp. curry powder

Wash and tear lettuce into bite-sized pieces. Slice the banana into thin slices and add, along with almond slivers, currants, and parsley, to lettuces. Make an oil and vinegar dressing by combining olive oil, red wine vinegar, salt, pepper, curry powder, and shallots. Toss gently.

## LAMB KEBOBS

2 lb. lean loin of lamb, cut into 1-inch cubes
3 large onions, chopped fine
1 clove garlic, chopped fine
3 tbsp. butter
2 cups fresh apricot pulp
1/4 cup dark brown sugar
3 tbsp. cider vinegar
2 tbsp. Madras curry powder
1 tsp. salt
dash of cayenne

Brown onions and garlic in butter. Add apricot pulp, brown sugar, vinegar, curry powder, salt, and cayenne. Simmer mixture gently; pour marinade over lamb. Let stand overnight. Drain the meat and place on skewers. Lay the lamb skewers on a rack over a dripping pan and broil until brown on all sides. Mix the marinade with the drippings, heat, and serve with lamb.

## SIMMONS GALLERY
## Louisville

*This is one of the finest restaurants in Kentucky and the nation as well. The cuisine is expertly prepared by chef de cuisine Doug DeMichael, and served in a gracious atmosphere.*

### ESCALLOPED SUMMER SQUASH WITH CHEESE

Wash and cut 1 3/4 lb. yellow summer squash into small pieces. Beat 2 egg yolks and beat in a little of 1 cup hot rich cream sauce. Beat the egg yolks into the remaining cream sauce with 2 tbsp. grated Swiss cheese and 1 tbsp. grated onion and season to taste with salt and a dash of cayenne. Add the squash, turn the mixture into a buttered baking dish, and sprinkle over the top enough grated Swiss cheese mixed equally with buttered bread crumbs to cover. Bake the dish in a slow oven (300°) for about 35 to 40 minutes, or until the top is lightly browned. Serve at once.

### BEEF WELLINGTON

2 lbs. prime beef tenderloin
1 lb. good puff pastry
1/2 lb. whole chicken livers
1/2 lb. small whole mushrooms
Pâté de Foie (see following recipe)
2 egg yolks
6 tbsp. milk

Sear beef in oil, remove from pan. Cover top and sides with pâté. Add whole chicken livers and mushrooms. Roll pastry to 1/8 inch and cover the tenderloin with it and seal sides. Make up a sauce consisting of 2 egg yolks and 3 tbsp. milk. Brush pastry with sauce.

Bake in 500° oven for 15 minutes or until golden brown.

### PÂTÉ DE FOIE

3/4 lb. chicken livers
1/2 cup rendered chicken fat
3 tbsp. minced shallots
1 tsp. dry mustard
1 tsp. salt
1/4 tsp. ground cloves
pinch of cayenne
pinch of fresh grated nutmeg
1 oz. truffles

Simmer chicken livers in water for 20 minutes. Drain. Run through finest blade of a food chopper twice. Mix paste with rendered chicken fat and all other ingredients. Pack in an air-tight container.

### CREAM OF CIDER SOUP

3 pts. apple cider
1/2 cup brown sugar
2 cups stale bread cubes
3 tbsp. butter
salt
3 eggs
2 tbsp. sugar
1 1/2 cups cream
3 tbsp. flour
pinch allspice
dark rum

Bring cider slowly to a boil, carefully skimming off the beads that appear on the surfaces. When boiling, stir in brown sugar. Then slowly sift in, while beating, 3 tbsp. flour. Set aside and keep warm. Sauté bread cubes in butter and salt to taste. Beat eggs lightly and add to them sugar, cream, and allspice. Pour mixture into hot cider, beating steadily. Pour into bowls and sprinkle bread cubes on top. Flambe with 1 tbsp. rum.

## ROASTED LAMB RACK WITH FRIED PARSLEY

1 3-lb. prime lamb rack
salt, crushed white pepper, marjoram,
   and rosemary
1 bunch curly parsley (top of stems
   only)
1/4 cup dry vermouth
1/2 stick butter

Have your butcher prepare the lamb rack in the French method. Preheat oven to 450°. Rub salt, white pepper, marjoram, and rosemary into meat and bone sides of rack. Coat with a little salad oil. Roast for 20 to 25 minutes. Allow to rest 10 to 15 minutes before carving. Pour vermouth in pan with natural juices to deglaze pan. Add butter and pour over lamb. Heat salad oil to 360°. Dry parsley well and place in fryer basket and slowly lower into hot oil. Fry for 8 seconds; remove, drain well, and salt slightly. Cover lamb rack with parsley and serve with natural sauce. Serves 2.

## BANANA FRITTERS

1/2 cup all-purpose flour
1 1/2 tsp. baking powder
1/4 tsp. salt
3 to 4 tbsp. milk
1 large egg

## LE RUTH'S
## Gretna

*This restaurant, housed in a century-old dwelling, is located across the Mississippi River from New Orleans in the city of Gretna and is run by owner/chef Warren LeRuth. The menu is composed of many regional specialties and includes such dishes as Crabmeat St. Francis, Redfish Termerau, Artichoke and Oyster Soup, and Trout Oliva. Excellent bread is also made on the premises.*

Sift flour, baking powder, and salt into bowl. Add egg and milk and mix to batter. Peel and cut several bananas in halves lengthwise, then in half again to make 4 pieces. Dip banana pieces in batter and then into heated salad oil (360°) and fry until brown. Drain well; sprinkle with powdered sugar. Serves 2.

## AVOCADO OLIVA

1 large, ripened avocado
1 14-oz. can baby artichoke hearts (20
   to 25), drained
1/3 cup olive oil
1 tbsp. tarragon wine vinegar
1 tbsp. lemon juice
salt and pepper to taste

Cut avocado in half. Fill cavity with marinated artichokes that have set in dressing overnight. Serves 2.

## PEAR ICE

1 cup pureed Bartlett pears
1 cup sugar
1 egg white
lemon juice to taste

Mix all ingredients well to dissolve sugar (a blender would be best). Pour into ice cube tray and freeze to heavy slush, stirring several times while freezing. Serve with vodka as refresher or after dinner. Serves 2 generously.

## PECAN PRALINES

pecans
2 tbsp. water
1 tbsp. cream
1 tsp. butter
1/4 tsp. salt
2 cups light brown sugar
1/4 tsp. vanilla extract

Stir together water, cream, butter, salt, and brown sugar over medium heat and bring to good boil. Boil 2 to 4 minutes. Add pecans and cook until rather thick (a few minutes). Add vanilla. Spread on wax paper and allow to set and cool. Makes 1 1/4 pounds.

## BANANAS FOSTER

1 1/2 oz. light brown sugar
1/8 tsp. cinnamon
2 pats butter
1 banana, sliced in quarters
1 large scoop vanilla ice cream
1/2 oz. creme de banana
1/2 oz. light rum

Melt butter in pan. Add brown sugar and cook to medium paste. Add cinnamon and stir well. Add creme de banana and stir to make syrupy. Add banana and cook on both sides until tender. Heat one side of pan over hottest part of fire. Add rum which will ignite into a high-rising flame. When flame settles, stir bananas into smaller flames. When flames go out completely, spoon bananas and sauce over ice cream. Serve immediately. Serves 1.

## CRABMEAT LAFITTE

1/4 lb. margarine
2 green onions
1/4 white onion
1 lb. lump crabmeat
2 oz. sherry wine
1/2 tsp. black pepper
1/2 tsp. salt
4 slices toast
1 dash paprika

Sauté white and green onions in butter until limp. Add crabmeat, salt, and pepper, and blend together. Add sherry wine and simmer. Spoon onto toast and overlay with Hollandaise sauce. Sprinkle paprika on center of sauce. Serves 4.

## THE ANDREW JACKSON RESTAURANT
### New Orleans

*This French Quarter restaurant serves excellent cuisine in elegant surroundings. Highly imaginative combinations of the best seafood obtainable are used in the preparation of such exotic dishes as Oysters 1812 and Crabmeat Lafitte.*

## HOLLANDAISE SAUCE:

4 egg yolks
2 oz. water
1/4 lb. melted butter
1 oz. tarragon vinegar
1/8 tsp. salt

Add vinegar to yolks and beat until light. Using double boiler, cook yolks slightly, then add butter slowly, beating continuously until firm. Add water if necessary to break heavy consistency. Lastly, add 3 dashes Tabasco.

## LOBSTER SAVANNAH

5 whole lobsters
1/2 lb. margarine
1 bell pepper
1 small white onion
1 oz. pimento
1 qt. milk
5 oz. flour
1/2 lb. mushrooms
5 oz. sherry wine

Sauté pepper and onion in margarine. Add mushrooms and flour. Heat milk separately and add, stirring to keep consistency smooth. Add pimento, salt, and white pepper to taste. While simmering, add sherry. Lobster should be cut in half and meat removed. Add meat to sauce and heat through and through. Stuff lobster shells with stuffing, top with grated Cheddar cheese, and put in oven to brown. Serves 10.

## VEAL KING FERDINAND

8 2-oz. pieces veal
2 eggs
3/4 tsp. salt
1/2 tsp. pepper
1 cup flour
8 asparagus tips
1/2 lb. crabmeat
1 green onion
1 oz. sherry wine
1/2 cup bread crumbs
1/2 cup margarine

Beat eggs well for egg wash. Salt and pepper veal. Pass veal through flour, egg wash, and bread crumbs in that order. Melt margarine in skillet and fry veal to golden brown. Melt margarine in skillet and sauté green onions until tender. Add crabmeat, salt, and pepper and blend together until warm. Add sherry and simmer. Place 2 pieces of veal on plate. Place 2 tbsp. crabmeat in center of veal. Place 2 asparagus tips on crabmeat and overlay with Bearnaise sauce. Serves 4.

## BEARNAISE SAUCE:

Same as Hollandaise sauce (see above) but add 1/8 tsp. chives, 1/2 tsp. parsley, and 1/8 tsp. dry tarragon leaves.

## TRIPE

1 1/2 lbs. tripe
1 small onion, finely chopped
1 stalk parsley
1 bay leaf
4 peppercorns
1/4 tbsp. salt
1/2 cup sliced mushrooms
3 tbsp. butter
1/2 tbsp. flour
1 egg yolk
2 tbsp. heavy cream
2 tbsp. sherry
1/2 cup tripe and beef stock

Cut tripe in 1-inch pieces. Save the stock. Sauté tripe, mushrooms, and finely chopped onions till mushrooms are tender. (Don't brown tripe.) Melt 1 tbsp. of butter, remove from heat, and blend in flour. Stir and cook for a few minutes, remove from heat, and add tripe and beef stocks. Stir and cook until sauce thickens. Mix egg yolk with cream and add to the sauce. (Don't boil.) Add sherry, heat 1/2 minute and serve over tripe and mushrooms.

## CHICKEN CURRY

2 2 1/2-lb. chickens
1/2 cup oil
1 cup chopped onions
1 cup chopped green peppers
1 cup chopped tomatoes
1 cup diced, cored apples
1/2 tsp. chopped garlic
2 tsp. chopped parsley
1 tbsp. curry powder
1 1/2 tbsp. flour
2 cups chicken stock
1 cup heavy cream
1 1/2 cups mango chutney
salt and ground pepper to taste

Debone and dice chicken into medium-size cubes. Sauté chicken in oil until golden (about 5 minutes) on a high flame. Remove from pan. In remaining oil, sauté onions, green peppers, garlic, and apples. Add curry powder and cook about 3 minutes. Keep stirring. Dust with flour. Add chicken, tomatoes, parsley, chicken stock, and heavy cream. Bring to a boil and simmer for about 5 minutes. Serve with rice or just French bread with the mango chutney on the side.

---

### BEGUE'S RESTAURANT
### Royal Sonesta Hotel
### New Orleans

*German-born Willy Coln is a classic European chef. His culinary talents have made this one of the finest restaurants in New Orleans —a city proud of its sophisticated palate.*

---

## ANDOUILLE JAMBALAYA

6 cups water
2 tsp. salt
1/2 tsp. saffron
1/2 cup butter
3 cups uncooked short-grain white rice
2 lbs. uncooked medium-size shrimp (about 20 to 24 per lb.)
6 lbs. cooked, unpeeled crawfish (yields 2 lbs. peeled tails)
6 tbsp. butter
1 cup finely chopped onions
1 tbsp. finely chopped garlic
2 cups peeled tomatoes, finely chopped with liquid
1/2 cup finely chopped green pepper
1/4 cup finely chopped celery
1 lb. sliced andouille sausage (or smoked sausage if andouille is unavailable)
Tabasco sauce
salt and pepper

In a heavy 5 to 6-quart casserole, melt butter over moderate heat. Add onions, garlic, green peppers, and celery. Sauté until soft and translucent but not brown. Add raw, peeled, and deveined shrimp and peeled, deveined crawfish tails and sausage. Sauté 4 to 5 minutes more. Add tomatoes, the tomato liquid, and seasonings. Mix in uncooked rice. Add water and stir. Cover casserole and place in 450° oven for 20 minutes or until the rice is cooked and has absorbed all liquid. Toss lightly and serve.

## MADAME BEGUE'S BREAD PUDDING WITH WHISKEY SAUCE

2 tbsp. softened butter
1 qt. milk
1 cup sugar
7 eggs
2 tbsp. vanilla extract
1/2 cup seedless raisins
nutmeg and cinnamon to taste
12-oz. loaf of day-old French bread
sweet rolls, thinly sliced (optional, for a really rich and decorative dessert)

Preheat oven to 350°. Spread softened butter evenly over the bottom and sides of a 13 X 9 X 2-inch baking/serving dish. Set the dish aside. Break bread into chunks. (If you use sweet rolls, slice the tops off and set aside, soaking them in a mixture of milk and 1 egg, breaking the remaining roll into chunks.) Drop bread into a bowl and pour milk over chunks. When the bread is softened, crumble it into small bits and let it continue to soak until all the milk is absorbed. In a small bowl, beat the remaining 6 eggs and sugar together until the mixture is smooth and thick. Stir in the raisins and vanilla extract, then pour the egg mixture over the bread crumbs, and stir until all the ingredients are well combined. Pour the bread pudding into the buttered dish, spreading it evenly and smoothing the top with the rubber spatula. (This is when you would place the milk-soaked tops of the sweet rolls in a decorative fashion over the top of the bread pudding.) Place the dish in a large shallow roasting pan set in the middle shelf of the oven and pour boiling water into the pan to a depth of about 1 inch. Bake for 1 hour, or until a knife inserted in the center of the pudding comes out clean.

## WHISKEY SAUCE:

4 oz. butter
1 cup sugar
1 egg
1/2 cup whiskey

Melt the butter in the top of a double boiler set over hot (but not boiling) water. Stir sugar and egg together in small bowl and add the mixture to the butter. Stir for 2 or 3 minutes, until the sugar dissolves completely and the egg is cooked, but do not let the sauce come near boiling or the egg will curdle. Remove the pan from the heat and let the sauce cool to room temperature before stirring in the bourbon. The bread pudding may be served cold or warm—and the whiskey sauce is served separately in a sauceboat or small bowl, preferably warm. (The whiskey sauce may be prepared in advance and reheated gently before serving.) Serves 8 to 10.

## REDFISH BON TON

1 8 to 10-oz. filet fresh redfish
1/2 stick butter
salt and pepper
lemon
parsley
paprika
1/4 cup crabmeat
white wine

Sprinkle lightly salt, pepper, and paprika on filet of redfish. Melt 1/4 stick of butter in a skillet over low flame. Place filet of fish (meat side down) in skillet until browned slightly. Turn fish over on skin side, add 1/2 cup water, cover, and allow to cook over low to medium flame until fish is cooked throughout (approximately 12 minutes). Remove cover, add juice of 1/2 lemon, add 1/4 stick of butter, and allow to remain over low flame until sauce thickens slightly. Sprinkle chopped parsley and baste fish with sauce. Place fish in serving plate and add Sautéed Crabmeat on top.

## SAUTÉED CRABMEAT:

Melt 1 tbsp. butter in small pot. Add 2 oz. white wine and 1/4 cup crabmeat. Allow to remain over flame until hot, then serve. Serves 1.

## SHRIMP ETOUFFEE

1/2 stick butter
2 cups small shrimp
1/4 tsp. chopped garlic
salt, pepper, and parsley
rice

Melt butter in skillet, add shrimp and garlic to melted butter, and salt and pepper to taste. Allow to simmer over low to medium fire until shrimp are cooked and butter-garlic sauce is thickened (approximately 10 minutes). Sprinkle chopped parsley and stir throughout. Serve with freshly cooked rice. Serves 2.

## THE BON TON RESTAURANT
### New Orleans

*The Bon Ton is a wonderful Cajun restaurant located in a converted red-brick store. Succulent crawfish are prepared in many delicious ways. The bread pudding is wonderful. This is a* Holiday *Award winner. Presented here are original recipes created by chef Alzina Pierce.*

## CRAWFISH NEWBURG

2 sticks butter
1 cup flour
2 cups milk
4 cups crawfish
parsley
1 egg yolk
Holland rusk
2 to 4 tbsp. sherry

Melt butter, add flour, and stir until well mixed. Then add milk, stir, and cook on low flame about 5 to 10 minutes. Sauté crawfish in 1 stick of butter for about 5 to 10 minutes over low flame. Add previously prepared cream sauce to crawfish, stir, add 1 egg yolk and stir more, then add 2 to 4 tbsp. sherry (can vary with taste) over low flame. Add chopped parsley and serve over Holland rusk. Serves 4.

## STUFFED EGGPLANT

6 medium eggplants
1 lb. small shrimp
1 lb. white lump crabmeat
4 bell peppers
4 medium onions
1/2 cup parsley
3 pods garlic
salt and pepper to taste
1/2 cup celery
bread crumbs

Boil eggplants till soft; then dig out meat. Save eggplant shells. While you are doing this, fry bell peppers, onion, celery, and garlic altogether till limp, then add eggplant meat. Let smother on medium fire till most water is cooked out, then add shrimp. Cook for another 20 minutes, then put all of this in another bowl, and fold in crabmeat and parsley. Let cool a little, then add enough bread crumbs to be firm enough to stuff shells. Sprinkle a little bread crumbs and paprika on top. Then sprinkle a little oil or oleo on top. Bake till done or brown in 350° oven.

## BREAD PUDDING

1 loaf French bread
1 qt. milk
3 eggs
2 cups sugar
2 tbsp. vanilla
3 tbsp. oleo
1 cup raisins

Soak bread in milk; crush with hands till well mixed. Then add eggs, sugar, vanilla, and raisins and stir well. Pour oleo in bottom of thick pan and bake till very firm. Let cool; then cube pudding and put in individual dessert dish. When ready to serve, add sauce and heat under broiler. Serve with Whiskey Sauce.

## WHISKEY SAUCE

1 stick butter or oleo
1 cup sugar (cream sugar)
1 egg

Cook sugar and butter in double boiler till very hot and well dissolved. Then add well-beaten egg and whip very fast so egg doesn't curdle. Let cool and add whiskey to taste.

## REDFISH J'AIME

1/3 cup butter
1/3 cup flour
2 cups fish stock
2 tbsp. paprika
1/2 cup finely chopped green onions
1 cup sliced mushrooms
1/2 tsp. finely chopped garlic
1/2 cup red wine
1/2 cup Lea & Perrins
1 1/2 cup crabmeat
4 4-oz. redfish filets

Melt butter and add flour. Add the butter and flour mixture to boiling fish stock. Add paprika, wine, Lea & Perrins, and salt and pepper to taste. Sauté onions and mushrooms in butter and let simmer for 10 minutes. Add onions, mushrooms, and crabmeat to sauce. Salt and pepper redfish filets. Dredge in flour and sauté in butter until brown. Pour sauce over filets. Serves 4.

## BEARNAISE SAUCE

4 egg yolks
juice of 1 lemon
2 cups melted butter
salt and pepper
2 tbsp. capers
1/4 cup chopped parsley
1 tbsp. tarragon vinegar

In top half of boiler, beat egg yolks and lemon juice. Cook slowly in double boiler over very low heat, never allowing water in bottom pan to come to a boil. Slowly add melted butter to above mixture, stirring constantly with a wooden spoon. Add salt, pepper (to taste), capers, parsley, and vinegar. Stir to blend. Makes 2 cups.

## CHICKEN PONTALBA

1/2 cup butter
1/2 cup thinly sliced white onion

---

## BRENNAN'S
## New Orleans

*Brennan's is famous around the world and the winner of practically every award possible. In the heart of the French Quarter, serving unparalleled food in an atmosphere of quiet dignity and elegance, Brennan's is truly one of a kind.*

1/4 cup chopped shallots
1 tbsp. minced garlic
1/2 cup chopped mushrooms
1/2 cup chopped ham
1 cup diced potato, deep-fried light brown and drained on absorbent paper
1/2 cup white wine
1 tbsp. chopped parsley
2 lbs. boned chicken leg, thigh, and breast
1 1/2 cups Bearnaise sauce (see above)

In a 10-inch skillet melt butter and sauté onion, shallots, and garlic until tender. Add mushrooms, ham, and potatoes and continue cooking about 5 minutes more. Add wine and parsley, heat through. Remove sauce from heat, keep warm. Dredge boned chicken pieces in seasoned flour and fry golden brown. To serve, arrange chicken pieces on bed of above sauce and cover chicken with Bearnaise sauce. Flank with warm toast triangles and sprinkle lightly with paprika. Makes 2 to 3 servings.

## HOLLANDAISE SAUCE

4 egg yolks
2 tbsp. lemon juice
1/2 lb. melted butter
1/4 tsp. salt

---

In top half of double boiler, beat egg yolks and stir in lemon juice. Cook very slowly in double boiler over low heat, never allowing water in bottom pan to come to a boil. Add butter a little at a time, stirring constantly with a wooden spoon. Add salt and pepper. Continue cooking slowly until thickened. Makes 1 cup.

## MARCHAND DE VIN SAUCE

3/4 cup butter
1/3 cup finely chopped mushrooms
1/2 cup minced ham
1/3 cup finely chopped shallots
1/2 cup finely chopped onion
2 tbsp. minced garlic
2 tbsp. flour
1/2 tsp. salt
1/8 tsp. pepper
dash cayenne
3/4 cup beef stock
1/2 cup red wine

In a 9-inch skillet melt butter and lightly sauté the mushrooms, ham, shallots, onion, and garlic. When the onion is golden brown, add the flour, salt, pepper, and cayenne. Brown well, about 7 to 10 minutes. Blend in the stock and the wine and simmer over low heat for 35 to 40 minutes. Makes 2 cups.

## EGGS HUSSARDE

2 large thin slices ham, grilled
2 Holland rusks
1/4 cup Marchand de Vin Sauce (see above)
2 eggs, soft poached
3/4 cup Hollandaise Sauce (see above)

Lay a large slice of ham across each rusk and cover with Marchand de Vin sauce. Cover next with egg and top with Hollandaise sauce. Garnish with sprinkling of paprika and serve with 1/2 grilled tomato. Serves 1.

## STRAWBERRIES CINELLI

6 cups fresh whole strawberries
2 1/2 tbsp. butter
8 tsp. sugar
2 cups orange juice
1 tsp. orange peel
1 tsp. lemon peel
1 cup Kirshwasser
1 cup Cointreau
1/2 cup brandy
1/2 cup rum
ice cream

Melt butter in large skillet over medium heat. Add sugar, stir, and add berries. Sauté a few seconds to blend with sugar. Add orange juice, orange and lemon peels, and simmer 1 minute. Heat all liquor in small pan and flame. Pour over berries. Have ice cream very cold in champagne glasses and add berries with sauce. Top with whipped cream and serve. Serves 8.

## SPAGHETTI AND TRUFFLES CARBONARA

2 lbs. spaghetti
6 truffles, cut julienne
8 slices bacon, cut julienne
1 cup Italian ham, cut julienne
2 tsp. black pepper
1 cup grated Parmesan cheese
4 cloves garlic, crushed
1/4 cup olive oil
1/2 cup chopped parsley
6 egg yolks

Heat oil in large skillet. Add garlic and heat. Add bacon and sauté till almost crisp. Add Italian ham, truffles, and black pepper and cook 2 minutes. Keep hot. Cook spaghetti in boiling water with salt till cooked but still *very* firm. Drain well. Put spaghetti in a warm bowl and add contents of skillet, cheese, and egg yolks. Briskly lift gently and mix quickly to blend egg yolks well. Sprinkle with parsley and serve. Serves 8.

## FUNGHETTI
*(Fresh Mushrooms)*

36 to 40 mushrooms
1/4 cup olive oil
salt and pepper to taste
1/2 tsp. cayenne or less
4 cloves garlic, crushed and chopped
4 or 5 medium fresh tomatoes, peeled and finely chopped
1/2 tsp. oregano

# COMMANDER'S PALACE
## New Orleans

*The bronze plaque on the front door says "Dedicated to dining in the grand manner." Keeping this promise has been a day-to-day tradition at Commander's since 1880. There are six exquisite dining rooms and a lovely dining patio, tinkling chandeliers, period wallpaper, and authentic Persian tile in the downstairs dining room. Dining at Commander's Palace, housed in a rambling Victorian mansion in the magnificent Garden District, is a tradition in New Orleans.*

1 tbsp. fresh basil or 1 tsp. dried basil
1 tbsp. chopped parsley
3/4 cup rose wine

Heat oil in skillet. Add garlic and sauté a few seconds. Add mushroom caps and cook over medium heat a few minutes. Add salt and pepper to taste, cayenne, and cook over high heat 2 minutes. Add wine and simmer for 5 or 6 minutes. Lastly, add parsley and serve. Serves 8.

## STRING BEAN SALAD WITH MINT DRESSING

2 lbs. green string beans
2 cloves garlic
1/2 cup fresh mint
1/2 tsp. oregano
1 1/2 tsp. salt
1 tsp. peppercorns
1/2 tsp. sugar
1/4 cup olive oil
juice of 1/2 lemon
2 tbsp. red wine vinegar

Trim ends of string beans and wash well. Cook in salted water till tender but still firm. Drain and set aside. Crush garlic, mint, peppercorns, salt, and sugar in mortar till mint leaves are completely mashed, or place in blender till combined. Add vinegar and lemon juice. Slowly add oil, beating constantly until well blended. Pour mixture over string beans and serve cold. Serves 8.

## PORK CHOPS À LA ANTONINA

8 loin pork chops, 1 inch thick, trimmed of fat
4 tbsp. olive oil
2 navel oranges
4 stalks celery
2 apples
4 cloves garlic, crushed
3 bay leaves
1 tbsp. rosemary
1 1/2 cups dry white wine
3/4 cup tomato sauce
salt and pepper to taste

Cut apples and oranges into quarter sections. Cut celery stalks on bias into 2-inch pieces and set aside. In large skillet, sauté chops in oil over medium heat until lightly browned. Add garlic, bay leaves, rosemary, and salt and pepper and sauté together 5 minutes longer to blend flavors. Remove everything except oil from skillet and set aside. Add fruit to skillet and sauté briskly, adding more oil if needed. Do not allow fruit to get too soft. Remove fruit and return chops to skillet. Place fruit mixture on top of chops and add wine and tomato sauce. Simmer gently for 10 minutes to blend completely.

## CHICKEN OLGA

4 chickens, 2 1/2 to 3 lbs. each
2 cloves garlic, crushed
16 artichoke hearts, canned or frozen
4 truffles, cut julienne
16 fresh medium-sized mushroom caps
1/2 cup olive oil
1 cup dry white wine (Rhine)
3/4 cup sweet Marsala wine
1 cup canned brown gravy
1 chicken cube diluted in brown gravy
salt and pepper to taste
dash of cayenne

Cut chickens in half and then cut each half into 4 pieces. Sauté in olive oil and garlic slowly, till lightly browned all over. Add salt and pepper to taste. Add mushrooms, artichokes, and sauté about 3 minutes to blend flavors. Add wines and allow to boil quickly for 2 or 3 minutes to reduce wine a little; then add brown gravy with chicken cube and cayenne. Taste for seasoning, adding salt and pepper as desired. Simmer slowly for 15 minutes and serve. Serves 8.

## DUNBAR'S SEAFOOD-OKRA GUMBO

1 1/2 lbs. fresh okra, cut into thin
    rounds
5 hard crabs
1/2 lb. shrimp
3 qts. water
shortening
1/2 small can tomatoes
1/2 small can tomato paste
1/4 cup chopped ham (optional)
1 small onion, ground
2 strips celery, chopped
1 clove garlic, chopped
2 sprigs thyme
1 bay leaf
2 cloves
flour to thicken
salt and pepper to taste

Brown okra, onion, garlic, tomatoes, and tomato paste in shortening, stirring constantly. Boil shrimp with salt, onion (using a small part of the ground onion), and celery about 5 minutes in 1 qt. water. Strain and save stock. Peel shrimp. Boil crabs in salted water. Save stock. Break crabs in half. Combine shrimp and crab stocks. Add okra mixture to stock. Add shrimp to crab and ham. Thicken with flour. Season with salt and pepper. Simmer for 2 1/2 hours, stirring frequently. Serve with boiled rice. Serves 10.

## OYSTERS CARNIVAL

2 doz. oysters, chopped and strained
    (save liquid)
1 1/4 large or 2 small onions, minced
1/2 bay leaf
pinch thyme
2 strips celery, minced
7 tbsp. butter
3/4 cup bread crumbs
6 oyster shells
6 strips bacon
6 lemon wedges
1 small clove garlic

Chop oysters and let drain. Mince onion, garlic, bay leaf, celery, and thyme. Fry in iron skillet in 3 tbsp. butter until brown. Add oysters. Moisten 1/2 cup bread crumbs with oyster liquid and add to above. Simmer for 20 to 30 minutes or until oysters have stopped drawing water. Add 2 tbsp. butter to mixture and cook until butter is melted. Boil and scrub oyster shells. Fill with oyster mixture, sprinkle with remaining 1/2 cup bread crumbs, and dot with another 2 tbsp. butter. When ready to serve, put in 375° oven for a few minutes until thoroughly heated. Serve at once, garnished with crisp bacon and lemon wedges. Serves 6.

---

## CORINNE DUNBAR'S New Orleans

*When dining at Dunbar's, one catches a glimpse of the style in which the Creole aristocrats of one hundred years ago lived. The menu includes such delicacies as Oiseau de Paradis, Huitres Dunbar, Daube à la Creole, Beignets aux Bananes, and Jambalaya Louisianaise.*

---

## BAKED CRABMEAT AND AVOCADO

1 lb. lump crabmeat
2 small cans cream of mushroom soup
    (undiluted)
2 avocados
1 cup evaporated milk
salt and pepper to taste
2 tsp. bread crumbs
1 can anchovies (flat)
1/4 lb. butter

Melt butter. Add soup and simmer 5 minutes. Add crabmeat. Add milk, salt, pepper, and simmer 5 minutes longer. Peel and slice avocados. Line baking dish with slices. Pour crabmeat mixture over slices. Sprinkle with bread crumbs and brush with melted butter. Heat until brown in 350° oven (approximately 15 minutes). Before serving, sprinkle a few drops of anchovy oil on top and garnish with anchovy strips. Serves 4 to 6.

## JAMBALAYA

2 onions, chopped
4 tbsp. butter
1 medium can tomatoes
1/2 small can tomato paste
1 clove garlic, chopped
2 stalks celery, chopped
1/4 sweet green pepper, chopped
1 tsp. parsley
1/2 tsp. thyme
3 whole cloves, chopped
1 lb. diced, boiled ham
2 lbs. peeled, boiled shrimp
3 cups cooked rice
salt, black pepper, and cayenne to taste

Sauté onions in butter 5 minutes. Add tomatoes, tomato paste, and cook 5 minutes, stirring constantly. Add all seasoning, chopped very fine. Cook 30 minutes, stirring frequently. Stir in ham and cook 5 minutes longer. Stir in shrimp and cook 5 minutes. Stir in rice, season to taste, and simmer 30 minutes longer, stirring frequently.

## SHERRIED BANANAS

6 half-ripe bananas
1 cup sugar
2 cups water
3 cloves
1/4 cup butter
1/2 lemon, sliced
2 tbsp. sherry
shortening for frying

Cut bananas in half lengthwise and fry in shortening until golden brown. Remove from skillet. Brown sugar in same skillet. Add water and cook until a thick syrup is formed. Add cloves, lemon, butter, and sherry and simmer 10 minutes. Add bananas and simmer 5 more minutes, gently. Serves 6.

## GUMBO Z'HERBES

1 lb. diced, boiled ham
1 lb. diced lean veal
2 tbsp. shortening
1 bunch collard greens
1 bunch mustard greens
1 bunch turnip greens
1 bunch spinach
1 bunch watercress
1 bunch beet tops
1 bunch carrot tops
1 bunch parsley
1 bunch chicory
1 bunch radish tops
1 whole green cabbage
1/2 bunch green onions
1 gal. water

### SEASONING:

1 large white onion, chopped
2 bay leaves
4 sprigs thyme
1 tbsp. chopped parsley
2 cloves
2 allspice
cayenne, salt, and pepper to taste

Wash all greens thoroughly, removing all stems or hard centers of leaves. Boil greens all together for 2 hours. Strain greens and save water. Chop greens finely. Simmer ham and veal in shortening for 10 minutes in deep iron skillet. Add onion and chopped parsley and sauté until onion is brown. Add greens and simmer 15 minutes. Add skillet contents back to water from greens. Add all seasonings and boil over low flame for 1 hour. Serves 10.

## CAFE DIABLE

18 cloves
3 cinnamon sticks
6 cubes sugar
6 oz. brandy
6 tsp. whipped cream
6 cups hot coffee
nutmeg
Cafe Noir (coffee liqueur)

Heat cloves, cinnamon sticks, and sugar. Flame with brandy. Add hot coffee, steep several minutes, and serve. Add whipped cream, sprinkle nutmeg, add several dashes Cafe Noir. Serves 6.

## MINT JULEP

2 oz. bourbon
mint leaves
sugar
12-oz. Collins-type glass

Muddle about 1 doz. medium-size mint leaves with 1 tsp. sugar. Add ice and fill glass, then add bourbon. Do not stir frappe until glass frosts. Garnish with cherry, pineapple chunk, and sprig of mint.

## NEW ORLEANS GIN FIZZ

3/4 oz. lemon juice
1/4 oz. lime juice
1/4 oz. simple syrup (or 1 tsp. sugar
    dissolved in 1 tsp. water)
dash orange flower water
white of 1 egg (or 1/4 tsp. powdered
    egg white)
1 oz. cream
1 1/4 oz. gin

Shake thoroughly or blend on slow speed for 20 seconds. Serve in chilled 8-ounce glass.

## SAZERAC
### (The Original Cocktail)

1/4 oz. simple syrup (tsp. sugar)
3 dashes Angostura bitters
4 dashes Peychaud bitters
1 1/4 oz. rye whiskey

Place ingredients in mixing glass and stir until cold. Strain into chilled 8-ounce tumbler that is lined with a few drops of absinthe. Add lemon twist.

## ABSINTHE SUISSESSE

1 1/4 oz. Herbsaint
1/4 oz. orgeat syrup
egg white (1/4 tsp. P.E.W.)
1 oz. cream (Half & Half)

---

# THE COURT OF TWO SISTERS
## New Orleans

*In many ways The Court of Two Sisters typifies the New Orleans of a bygone era. It has a charming terrace shaded by picturesque trees where diners can enjoy the special ambiance and cuisine of this excellent restaurant.*

Shake thoroughly or blend for 20 seconds on slow speed. Serve in chilled 8-ounce Old-Fashioned tumbler.

## FLAMINGO
### (Court of Two Sisters Original)

dash of red grenadine
1 oz. cherry liqueur
2 oz. rum
2 oz. lemon juice

Fill 10-inch Hurricane glass with ice and stir vigorously. Add more crushed ice and float a collar (2 inches) of orange juice. Garnish with cherry and slice of orange.

## DIRTY RICE

1 cup rice
6 chicken gizzards
3 chicken livers
1 tbsp. finely chopped celery
1 heaping tbsp. chopped shallots
1 tbsp. chopped onion
2 bay leaves
1 tbsp. chopped parsley
1 tsp. salt
1/2 tsp. black or white pepper
2 tbsp. cooking oil

Cook rice until 3/4 done. Boil gizzards in seasoned water with bay leaves and pieces of celery until tender. Add livers for 5 minutes, then take out. Chop fine and sauté onions, shallots, celery. Add liver and gizzards, stir well. Add rice, stir well. Add parsley, stir well. Cover and let simmer for 10 minutes or until rice is tender and dry. Add salt and pepper, stir well. Serves 8.

## STEAMBOAT WET HASH

1 lb. cold, cooked roast beef or cooked
    steak diced in 1/2-inch cubes
1 cup chopped shallots
1/2 cup chopped onions

---

1 tsp. finely chopped garlic
1/4 cup cooking oil
2 lbs. 1/2-inch diced potatoes
1 tsp. salt
1/2 tsp. ground pepper

Sauté meat in cooking oil until brown and crisp outside. Add onions and garlic. Let cook for 5 minutes. Add potatoes and shallots. Add hot water until ingredients are covered by a half inch. Add salt and pepper, stir, cover, and let simmer on low fire until potatoes are tender and cooked. Serve with creamy grits, hominy, or on toast bread.

## SHRIMP SOUFFLE

1/8 lb. butter
1/2 cup chopped onion
2 tbsp. flour
1 cup hot milk
1 cup apple sauce
1/2 cup tomato soup
1 oz. curry powder
1 cup chopped shrimp
1/2 cup cooked rice
4 eggs
salt
pepper

Draw butter, sauté onions, add flour, and stir well to make a roux. Add curry, stir well. Add tomato soup, apple sauce, chopped shrimp, rice, and egg yolk whipped. Salt and pepper to taste. Simmer 15 minutes. Fold in whipped egg white. Pour in greased pan, bake until firm at 350°. Serves 6.

## DECATUR SAUCE

1/4 lb. butter
1/4 cup chopped green peppers
1/4 cup chopped celery
1/4 cup chopped shallots
2 cups chopped tomatoes, fresh or
    canned
1 cup tomato puree or 1 tbsp. tomato
    paste
2 bay leaves
1 lb. peeled and deveined shrimp
1/4 lb. lump crabmeat
juice of 1 lemon or 1 oz. lemon juice
salt and pepper to taste
1 cup dry red wine
1/4 cup chopped parsley

Draw butter and sauté peppers, celery, shallots, tomatoes, and puree or paste. Add shrimp, bay leaves, lemon juice, and simmer for 15 minutes. Add salt and pepper to taste, red wine, chopped parsley, and simmer 10 minutes. Add crabmeat. Serve over any broiled fish.

## CAFE BRÛLOT

1/2 lemon peel
1/2 orange peel
12 cloves
3 pieces cinnamon bark
9 lumps sugar
12 oz. brandy or cognac

Place all of these ingredients in a silver bowl that has been warmed. Light it and burn slowly for 3 minutes, then gradually add about 12 oz. of strong coffee. Serves 6.

## CHICKEN CLEMENCEAU

Peel and dice a large potato and fry in deep fat. Select a young chicken about 2 lbs. Cut into pieces and sauté in butter until brown. Drain off excess butter, then add diced potatoes, a little mashed garlic, and cook for about 20 minutes longer on very low fire. Then add some sliced mushrooms and little green peas. Serve with chopped parsley.

---

# GALATOIRE'S RESTAURANT
## New Orleans

*This* Holiday *Award-winning restaurant is a well-established location for fine dining in this romantic city. In spite of the fact that reservations are not accepted, patrons stand outside in long lines because dining at Galatoire's is well worth the wait. The cuisine is the finest to be had anywhere.*

## EGGS SARDOU

Boil 12 large artichokes. Remove some of the leafage and spikes of the heart. Fill heart with creamed spinach. Place 1 poached egg on each artichoke and pour 1 tbsp. of Hollandaise sauce over each. (This dish is named after M. Victorien Sardou, French playwright of the nineteenth century.) Serves 6.

## CRABMEAT YVONNE

Sauté in butter 1 sliced mushroom, 1 sliced artichoke heart, and 1/3 lb. lump crabmeat. Cook for 3 to 5 minutes over medium heat; add chopped parsley and serve with toast points.

## CRABMEAT AU GRATIN

Sauté lightly in butter some fine chopped green onions, then make a cream sauce using a little milk. To the cream sauce add the crabmeat and cook on very low fire for 3 minutes. Add the onions to this and remove from fire. Pour into oven-proof dish and sprinkle with bread crumbs, grated cheese, and a little melted butter. Place in hot oven until golden brown.

## HOT CRABMEAT RAVIGOTTE

Chop fine: parsley, green onions, and a few pitted olives. Sauté lightly in butter with lump crabmeat that has been previously seasoned with salt and pepper and a little cayenne. Just before serving, add a little Hollandaise sauce. Garnish with slices of toast.

## KOLB'S HOUSE DRESSING

3 cups salad oil
2 cups creole mustard
1 cup water
1 cup cider vinegar
3 tbsp. sugar

Combine all ingredients and mix well. If desired, increase or decrease mustard and/or sugar to taste.

## TROUT VERONIQUE

6 trout filets, skin removed (about 6 oz. each)
2 cups water
1 cup dry vermouth
1 lemon, in wedges
salt and white pepper to taste
small bunch, tiny seedless white grapes
3 cups Hollandaise sauce

Place filets in shallow baking dish or pan. Cover with water and vermouth. Squeeze lemon wedges over fish and season to taste with the salt and pepper. Place in moderate oven for 10 to 12 minutes until fish is white and flaky. Remove from water/wine mixture and put aside in warm place. When ready to serve, place fish on oven-proof plate. Cut tiny, green, seedless grapes in half and place 10 to 12 halves on each portion of fish. Cover with scant 1/2 cup Hollandaise sauce (below) and place under broiler to set sauce.

## HOLLANDAISE SAUCE:

6 egg yolks
1 lb. melted butter
dash Tabasco sauce

# KOLB'S RESTAURANT
## New Orleans

*A landmark in New Orleans, this internationally known restaurant was founded by the late Konrad Kolb in 1899 and has remained in the same location since. Its aim has always been to serve the finest of foods in an atmosphere dedicated to good dining.*

2 tbsp. tarragon vinegar
juice of 1/2 large lemon (or 1 small lemon)

In double boiler over low heat, beat egg yolks until creamy. Continue beating and slowly add melted butter, then balance of ingredients. Remove to warm, *not hot* place. Never refrigerate.

## LOUISIANA JAMBALAYA À LA KOLB'S

1/4 lb. melted butter or margarine
1 lb. raw long-grain rice
1/2 tsp. paprika
1 lb. small peeled, and deveined shrimp
2 oz. claw crabmeat
1 cup tomatoes
1/4 cup tomato paste
1 small onion, chopped fine
1 small green pepper, chopped fine
1 cup finely chopped celery
2 green onions, chopped fine
1 tbsp. chopped parsley
1 tsp. Lea & Perrins
dash Tabasco sauce to taste

Melt butter, add raw rice and paprika, and cook over low flame until rice is lightly browned. In separate pot, combine shrimp, crabmeat, tomatoes, tomato paste, chopped onions, peppers, and celery. Cook 20 minutes gently. Combine with brown rice and simmer, covered, 20 to 30 minutes or until rice is tender. Stir in green onions, parsley, and seasoning.

## KOLB'S SAUERBRATEN

In a covered bowl place a 4-lb. bottom beef round, cover with following marinade, and let stand in refrigerator for 7 days, turning occasionally.

3 cups tarragon vinegar
4 cups water
1/2 cup sugar
1/4 cup salt
4 bay leaves
12 whole cloves
1/2 tsp. ground allspice
2 medium carrots, sliced
2 medium onions, sliced
1 bell pepper, sliced
1 stalk celery, diced
1/4 bunch chopped parsley

After soaking for 7 days, remove meat from marinade. Wipe dry with paper towels. Sear on all sides in hot oil in Dutch oven. Pour marinade back over meat. Cover and cook slowly until tender. Remove meat, strain liquid, and thicken with mixture of 1 tbsp. flour and 1 tbsp. ginger plus any necessary vinegar and/or sugar to balance flavor of sweet and sour gravy. Slice meat and serve covered with the hot gravy. Serves 8 to 10.

## LOBSTER MARINADE

2 tsp. salt
1/4 tsp. pepper
1 clove garlic
1/4 cup wine vinegar
1 cup olive oil
1/2 cup chopped green onions
2 tbsp. chopped parsley
1 lb. cooked lobster meat

Mash garlic in wooden bowl with salt and pepper. Add vinegar and mix well. Add oil, green onions, and parsley. Mix well. Pour over lobster meat and toss lightly. Refrigerate for 2 to 3 hours before serving.

## TOURNEDOS SAUCE PROVENCE

8 3-oz. tenderloin slices
1 cup cooking oil
2 large onions, cut rough
1 carrot, cut rough
2 cloves garlic
1/2 bunch parsley
1/2 cup flour
2 tbsp. tomato paste
1 cup dry red wine
4 cups light beef stock or 2 cups beef
    consommé
2 cups water
4 tbsp. olive oil
2 cloves garlic, chopped
2 tbsp. chopped parsley

Sauté onions, carrots, garlic, and parsley in oil until brown. Add flour and cook 5 to 8 minutes. Add tomato paste and cook 3 to 4 minutes. Add wine and beef stock with 2 cups water. Simmer until volume reduces by one-half. Strain through a fine-mesh strainer. Sauté chopped garlic in olive oil until soft (do not brown). Add strained mixture to this and stir. Add chopped parsley. Salt and pepper tenderloins. Sauté in pan with 1 tbsp. olive oil to desired doneness. Pour stock over and serve 2 to a person.

## MASSON'S RESTAURANT FRANÇAIS
### New Orleans

*The style of cooking at Masson's is French Provincial with the seasoning influenced by the Creole tradition. The cuisine makes the drive to this* Holiday *Award-winning restaurant on Lake Pontchartrain well worth the effort.*

## CREAM OF ARTICHOKE SOUP

1/8 lb. butter
1/2 cup chopped green onions
1 bay leaf
1 stalk celery, chopped
1 medium carrot, chopped
pinch thyme
1 qt. chicken consommé
1 cup sliced, cooked artichoke hearts
2 egg yolks
1 cup heavy cream

Sauté green onions, celery, carrots, bay leaf, and thyme in butter. Add consommé. Simmer 10 to 15 minutes. Add artichoke hearts. Simmer 5 to 10 minutes. Remove from fire. Add beaten yolks and cream. Salt and pepper to taste.

## OYSTERS ALBERT

1/2 lb. butter
1/4 cup chopped, cooked shrimp
1/2 cup chopped green onions
pinch thyme, cayenne, and garlic powder
1/4 cup bread crumbs
2 tsp. cognac

2 doz. raw oysters
1/8 cup white wine

Sauté green onions, thyme, cayenne, and garlic in butter. Cool. Separate one-half of this and add to it the bread crumbs and cognac. Shape into roll and refrigerate. Cook oysters and white wine in remaining one-half of butter and shallots until edges curl. Place 6 oysters in ramekin and top with slices of butter mixture. Bake 8 to 10 minutes at 350°.

## SUPREME OF TROUT, CRABMEAT SAUCE

4 filets trout, 6 to 8 oz. each
1/4 lb. butter
1/2 cup chopped green onions
1/2 cup white wine
2 cups heavy cream
2 or 3 egg yolks
salt and pepper
1 1/2 lb. cooked crabmeat

Salt and pepper trout filets. Squeeze one-half of lemon over each. Broil until done. Sauté onions in butter until soft. Add wine and cream. Simmer 5 to 8 minutes. Salt and pepper to taste. Remove from fire and stir in beaten yolks. Fold in crabmeat. Spoon over cooked filets.

## SABAYON

6 eggs, separated
3/4 cup sugar
3/4 cup cream sherry
3/4 cup heavy cream
1 tsp. vanilla

Beat yolks with sugar until creamy. Add sherry and cook in double boiler until thick. Cool in bowl for 10 to 15 minutes. Add whipped cream and vanilla. Fold in stiffly beaten egg whites. Divide into 4 small ramekins and chill 2 to 3 hours.

## CAFÉ BRÛLOT

Put a 2-inch piece of cinnamon stick, broken in half, 1/2 doz. cloves, 8 or 10 lumps of sugar, a piece each of lemon and orange peel, and 3 jiggers of brandy or cognac in a warm silver bowl. Light and let burn until sugar is dissolved, stirring all the time. Pour in about 4 half cups of freshly dripped, strong, hot, black coffee, and stir with ladle until flame is quenched. Serves about 4 or more.

## CAFÉ ROYALE

For each cup of coffee, place 2 lumps of sugar on spoon. Put spoon into cup. Pour 2 tsp. cognac or brandy over the sugar. Ignite. Pour hot coffee in slowly.

## CRAWFISH BISQUE

6 or 8 doz. large crawfish
2 tbsp. flour
2 onions
2 branches celery
2 tomatoes
1 bay leaf
2 sprigs thyme
3 cloves
2 qts. oyster water or beef stock
piece hot pepper
dash cayenne
1 tbsp. minced garlic and parsley
2 tbsp. butter or good lard
salt and pepper
1 cup wet bread that has been soaked and squeezed
1 egg

Wash and cleanse crawfish after they have soaked in salt water to make them emit all sand. Boil in about a gallon of water. Remove crawfish and save the water. Select one-third of the largest fish, remove tails, and clean out inside of heads, then free heads of claws, feet, and eyes, etc. Shell the tails and rest of crawfish. Make a roux of the flour and one-half of the lard or butter. Brown 1 minced onion and 2 tomatoes well, then pour in the crawfish water with warm oyster water, if to be used for a fast dinner, otherwise substitute beef stock for oyster water. Insert broken fish meats and seasonings and let come to a boil, then let simmer while heads are being prepared. Take reserved crawfish meat and make a stuffing as follows: Mince the other onion and fry in melted butter. Then add minced crawfish tails and squeezed, chopped bread with leaves from a sprig of thyme, salt, and pepper. Mash all well and add beaten egg after having cooled same a little. Stuff heads, roll lightly in flour, and brown in oven. Then add to soup and simmer for half an

hour. This is a soup which demands time to make, but one is rewarded for the trouble when partaking of a bisque made of these crustaceans. Serve with boiled rice or croutons.

## JAMBALAYA À LA CREOLE

This is a popular Spanish-creole dish, and a great favorite in New Orleans.

1 1/2 cups Louisiana rice
1 tbsp. butter
1 slice raw, fat ham
1 doz. chaurice (hot pork sausage)
1 cup boiled shrimp
1 onion, minced
2 creole tomatoes
1 sweet green pepper
sprig thyme
1 bay leaf
2 cloves
1 tbsp. minced garlic and parsley
1 1/2 qts. each beef stock and water
salt and pepper to taste
cayenne, if desired very hot

Cut ham into small pieces. Fry ham, shrimp, and chaurice in butter. Add onion and green pepper, then tomatoes. Add herbs, garlic, and parsley, then hot beef stock and water, salt and pepper, and boil a few minutes. Add rice that has been carefully washed. Cayenne may be added. Cook until rice is done or swelled, but not mushy, and serve hot.

## CREOLE BOUILLABAISE

4 or 6 slices each red snapper and redfish
4 large creole tomatoes or equivalent in can
1 bell pepper
2 onions
1 large bay leaf

### MAYLIE'S
### New Orleans

*When you dine at this wonderful restaurant, you can tell immediately that you have found true Southern Creole cuisine, for the chefs here know but one way to prepare their delectable dishes—in the time-honored tradition of their forefathers, who were responsible for the initial creation of many Creole dishes generations ago.*

1 large sprig thyme
4 allspice
1 herb bouquet
1/2 lemon
2 tbsp. olive oil
1 heaping tbsp. minced garlic and pepper
salt, pepper, and cayenne to taste
1 glass white wine

Buy fish small so as to have no waste. Cut heads off, rinse, and boil in one qt. of water, with the bouquet of herbs and a generous slice of onion. Let reduce to half so as to make a fish stock. Strain and set aside. Rinse whole fish and cut into slices of amount desired. Rub well on both sides with thyme, parsley, garlic, bay leaf, and allspice, that have been minced or ground well. See that every part of fish is well saturated. Heat olive oil in a roomy saucepan so that when placing fish, the slices will lie flat. Mince rest of onion and fry in hot oil. Place slices of fish side by side and cover to smother, for about 15 minutes. Turn fish over carefully to fry on other side. Remove fish carefully so as not to break slices, and set aside to keep warm. Add tomatoes that have been skinned, and seeded rings of green sweet pepper, and let fry well. Add thin slices of lemon, hot fish stock, white wine, salt, pepper, cayenne, or other hot pepper. Let all boil well until reduced to about half. Place fish in this gravy, without overlapping, and boil about 5 minutes or more. Serve fish on buttered slices of toast and pour sauce over. Serve immediately or toast will become soggy.

## CREOLE SALAD BOWL

2 heads creole or Romaine lettuce
1 Bermuda onion, sliced
4 creole tomatoes, skinned and seeded
1 cucumber, peeled, scored, and sliced very thin
1 doz. radishes, peeled, leaving on a little of the red skin
1 small sweet pepper, cut in rings
tender watercress
garlic to rub bowl

Make a French dressing of 1 tbsp. each of vinegar and lemon and 4 to 6 tbsp. olive oil (if a rich salad is desired, otherwise use vegetable oil). Salt and pepper to taste. Place all ingredients except greens in salad bowl that has been rubbed with garlic. Pour French dressing over all and toss well. Then place lettuce, Romaine, and watercress around sides and on top. Place in refrigerator to marinate a while and when ready to serve, mix again so that greens will absorb some of the dressing but will still retain their crispness.

## SHRIMP DE JONGHE

**10 shrimp (21 to 25 per lb., with tails), peeled and deveined**
**1 pinch freshly crushed garlic**
**1 pinch salt**
**1 pinch white pepper**
**1 pinch thyme leaf**
**1 tbsp. finely chopped green onion**
**1/4 cup bread crumbs**
**4 oz. clarified butter**
**1 oz. straight sherry**

Sauté shrimp in butter with garlic, salt, pepper, and thyme. Prevent shrimp from sticking to pan, allowing natural curl. Shrimp should not be completely cooked, but should curl. Pour sherry into small casserole-type dish and arrange shrimp uniformly in the sherry. Return the sauté pan to heat and turn up the flame. Add green onion and bread crumbs to the pan drippings. Shake or stir the pan and allow paste to bubble evenly. Spoon the seasoned butter and bread-crumb paste evenly over the meat of the shrimp (leaving tails exposed) while still bubbling in the hot pan. Last and just before serving time, place the casserole in preheated 500° oven to finish cooking shrimp and sherry. Sherry should bubble in the dish before removing from oven.

## SHRIMP MARTINO

**10 shrimp, peeled and deveined, tails on**
**12 or more seedless white grapes**
**1 pt. Sauterne wine (nonvintage)**
**1 bay leaf**
**1 level tbsp. coarsely chopped Bermuda onion**
**1 level tbsp. coarsely chopped green pepper**
**Approximately 1 cup Hollandaise sauce (Salt and pepper should be called for in your Hollandaise recipe.)**

Poach shrimp in a small pot (quart size) with bay leaf, onion, and green pepper. Bring to a slow boil and simmer briefly. Remove shrimp and allow to cool. Arrange shrimp on a plate or in an 8-oz. individual casserole dish, with tails pointing in, out, or up. Place the grapes between the shrimp and place a cluster of 3 or 4 directly in the center. Pour Hollandaise sauce carefully over the shrimp, leaving the tails and the center grape cluster exposed. Bake the dish until it browns and bubbles on the top and serve from the oven. Garnish with a sprinkle of chopped parsley.

---

**LE PETIT**
**The Saint Louis Hotel**
**New Orleans**

*The winner of many awards, this tiny, intimate dining room off the beautiful St. Louis Hotel court- yard is decorated in delicate shades of dusty pink, with rich green tropical plants all around. The cuisine is French and pleases the most discriminating palate.*

## BAKED EGGPLANT SUPREME

Sauté 3 round slices, 1/4 inch thick, of eggplant coated in flour batter and fine bread crumbs until golden brown but not completely done. In another pan sauté 4 oz. of lump crabmeat in 2 tbsp. of clarified butter with 1 finely chopped green onion (green only), a pinch of freshly crushed garlic, salt and white pepper to taste, and 1/2 oz. of straight sherry. Do not overcook the crabmeat. Hold eggplant and crabmeat to the side while making cheese sauce for topping.

Make a roux with 1 tbsp. butter and 1 tbsp. flour. Add 1 cup scalded milk and just a touch of salt and white pepper to taste. Whip smooth. Pour into top of double boiler with 1/2 lb. of grated or shredded aged English Cheddar and 1/4 lb. of grated or shredded American cheese. Melt slowly, whipping continuously until completely smooth. Add 2 dashes of bitters. Makes approximately 1 qt. of cheese sauce.

To stack the eggplant, place 1 slice of eggplant on a plate, spread 1/2 tsp. of tomato paste on top of it, and lightly sprinkle a small pinch of chervil over the paste. Place the second slice of eggplant atop and load it with the prepared crabmeat, pushing it in place. Press the third slice of eggplant firmly over it and place a fluted mushroom cap on the top. Spoon over enough cheese sauce to blanket the stack entirely and then place it in a preheated 400° oven for 10 or 15 minutes until the cheese has sealed off the sides and is bubbling in the plate. Garnish with a light sprinkle of paprika and a sprig of parsley.

## MOUSSE AU CHOCOLAT

**1/2 lb. semisweet chocolate**
**1/2 oz. bitter chocolate**
**1/4 cup water**
**5 eggs, separated**
**1 tsp. vanilla extract**

---

Combine water and both types of chocolate in top of double boiler, stir mixture until smooth, and remove from heat. Add well-beaten egg yolks and vanilla extract. Beat egg whites until they are stiff and gently fold in the chocolate mixture. Pour directly into 6 individual serving glasses and chill for 8 hours.

To serve as mold, pour into ring mold and freeze. Unmold after frozen onto platter, using warm water and toweling the top of the overturned mold. Garnish with whipped cream and sprinklings of grated bitter chocolate.

## CRABMEAT BENEDICT

**4 oz. fresh lump crabmeat**
**pinch crushed garlic**
**pinch salt**
**pinch pepper**
**1 oz. clarified butter**
**1 tbsp. chives**
**2 tbsp. straight sherry**
**1 Holland rusk**
**2 eggs, poached**
**2 oz. Hollandaise sauce**

Sauté crabmeat in butter with garlic, salt, pepper, and chives. Use wooden utensil to prevent breaking lump meat. Cook sherry to reduce by 1/2 and add remaining 1 tbsp. to sautéed crabmeat. Place crabmeat over Holland rusk and place 2 poached eggs gently on the crabmeat. Then cover with Hollandaise. Place in preheated 400° to 450° oven and brown and serve.

## CANADIAN BACON AND FRESH MUSHROOMS

**4 slices Canadian bacon**
**3 sliced mushrooms with stem**
**1 tbsp. clarified butter**
**1 pinch freshly crushed garlic**
**1/4 tsp. chopped parsley**
**1/2 tsp. chopped Spanish onion**
**1 pinch each cayenne pepper, ground coriander, ground cuminseed, and ground ginger**
**1/2 oz. French brandy**

Heat butter in sauté pan. Add garlic, onion, pepper, cuminseed, coriander, and ginger. Decrease heat and add Canadian bacon, mushrooms, and parsley. Sauté gently until mushrooms brown. Turn the flame to high for a few seconds, then add brandy. Leave on high heat until brandy ignites, then lower heat. Continue simmering until flame has gone. Salt to taste. Serve at once with almond rice and petit pois. Serves one.

## ROCKEFELLER SAUCE

6 oysters on the half shell per serving
1 lb. freshly boiled spinach, chopped
fine
1 tbsp. chopped parsley
3 cups oyster water
1/2 doz. chopped oysters
1 tsp. Lea & Perrins
Tabasco sauce (few drops)
salt and pepper to taste
1 pinch fennel
2 tbsp. flour

Sauté with butter the spinach and parsley. Add flour and mix with oyster water and chopped oysters. Cook one-half hour, add seasoning and fennel. Cook another one-half hour, take from fire, and add 1 tbsp. of Herbsaint. Place over oysters on the half shell and bake for 25 minutes at 380°. Serves 4.

## TURTLE SOUP

6 oz. turtle meat
1 medium onion, chopped
1 tsp. chopped parsley
1/2 cup celery
2 cloves garlic
1 medium green pepper
3 oz. butter
2 tbsp. tomato puree
1 tsp. tomato paste
1 tsp. beef stock
2 tbsp. flour

Grind turtle meat together with above chopped vegetables. Cook for 30 minutes. Add butter, tomato paste, tomato puree, and 12 cups of water. Cook for 1 1/2 hours slowly. When finished, add 1/2 lemon.

1 egg, hard boiled
1 tsp. chopped parsley
2 cups sherry wine
1 pinch oregano
1 pinch rosemary
1 pinch sage
1 pinch Coriander
2 pinches thyme
2 bay leaves
1 lemon

---

## RIB ROOM
## The Royal Orleans
## New Orleans

*The dining room of the elegant Royal Orleans, located in the French Quarter, has the atmosphere of an old English inn. Chef Luis Caner creates excellent Creole, French, and American dishes.*

Add all the spices to the wine and cook until the liquid is reduced by half. Add eggs and chopped parsley. Ready to serve. If desired, add more sherry. Serves 8.

## CHORON SAUCE

4 egg yolks
8 oz. clarified butter
1 tsp. dry shallots
1 tsp. dried tarragon leaves
1 tbsp. white tarragon vinegar
1 tbsp. tomato ketchup

Combine tarragon vinegar and shallots. Reduce to one-half liquid. Add egg yolks and 1 tbsp. of water. Whip all ingredients in round pot set in another pot of hot water until thick. Add clarified butter slowly and ketchup, tarragon, and salt and pepper to taste. Keep in warm place because change of temperature will break sauce. This is a rich sauce and is best served with broiled beef.

## ROAST DUCKLING BIGARRADE

Salt and pepper 5 lb. duck and arrange orange and lemon skins around. Roast. After duck has roasted save gravy; you will need 10 oz. In another pot mix 1 tsp. of sugar with a little water and cook until caramelized. Add 1/2 cup of

---

wine vinegar and reduce. To this add 1 cup of fresh orange juice. Cook 5 to 10 minutes. Add gravy and cornstarch to thicken and salt and pepper to taste. Strain and add to this parched julienne orange and lemon skins and 1 tsp. of butter and mix. This sauce is best with strong meats, such as duck and venison.

## CRAB BISQUE

1 lb. blue crab
1 small onion
2 tbsp. chopped celery
3 cloves garlic
2 or 3 parsley stems
3 tomatoes
2 bay leaves
1/2 coffeespoon whole black pepper
1 pinch thyme
1 pinch rosemary
4 cups beef consommé
1/2 cup brandy
1 cup Chablis wine
2 oz. butter
2 soupspoons flour

Cut crab into small pieces and add chopped vegetables. Brown lightly. Add brandy and wine, tomatoes, beef consommé, 6 cups of water, and spices. Cook slowly for 40 minutes. Salt and pepper to taste, strain, and garnish with a little rice and crabmeat lumps. Serve very hot. Serves 8.

## CHOCOLATE MOUSSE

8 1/2 oz. melted chocolate
1/4 cup hot water
2 egg yolks
2 egg whites
2 oz. sugar
vanilla to taste

Whip egg whites with sugar. Mix chocolate with water and yolks with vanilla to taste. Add a pinch of salt and 1 qt. of cream (whipped); fold. Place in refrigerator and cool for 1 hour. Serve with shredded chocolate to garnish. Serves 8.

## RS AU CHAMPAGNE

**fresh pears**
**3 lbs. sugar**
**2 qts. water**
**4 cinnamon sticks**
**1/4 oz. cloves**

Peel and core pears. Put all ingredients together in saucepan and bring to full boil, then simmer until pears are tender to the touch. Do not overcook. Let cool. When ready to serve, place 1 pear each in champagne glasses, cover with juice, then add 3 oz. of champagne over each pear.

## PHEASANT VERONIQUE WITH GRAPES AND PINE SEEDS

**1 14-oz. pheasant**
**2 oz. butter**
**1 1/2 oz. gooseliver pâté**
**20 fresh white seedless grapes, peeled**
**1 tsp. toasted pine seed**
**3 oz. heavy cream**
**3/4 oz. cognac**
**salt, white pepper**
**1 tsp. chopped onion**
**1 tsp. chopped celery**
**1 tsp. diced carrot**
**4 pieces juniper berries**
**3 oz. dry white wine (Chablis)**

Bone pheasant by cutting from the back, leaving in drumstick and wing bone only. Season lightly with salt and pepper and lay butterflied pheasant inside out on table. Add 1 oz. butter, 3/4 oz. gooseliver, and roll bird back to original shape to hold together. Best to tie with fine butcher cord. Add 1/2 oz. butter to saucepan and sauté pheasant from both sides until golden brown. Place in oven and roast for approximately 30 minutes at 350°. To make the pheasant stock, combine the pheasant bones, celery, onion, and carrots and sauté with 1/2 oz. butter in pan until golden brown. Fill up with wine and 1 cup of water or chicken stock. Add juniper berries and cook over slow heat for 1 hour. When bird is roasted, take from oven and flame with cognac by pouring cognac over the bird and lighting with a match. Then place bird in serving dish. Put stock into same saucepan. Add cream and 3/4 oz. of the gooseliver. Cook until sauce reaches correct thickness. Season with salt. Add grapes and pour sauce over pheasant. Top with pine seed and serve. Serves 1.

## SAZERAC RESTAURANT
## The Fairmont Hotel
## New Orleans

*Named after the storied Sazerac cocktail that was born in New Orleans in the eighteenth century, this beautiful restaurant serves magnificent cuisine. The service, the decor—everything—is impeccable.*

## FISH PÂTÉ

**FISH MOUSSE:**

**3 lbs. fresh trout or redfish**
**6 egg whites**
**1 lb. butter**
**1 qt. whipping cream**
**salt, pepper, and cayenne**

Grind fish. Put in mixing bowl and add seasonings to taste. Add egg whites, one at a time, and beat in until well blended. When butter has reached room temperature, thoroughly blend it into mixture. Now add whipping cream and beat until mixture is stiff. This bowl must be placed in a bowl of ice during the whole procedure.

**BREAD CRUMB FILLING:**

**2 cups bread crumbs**
**1/2 cup chopped parsley**
**2 eggs**
**Half & Half**
**salt and pepper to taste**

Mix all ingredients together and use just enough Half & Half so that mixture will spread. Blend well.

**SAUCE:**

**1/4 cup chopped dry shallots**
**1/2 lb. sweet butter (do not melt in advance)**
**1 cup white wine**
**2 cups whipping cream**

Cook shallots and wine until reduced by half. Add cream and bring to boil. Add butter and allow to reach boil again.

Correct taste with salt, cayenne pepper, and a few drops of lemon juice.

In buttered loaf pan, put a layer of fish mousse, then a layer of bread crumb filling, and continue layer on layer ending with mousse on top. Place pan in another pan with water and cook in 380° oven for 1 hour. Cut in 1-inch slices and top with sauce. Serves 12 to 15.

## FAIRMONT SPINACH SALAD

**1 pkg. fresh spinach**
**5 strips bacon**
**2 tbsp. olive oil**
**3 tbsp. red wine vinegar**
**1 tsp. Worcestershire sauce**
**1 tsp. Dijon mustard**
**2 tsp. sugar**
**1 tsp. herb mixture (consisting of rosemary, tarragon, and oregano)**
**black pepper to taste**

Wash and dry fresh spinach. Remove stems. Place in bowl. Cut bacon into 1-inch pieces. Crispen in saucepan. Drain grease. Add rosemary, tarragon, and oregano and mix well. Add oil, vinegar, Worcestershire, mustard, sugar, and mix well. Let heat. Add pepper to taste from pepper mill. Pour hot dressing over salad, cover with pan, and let steam for 15 seconds. Toss salad, dish out, and pour remaining dressing with bacon over salad. Serves 2.

## STEAK TARTARE

**8 oz. ground lean beef**

**DRESSING:**

**1 demitasse spoonful mashed anchovies**
**1 demitasse spoonful Dijon mustard**
**2 demitasse spoonfuls red wine vinegar**
**4 demitasse spoonfuls olive oil**
**1 egg yolk**
**2 dashes Worcestershire sauce**
**1 dash Tabasco sauce**
**2 dashes brandy**
**1/2 dash paprika**
**1 1/2 dashes onion**
**1 gherkin, chopped**
**3 capers**
**salt and pepper**

Mix everything together well until you get a smooth liquid dressing. Then add beef and mix very well. Garnish with fresh parsley and serve with rye bread.

## STUFFED OYSTERS BERNARD

24 oysters on half shell, in tray on rock salt

STUFFING:

16 oz. chopped raw mushrooms
4 oz. chopped, cooked shrimp
6 filets of anchovies, chopped fine
3 oz. chopped shallots
1 pinch thyme leaves
salt and pepper to taste
2 egg yolks

Sauté the shallots in butter, add mushrooms, and cook for 10 minutes. Add shrimp, anchovies, thyme leaves, salt, and pepper. Stir in egg yolks and remove mixture from heat. Mix thoroughly. Top each oyster with stuffing, cover with Mornay sauce, and sprinkle Gruyere or Parmesan cheese on each. Bake at 375° for about 15 minutes or until brown. Serves 4.

## SEAFOOD DIVAN

Sauté shrimps, scallops, crabmeat, and lobster meat in clarified butter. Add sherry wine. Bring to a boil. Cover a casserole with several stalks of cooked broccoli. Add sautéed seafood. Cover with Mornay sauce. Sprinkle with Gruyere cheese and brown under broiler.

## CRAB CAKES

1 lb. picked-over jumbo crab lumps
2 tbsp. mayonnaise (heavy)

## DANNY'S
## Baltimore

*Danny Dickman continues to do his own marketing for the ingredients for such delicacies as Danny's Crab Cakes, Plume de Veau, Baked Stuffed Oysters, and Dover Sole. He is a master of the art of gueridon—or tableside—cooking. Danny's wins the coveted* Holiday *Award year after year.*

1 tsp. Lea & Perrins
1/4 tsp. Old Bay seafood seasoning
2 whole eggs
1/4 cup flour

Mix all ingredients except the crabmeat thoroughly. Pour over crabmeat and mix carefully as not to break the crab lumps. Fry in skillet using Wesson oil (keep flame about medium) approximately 2 to 3 minutes on each side or until golden. Should make 3 crab cakes (Danny's size).

## STEAK DIANE, FLAMBE

3 oz. clarified butter
2 8-oz. mignonettes of beef
4 oz. sliced mushrooms
2 tbsp. chopped shallots
1/2 tsp. chopped chives
1 tsp. chopped parsley
1/4 tsp. Lea & Perrins

1 tbsp. sauce Robert (Escoffier)
1/2 tsp. salt
1/4 tsp. freshly ground black pepper
2 oz. beef stock
2 oz. cognac
1 oz. Madeira wine

Pour butter into blazer of a chafing dish. When very hot, but not brown, add the sliced mushrooms. Next, add the shallots, chives, and parsley. Cook for 2 minutes. Add the mignonettes of beef, and cook 2 minutes on each side. Add the cognac and set aflame; when the flame is extinguished, add the Lea & Perrins and sauce Robert. Then add the beef stock and Madeira wine; cook for 2 minutes. Season to taste with salt and pepper, and serve accompanied with wild rice.

## CAESAR SALAD

6 oz. washed inside leaves of Romaine lettuce
2 oz. croutons
3 oz. garlic olive oil
1 tsp. freshly ground pepper
4 large flat Spanish anchovies
1/2 tsp. Lea & Perrins
1 lemon
1 egg, coddled
2 oz. Parmesan cheese
dash salt

Pour olive oil over Romaine lettuce in wooden salad bowl rubbed with garlic. Add Lea & Perrins, salt, and pepper. Add egg and roll lightly. Add juice of lemon and roll again lightly. Add croutons and Parmesan cheese and roll. Cut anchovies up into bite-size pieces and add to salad. Toss salad and serve.

## LOBSTER SALAD

1 lb. cooked lobster meat
1/3 cup mayonnaise
2 tbsp. lemon juice
1/4 tsp. salt
lettuce
3 tomatoes

Cut lobster into small pieces. Add mayonnaise, lemon juice, and salt. Serve on lettuce and garnish with tomato wedges. Serves 6.

## CRABMEAT GUMBO À LA MARYLAND

1 lb. Maryland backfin lump crabmeat
1 can whole tomatoes (28 oz. size), chopped into small chunks
1 can cut okra (15 1/2 oz. size)
1 can tomato sauce (8 oz. size)
1 1/2 cups chopped celery
1/2 cup chopped onions
1/2 cup green peppers
4 oz. butter or margarine
2 oz. seasoned chicken base
3 pts. water
2 tbsp. basil
1 tbsp. salt
1/2 tsp. chili powder
1 tbsp. garlic powder
1 tsp. black pepper

Sauté green peppers, onions, and celery in a 4-quart pot until almost tender (about 10 minutes). Add to this all ingredients except crabmeat. Allow to cook for 30 minutes over small flame, stirring occasionally. Pick over crabmeat for any excess shells or cartilage. Add crabmeat to soup and simmer for 5 minutes. Serves 8 to 10.

## MARYLAND ROCKFISH SALAD

1 lb. cooked filet of rockfish
1 tbsp. diced onion
1/4 cup chopped green pepper
1/4 cup salad oil
2 tbsp. wine vinegar
1/8 tsp. oregano
1 tsp. parsley flakes
1/2 tsp. salt
1/4 tsp. pepper
2 tbsp. mayonnaise

Cut fish into small pieces and place in a bowl; mix with all other ingredients. Makes about 1 pound salad.

---

### GORDON'S OF ORLEANS STREET
### Baltimore

*Gordon's is a crab house that is simplicity itself. It has great charm, with its wall photographs that detail how to eat a steamed crab. Mrs. Gordon, the owner, has a flair for having everything "just right." Not only is the seafood the very finest, but so are the many other delectable items on the menu.*

---

## MARYLAND CRAB CAKES

1 lb. backfin or regular crabmeat
1/2 cup bread crumbs
1 large egg
1/4 cup mayonnaise
1/2 tsp. salt
1/4 tsp. black pepper
1 tsp. grated horseradish
1/4 tsp. dry mustard
fat or oil for frying

Remove any remaining shell or cartilage from crabmeat. In another bowl mix mayonnaise, egg, seasonings and bread crumbs. Pour this mixture over crabmeat and blend thoroughly. Shape into 6 crab cakes. Fry in hot fat or oil approximately 2 or 3 minutes at 350°. They may also be pan-fried in butter or oil for approximately 1 1/2 minutes on each side.

## LOBSTER STEW

1 lb. cooked lobster meat
1 tsp. salt
1/4 tsp. paprika
dash nutmeg
1/4 cup melted butter
1 pt. table cream
chopped parsley

Cut lobster meat into 1/2-inch pieces. Add seasonings and lobster meat to butter; sauté 5 minutes. Add cream and simmer for 3 minutes (do not boil). Garnish with parsley sprinkled over the top. Serves 6.

## SWEET AND SOUR SHRIMP

1 lb. small, cooked, peeled, deveined shrimp
1 8-oz. jar sweet and sour sauce
3/4 cup diced celery
2 tbsp. sour cream
1 tbsp. grated horseradish
1 tsp. salt
1/2 tsp. black pepper
1/2 tsp. celery seed

Mix all ingredients thoroughly in a bowl. Refrigerate. Serve over shredded lettuce in deep cocktail dishes. Serves 3 to 4.

## CRAB MORNAY

1 lb. Maryland backfin crabmeat
1 pt. table cream
2 tsp. lemon juice
6 tsp. sherry wine
nutmeg
1 pkg. sharp Cheddar grated cheese
paprika

Pour a small amount of sauce into each casserole. Divide the crabmeat in equal amounts in the casseroles. Add 1 tsp. sherry on top of crabmeat. Sprinkle a dash of nutmeg on each casserole. Add cream sauce to casserole. (Don't fill to top of casserole.) Now, fill 6 6- to 7-oz. casserole dishes with Cheddar cheese and sprinkle with paprika. Place in oven at 350° for 8 to 10 minutes.

## SIMPLE CRABMEAT AU GRATIN

1 lb. Maryland backfin crabmeat
1 can condensed Cheddar cheese soup (10 1/2 oz. size)
1/4 cup table cream
1/4 lb. pkg. shredded sharp cheese
1/8 tsp. nutmeg
paprika

Empty can of Cheddar cheese soup and cream into a saucepan. Stir over moderate flame until it simmers. Remove from heat. Add crabmeat. (Pick over crabmeat and discard any shells or cartilage.) Add rest of ingredients except shredded cheese and paprika. Divide this mixture into 5 6-oz. baking casseroles. Use all the content of shredded cheese on top of casseroles. Sprinkle with paprika. Bake in oven at 400° for 10 minutes. Serve immediately. Serves 5.

## CHICKEN LIVERS WITH RED WINE

12 chicken livers (about 1/2 lb.)
2 tbsp. butter
2 tbsp. chopped onion
1/4 lb. mushrooms
2 tbsp. flour
1/2 cup dry red wine
1/2 cup chicken stock
1/2 tsp. thyme
1/2 tsp. parsley

Cut livers in half. Melt butter and sauté onion and mushrooms. Add livers and sauté 3 minutes longer. Stir in flour. Slowly add chicken stock and wine, stirring until mixture is very smooth. Add thyme and parsley and simmer gently for 10 minutes. Stir occasionally. Add salt and pepper to taste. Serve on toast or rice. Serves 4.

## SOUTH MOUNTAIN SWEET POTATOES

4 cups cooked, mashed sweet potatoes
1/2 cup sherry wine
1/4 tsp. salt
1/2 cup sugar
1/2 cup melted butter
2 eggs, beaten

Whip all ingredients together until fluffy. Fold into buttered pan and bake in moderate oven until golden brown.

## DEEP DISH PEACH PIE

Arrange whole, peeled peaches in deep baking dish. It is best to use a very sweet variety and they should be very ripe and mellow. Sprinkle liberally with sugar. Cover with a pastry crust, prick with a fork, and bake in 450° oven for 10 minutes. Reduce heat to 350° and bake for 30 or 40 minutes longer.

# OLD SOUTH MOUNTAIN INN
## Boonsboro

*This is a romantic inn located in a beautiful section of Maryland. It serves excellent food in its delightful dining room under the able leadership of owner Charles Reichmuth.*

## POTATO SOUP

4 cups cubed, peeled potatoes
1 cup sliced onion
1/2 green pepper
3 cups water
1 ham bone (with bit of meat left on)
1 tsp. celery salt
1 1/2 cups milk
1/2 cup cream
dash red pepper
black pepper
salt to taste
3 tbsp. butter or margarine
parsley

Boil potatoes, onion, and green pepper in water with ham bone. As vegetables become tender, remove ham bone and press all through a colander. Add celery salt, heated milk, cream, seasoning, and butter or margarine. When hot and blended, serve with parsley leaf atop each serving.

## SOUTH MOUNTAIN BREAD PUDDING

4 cups milk
2 cups bread crumbs
1 tbsp. butter
1 cup sugar
4 eggs
rind and juice of 2 lemons
4 tbsp. powdered sugar

Heat milk and pour over bread crumbs. Add butter. Cover and set aside to cool. Then beat sugar and egg yolks together and add grated lemon rind. Add to first mixture and pour all into a buttered pudding dish. Bake for about 1/2 hour in a 375° oven, until firm and slightly browned. Remove from oven and spread with a meringue made with the egg whites whipped to a froth, to which have been added the powdered sugar and lemon juice. Brown in a slow oven to a light straw color. Serve warm with Lemon Pudding sauce or cream.

## ROAST LOIN OF PORK

1 4 or 5-lb. center cut loin of pork
flour
salt and pepper
2 medium onions
1 carrot
1 stalk of celery with leaves
sprigs of parsley
thyme or marjoram
1 bay leaf
1 cup boiling water or more
brown sugar

Rub the loin of pork with salt and pepper and dust well with flour. Make a bed of chopped onions and carrot in a roasting pan. Then tie together celery, parsley, and herbs and place them in pan to flavor basting juices. Place pork loin, fat side up, in the bed of vegetables and pour the cup of boiling water into the pan. In a moderate oven, roast for 2 1/2 hours or more until the pork is tender. Baste often with juices in pan. Add more water if it is needed. In the last quarter hour of roasting, sprinkle the top of the loin with enough brown sugar to make a nice glaze. Let it color in a fairly hot oven.

To make sauce, remove bunch of herbs and excess fat. Thicken this with flour. Leave vegetable bits in the gravy. Serve with apple sauce, sweet potato pone, and a green such as kale, collards, or spinach.

## AU PETIT PARIS SALAD DRESSING

1 cup salad oil
1/3 cup Burgundy wine
1/3 cup vinegar
1 tsp. poppy seed
1 tsp. coriander
1 tsp. sesame seed
1 tsp. celery seed
1 tsp. dry mustard
1 small clove garlic, crushed

Combine all ingredients, place in jar, and shake well.

## STEAK AU POIVRE AU PETIT PARIS
### (Pepper steak)

Choose a nice cut of New York sirloin strip. Rub meat both sides with a clove of garlic in garlic press. Use fresh ground black pepper and press pepper in meat with back side of a large knife. Season with salt. Broil to desired taste. Place on platter and top with 1 pat of butter. Then flame with 3/4 oz. of heated cognac.

## LES ESCARGOTS BOURGNINNONE

In a mixer, cream 1 lb. of butter. Add 2 tbsp. minced parsley, 2 cloves of garlic, 1/2 tsp. salt, 2 tsp. ground nutmeg, and 1/2 tsp. of fresh ground black pepper. Use this butter to stuff snail shells.

### PREPARATION OF SNAILS:

Use 1 small can of snails. Drain well. Pack snail shells with some of the butter prepared, then a snail, then more of the butter. Cook in hot oven until butter bubbles in shell.

---

## AU PETIT PARIS
## Frostburg

*This French restaurant, located two hours away from Pittsburgh, is first class in every respect. The brick building and basement were converted into a beautiful restaurant by M. St. Marie, the French-Canadian owner and chef.*

## POULET ST. MARIE

1 large chicken breast
onion-flavored cheese
2 to 3 strips crisp bacon
bread crumbs
egg and milk mixture
clarified butter

Chicken breast must be deboned and skinned. Keep hold of chicken breast, and flatten with back side of a cleaver, between 2 sheets of freezer wrap or wax paper. Stuff chicken breast with 1 square of cheese and chopped, crisp bacon. Fold together, keeping seams at bottom. Season with salt and white pepper. Dust with flour. Dip in egg and milk mixture, then in bread crumbs. Sauté in clarified butter, bottom of chicken first, approximately 10 minutes each side.

## POULET MADEIRA

1 whole chicken breast, deboned and skinned

---

Flatten each side of breast between 2 sheets of freezer wrap or wax paper with the flat side of a cleaver. Season lightly with salt and white pepper and powdered rosemary. Dust with flour; then sauté in clarified butter. Serve the breast on white or wild rice. Then top each breast with Sauce Madeira.

### SAUCE MADEIRA:

1 cup Madeira wine
1 sprig parsley
1 small carrot, thinly sliced
1/2 tsp. lemon juice
grated zest of 1 orange and the juice of 1 orange
2 pinches powdered thyme

Cook ingredients over low heat until reduced by approximately one half. Strain the sauce through fine cheesecloth and add 3/4 cup of brown sauce.

### BEIGNETS

1/4 lb. butter
1/2 cup water
1 cup flour
1 tsp. sugar
1 dash salt
4 eggs

In a saucepan melt butter with the water. After butter is completely melted, add sugar and salt. Briefly over the heat, add flour and stir rapidly until the ingredients form a ball. Remove from heat. Place dough in large mixing bowl and beat in with wooden spoon 4 eggs one at a time, until completely absorbed within the dough. Using a spoon to dip out batter, drop in deep fat 375° to 400°. Cook until puffed and golden brown. Then dip in powdered sugar.

## STRAWBERRIES ROMANOFF

1 qt. strawberries
1/3 cup powdered sugar
1/2 lemon, squeezed and strained
1 1/2 oz. Grand Marnier
1 1/2 pts. heavy whipping cream

Thoroughly wash and strain strawberries. Remove stems; slice in half. Place strawberries in a bowl. Add sugar, lemon juice, and Grand Marnier. Marinate for about 30 minutes. Fold strawberries into whipped cream. Serve in champagne glass or a deep glass dessert dish. Garnish with a large fresh strawberry on top. Serves 4.

## SHRIMP CURRY MAHARADJA

20 large shrimp
1/4 cup onions
1/4 cup leeks
1/4 cup celery
1/4 cup mushrooms
1/4 cup pineapple and 4 pineapple rings
1/4 cup apples
1/4 cup bananas
1 tbsp. mango chutney
2 tbsp. lemon juice
1 tsp. Worcestershire sauce
1 tsp. salt
1 tsp. pepper
6 tsp. curry powder
2 tbsp. flour
1/4 cup white wine
1/4 cup pineapple juice
1 pt. heavy cream

Sauté onions, leeks, celery, mushrooms, pineapples, apples, and bananas in butter. Add flour and curry powder.

## SAMUEL OWINGS 1767
## Owings Mills

*This is one of America's best restaurants, with elegant dining in elegant surroundings. The very finest cuisine is lovingly prepared and served. Samuel Owings 1767 is the winner of many coveted awards.*

Add white wine, pineapple juice, and heavy cream. Bring to boil and add rest of seasonings. Serves 4.

## FRESH MUSHROOMS STUFFED WITH CRABMEAT

24 medium-size fresh mushrooms
16 oz. Alaskan king crabmeat
2 pts. heavy whipping cream
2 lemons
2 oz. white wine
1/2 oz. Pernod
salt, white pepper, cayenne pepper, and Worcestershire sauce
1/4 lb. melted butter and 1/4 lb. flour mixed together (roux)

Take stems out of mushrooms. Boil caps for 20 minutes; then chop stems very fine. Place in stainless pot with 1 tbsp. butter and sauté for 5 minutes. Add white wine, crabmeat, and heavy cream. Bring to boiling point. Bind mixture with roux, season with lemon juice, salt, white pepper, a pinch of cayenne pepper, Worcestershire sauce, and Pernod. Fill mushroom caps and place in hot oven until golden brown. Serves 4.

## SPINACH SALAD WITH CRISP BACON

1 lb. thoroughly washed leaf spinach (without stems)
4 large mushrooms
4 shallots
6 slices bacon
1 oz. red wine, vinegar, oil, salt, pepper, thyme, oregano to taste

Place raw spinach leaves in large wooden bowl. Add sliced raw mushrooms and chopped shallots. Mix with oil and vinegar dressing. Place fine diced bacon in frying pan and cook until crisp. Pour hot bacon and fat over spinach. Toss and serve immediately. Serves 4.

## MARINATED HERRING BONNE FEMME

8 marinated herring
1 apple
1 onion
1 cucumber pickle
1 cup sour cream
1 pt. heavy whipping cream
1/2 lemon, squeezed and strained
salt, pepper, and Worcestershire sauce

Place herring filets on a bed of lettuce leaves. Slice apple, onion, and pickle very thin. Mix with sour cream. Add heavy whipping cream. Season with lemon juice, salt, pepper, and Worcestershire sauce. Pour over herring filets. Garnish with hard-boiled egg slices, black olives, and tomato wedges.

## SCALLOPED OYSTERS

1 pt. oysters
1/2 cup oleo
2 cups cracker crumbs
1 pt. sweet milk
salt and pepper to taste

Drain oysters in colander. Place a layer of oysters, then a layer of cracker crumbs in casserole. Add 1/4 stick oleo. Pour milk over this and bake 15 minutes.

## RICE CASSEROLE

Melt 1/4 lb. of butter in a pan. Sauté 4 chopped green onions in butter until they are light brown. Add 2 cans mushroom soup and juice from a 4-oz. can of mushrooms. Blend together. Pour this mixture over 4 cups of cooked rice in a casserole. Then add a layer of 10 oz. of grated sharp cheese, a drained 4-oz. can of mushrooms, and 1 cup of chopped, toasted almonds. Bake in 350° oven until casserole is heated through. Serves 10.

## CELERY CASSEROLE

2 cups chopped celery
1 can chicken broth
1/4 cup chopped pimento
5-oz. can mushrooms
slivered water chestnuts
1 can cream of chicken soup

Boil chopped celery and chicken broth for 8 minutes. Mix in chopped pimento, mushrooms, chestnuts, and cream of chicken soup. Put in casserole dish. Cover top with bread crumbs and dot with oleo. Bake 20 minutes at 350°.

## TURKEY CASSEROLE

2 pkgs. noodles
1 cup chopped green pepper
1 cup chopped celery
4 tbsp. grated onion
garlic
1/2 cup oleo
1/2 cup flour

---

## MENDENHALL HOTEL DINING ROOM
## Mendenhall

*Southern hospitality reigns here. The dining room is known as "home of the revolving tables." An expansive porch with big old-fashioned rocking chairs greets the guests as they enter this unusual hotel of the Old South.*

2 tsp. salt
1/4 tsp. pepper
5 cups milk
4 cups diced turkey
1 cup grated cheese
8 eggs, hard boiled and sliced
2 cans mushrooms
2 cups corn flakes

Cook noodles. Drain. Cook pepper, celery, onions, and garlic in oleo till tender. Blend in flour and seasoning. Add milk and cook till thick. Add turkey, cheese, eggs, and mushrooms. Put half of noodles in casserole. Add half of sauce. Add more noodles, then sauce. Top with corn flakes or bread crumbs. Bake in 350° oven about 30 minutes.

## REMOULADE SAUCE FOR SHRIMP

1 cup French dressing (orange)
1 cup creole mustard
2 tbsp. paprika
1 tbsp. horseradish
1 tbsp. grated onion
small clove garlic, crushed
juice of 1 lemon
1 tsp. Worcestershire sauce
1/2 tsp. celery salt

Combine ingredients in a jar and shake well. Serve over cold boiled shrimp.

---

## HARVARD BEETS

1 #2 can sliced beets, drained
1/2 cup white sugar
1/2 cup white vinegar
1 level tbsp. cornstarch

Dissolve cornstarch in beet juice. Add to remaining ingredients and cook over slow heat until glazed, about 30 minutes. Serves 6.

## CARAMEL PIE

1/2 cup browned sugar
1 cup sugar
2 heaping tbsp. cornstarch
pinch salt
3 eggs, separated
2 cups sweet milk
1/2 stick butter or oleo
1 tsp. vanilla

Caramelize 1/2 cup sugar in skillet. Mix other sugar, cornstarch, salt, egg yolks, and warm milk. Add to browned sugar in skillet. Add butter and cook until thick. Add vanilla. Pour in baked pie crust and top with meringue from 3 egg whites. Bake in 300° oven until meringue browns.

## CHOCOLATE PIE

1/3 cup flour
3/4 cup sugar
2 heaping tbsp. cocoa
1/4 tsp. salt
2 cups milk
2 eggs, separated
3 tbsp. butter or oleo
1 tbsp. vanilla

Combine flour, sugar, salt, and cocoa. Add a little milk to thin the egg yolks. Beat milk and egg mixture and add to dry ingredients. Put on stove and add remaining milk and butter. Cook until thick and add vanilla. Pour in baked pie crust and top with meringue. Bake in 300° oven until meringue browns.

## OLD SOUTHERN STUFFED BAKED HAM
*(Recipe over 100 years old)*

10 to 12-lb. ham
1 tbsp. vinegar
2 tbsp. brown sugar
steaming water

Cut off ham hock. Add vinegar and brown sugar to water and steam ham until meat is tender enough to feel loose at the bone. Remove bone and all fat. Reserve a cup of the fat. Fill bone cavity with dressing. Cover outside of ham about 2 1/2 inches thick with remaining dressing. Wrap securely in cheesecloth and tie tightly with cord. Bake at 300° for one-half hour. Chill 24 hours and slice very thinly.

## DRESSING:

1 cup ground ham fat
1 lb. ground, toasted crackers
1 small loaf toasted bread, ground
2 tbsp. sugar
1 tsp. mustard seed
1 tsp. dry mustard
1 stalk celery, ground
2 medium onions, ground
1/2 cup pickle relish
1 tbsp. chopped parsley
4 eggs, beaten
1 cup sherry wine
4 dashes Tabasco sauce
vinegar to make pastelike consistency, not too soft

Thoroughly combine all ingredients. Stuff the ham as directed.

## TWENTY-FOUR HOUR COCKTAIL

1/2 cup lemon juice
2 qts. orange juice
1 qt. pineapple juice
1 qt. grapefruit juice
1 cup grenadine
1 qt. good bourbon whiskey

Stir mixture. Put in refrigerator overnight or longer. Shake a little before serving. No ice. Add another cup of whiskey if you like the drink stronger.

---

# OLD SOUTHERN TEA ROOM
## Vicksburg

*This quaint tea room carries on the traditions of delicious Southern cooking and gracious hospitality. Waitresses in bright costumes serve steaming shrimp gumbo, crisp fried chicken, and luscious hot biscuits. This is the place for authentic, old-fashioned Southern cooking.*

## TOMATO ASPIC SALAD

46-oz. can or 6 cups tomato juice
3 medium onions, quartered
3 strips celery
3 tbsp. vinegar
1 tbsp. Worcestershire sauce
juice of 2 lemons
3 bay leaves
1 tsp. sugar
salt, red pepper, and Tabasco sauce
5 tbsp. gelatin added to 1 cup water

Put all ingredients except gelatin onto heat. Let come to a boil. Then take off fire and add gelatin that has been in 1 cup water. Strain into molds. After this has cooled to lukewarm, drop in each mold a cheese ball, which has been made by mixing the following ingredients:

2 3-oz. pkgs. Philadelphia cream cheese
1 tsp. grated onion
2 tsp. pickle relish
2 tbsp. mayonnaise
2 tsp. chili sauce
red pepper sauce, to taste

Mold into shape of balls. Let molds set in refrigerator for at least 6 hours. Unmold. Serve on lettuce leaf with dab of mayonnaise. Decorate with sprig of parsley and carrot curls.

---

## VICKSBURG CHRISTMAS EGG NOG

1 doz. eggs
1 qt. whipping cream
3/4 qt. whiskey
24 oz. powdered sugar

Beat yolks with electric mixer, or until very light; add sugar gradually. Add whiskey slowly a little at a time until it gets thin, then increase. This can be done the day before and the whipped cream and stiffly beaten egg whites added just before serving.

## WHISKEY BALLS

small pkg. Vanilla Wafers
1 cup powdered sugar
1/4 cup whiskey
1 cup pecans
3 tbsp. white Karo

Crush wafers, and add other ingredients as they are listed. Roll into small balls, then roll in sifted powdered sugar.

## STUFFED BELL PEPPERS CREOLE

16 large peppers
2 cloves garlic, chopped
4 onions, chopped
1/2 cup butter or margarine
1 cup chopped ham
1 cup water
1 cup tomato juice
1 #2 can tomatoes
2 eggs, well beaten
4 cups cracker crumbs
salt and pepper to taste
1 tsp. sugar
bread crumbs
melted butter or margarine
dash of paprika

Chop 4 of the peppers, leaving in seeds. Sauté in butter with garlic and onions until tender. Add ham, water, tomato juice, and tomatoes. Cook until liquid is absorbed. Stir in eggs and cracker crumbs. Season to taste. Cut off tops and remove seeds from remaining 12 peppers. Parboil with sugar until slightly tender. Stuff with tomato mixture. Cover lightly with bread crumbs, butter, and a sprinkle of paprika. Bake at 350° for about 20 minutes until peppers are piping hot. Serves 12.

## RAVIOLINI ALLA PANA

1 lb. raviolini
1/2 stick butter
4 whole mushrooms, sliced
1/2 shot cognac
1 pt. half-and-half
2 oz. prosciutto ham, sliced thin, then diced
1 pinch nutmeg
2 tsp. chopped parsley
3/4 cup Parmesan reggiano cheese
salt and fresh ground pepper to taste

In medium skillet, melt butter. Add mushrooms and ham and sauté for 2 minutes. Add other ingredients except cheese. Let simmer until hot. Do not boil. Set aside. In medium pot, boil lightly salted water; add raviolini. When raviolini comes to the top, drain water from pot. Add other ingredients. Blend well, add cheese, and serve hot. If raviolini becomes too thick, add more warm cream. The dish should be creamy. Serves four.

## RED SNAPPER ALLA LIVORNESE

24 oz. fillet snapper
2 large ripe tomatoes, peeled and chopped
1 medium clove garlic, mashed
1 small onion, chopped
2 oz. capers
4 whole mushrooms, chopped
1 oz. olive oil
1/2 cup white wine
chopped parsley
salt to taste
red pepper to taste

In medium skillet, sauté onion in oil to golden color. Add all ingredients and let simmer for about 8 minutes. Place snapper in baking dish and pour sauce over the fish. Cover with foil and bake for 10 to 15 minutes in 500° oven. Italian rice goes well with this dish. Serves four.

## APPLE FLAMBÉ

3 apples, cored, peeled and thinly sliced
1/4 stick butter
juice of 1 lemon plus half of lemon rind, grated

---

# DOMINIC'S
## St. Louis

*Owner Dominic Galati is the prime reason for the great success of this elegant restaurant. "Unsurpassed for sheer mood and elegance," praise the critics. It is often rated one of the outstanding restaurants of the world. The entry area is covered with major awards bestowed upon this exceptional gourmet restaurant. Menu selections are prepared tableside, enticing the diner's eye and palate. Dominic's intimately romantic yet exciting atmosphere combines with great food and service to create an unquestionably superior dining experience.*

3/4 cup water
4 tsp. sugar
1 cinnamon stick
2 oz. apple liquor
1 oz. brandy

Melt butter in large skillet. Add apples and sauté for 2 minutes. Add all ingredients and reduce heat until sauce becomes a syrup. Serve hot over vanilla ice cream. Serves four.

## SPAGHETTI ALLA CARBONARA

1 1/2 lbs. spaghetti
3 eggs
4 tbsp. unsalted butter
1/2 cup warm heavy cream
8 oz. pancetta, chopped
1/2 cup grated parmigiana cheese
1 small onion, chopped
1/2 cup dry white wine
pepper to taste

In skillet, melt butter and sauté onion and pancetta until golden. Add wine. Simmer 2 minutes. In a bowl, beat eggs, cheese, parsley, and pepper. Set aside. Using a large pot, boil water and cook spaghetti for 8 minutes. Strain water and

---

combine ingredients that were sautéed in skillet and mix thoroughly. Then pour in egg mixture and blend together. Serves six.

## CHICKEN CARDINALE

12 boneless chicken breasts
1/4 cup olive oil
1/2 stick unsalted butter
1/2 medium onion, thinly sliced
1 1/2 cups green peas
2 oz. chopped prosciutto
1/2 cup dry white wine
1 cup chicken broth
1/2 cup grated mozzarella cheese
1 pinch saffron
salt and pepper to taste

In skillet, sauté onion in oil until golden. Add ham, peas, saffron, and broth. Simmer 8 minutes. In another skillet, melt butter and sauté chicken breasts about 3 minutes on both sides. Add wine and simmer 3 minutes. In baking dish, place chicken and add the above ingredients over breasts. Top with cheese and bake for 8 or 9 minutes at 475°. Note: This dish should accompany Risotto alla Milanese (see recipe). Serves six.

## RISOTTO ALLA MILANESE

1 lb. Italian rice (rinsed in cold water)
1/2 onion, thinly sliced
1/2 stick unsalted butter
1/2 cup fresh mushrooms, sliced
1/2 cup grated parmigiana cheese
2 qts. chicken or beef broth (boiling hot)
2 oz. bone marrow, chopped
1 pinch saffron
salt and pepper to taste

In casserole, melt one tbsp. of butter and add marrow and onion. Cook slowly to a golden color. Do not burn. Add mushrooms and rice, stirring with a wooden spoon. Slowly add broth. As rice begins to swell and becomes dry, continue to gradually add broth and saffron until rice is cooked and creamy. Add remaining butter, cheese, and parsley. Stir and serve at once. Serves six.

## ARTICHOKES FLORENTINE

4 cups frozen leaf spinach, defrosted
  and well drained
2 tbsp. minced onion
1 tbsp. lemon juice
4 tbsp. melted butter
salt and pepper to taste
nutmeg to taste
2 large artichokes
pinch salt
1 bay leaf
2 tbsp. vegetable oil
juice from 1/2 lemon
1 hard-cooked egg

Chop spinach very fine in a chopper or blender. Combine with onion in mixing bowl. Add lemon juice, 3 tbsp. butter, salt, pepper, and nutmeg to mixture. Adjust seasoning if necessary. Place artichokes in a pan and cover with cold water. Add salt, bay leaf, oil, and lemon juice. (The lemon juice flavors the artichokes and helps preserve the color.) Bring water to slow boil and cook 20 to 40 minutes or until leaves pull out easily. Remove artichokes from water and plunge into cold water to cool quickly and preserve the color. Preheat oven to 350°. Split artichokes into 2 sections from top to bottom and remove the choke (purple, hairy area) with a spoon or your fingers. Fill each half with the spinach mixture and bake in preheated oven approximately 20 minutes. Baste with remaining melted butter after 10 minutes. Garnish with a slice of hard-cooked egg.

## LETTUCE AND SPINACH SALAD

6 oz. fresh spinach, washed and with
  stems removed
2 heads Bibb or Kentucky limestone
  lettuce, broken in pieces
4 slices fresh bacon, cooked and crumbled
2 hard-cooked eggs, chopped
3 oz. fresh bean sprouts
12 cherry tomatoes
Creamy Anchovy Dressing (see recipe)

Combine spinach and lettuce and portion onto chilled plates. Garnish with remaining ingredients. Serve with dressing.

## CREAMY ANCHOVY DRESSING

1 1/2 cups salad oil
1/2 cup cider vinegar
1 tsp. garlic powder

## ALAMEDA PLAZA
## Kansas City

*This elegant hotel is on one side of the street while the Alameda's sister, the Raphael, is on the opposite. Both are on The Country Club Plaza in the heart of this great city. The atmosphere is just as exciting as the cuisine. The recipes on this page are from Executive Chef Jess Barbosa.*

1/2 tsp. dry English mustard
salt and white pepper to taste
oregano to taste
garlic powder to taste
chopped parsley to taste
2 eggs
2 tsp. anchovy paste

In a bowl, combine all ingredients except eggs and anchovy paste. Beat eggs and anchovy paste together and then beat into the mixture until smooth. This dressing is quite spicy, and it can be used on a variety of greens. Makes 4 cups.

## LEMON SHERBET WITH KIWI

This icy treat cleanses and refreshes the palate. Another name for this type of sherbet is Spoom.

sugar
fresh lime
1 small scoop lemon sherbet
1/2 kiwi fruit, skinned
dash Guyot's Creme de Cassis
1 sprig fresh mint (candied violet can
  be substituted for this, if desired)

Rim a 5- or 6-oz. champagne saucer in sugar, wetting the edges first with a lime. Scoop the lemon sherbet into the glass. Cut the kiwi into slices, cut each slice in half again, and arrange a border around the sherbet. Dot the sherbet with creme de cassis and garnish with fresh mint sprig. (Indent the top of the sherbet with the bowl of a demitasse spoon to collect some of the liqueur on top.) Serves one.

## CHILLED POTAGE SINGAPORE

9 oz. cream cheese, softened to room
  temperature

2 cups canned, undiluted beef consommé
pinch garlic powder
2 tsp. curry powder
light cream as needed
8 sprigs fresh watercress

Place cream cheese in blender and slowly blend in 1 cup consommé. Mix well. Add remaining 1 cup beef consommé, garlic powder, and curry powder. Mix for 1 minute. Chill overnight or at least 2 to 3 hours in a plastic container. The mixture should thicken to consistency of yogurt. Just before serving, thin with cream to the texture of a potage or cream soup. Serve in a champagne saucer or a margarita glass. Garnish with 2 sprigs of fresh watercress. Note: This recipe contains very simple ingredients but the potage ends up tasting quite exotic. It is important to add the consommé very gradually to the softened cream cheese. Makes three cups.

## LOBSTER AMERICAINE

8 tbsp. butter
1/4 cup finely chopped carrots
1/4 cup finely chopped onions
1/4 cup finely chopped celery
2 tbsp. finely chopped fresh parsley
1/2 tsp. saffron
1 bay leaf
2 large tomatoes, peeled, seeded, and
  coarsely chopped (about 3 cups)
1 cup seasoned flour (add 1 tbsp.
  Parmesan cheese)
1/4 cup finely chopped shallots or scallions
1 cup dry white wine
3 oz. tomato juice
4 4-oz. lobster tails
1/2 tsp. lemon juice
1 cup milk

In heavy saucepan, melt 4 tbsp. of the butter over moderate heat. When foam subsides, stir in carrots, onions, and celery. Cook about 5 minutes, then add scallions. Continue cooking another 3 minutes. Add parsley, saffron, which has been soaking in wine. Cook 2 minutes. Set aside. Split lobster tails in half lengthwise and pull meat out. Dip in egg and milk mixture, then dredge in flour. Shake off excess flour. In the skillet cook the tails on one side for about 3 to 4 minutes at moderate heat. Then turn and do the same on the other side until golden brown. When done, pour sauce over and serve. Serves four.

## CHOPPED CHICKEN LIVERS

3 lbs. chicken livers
2 medium onions, chopped
4 hard-boiled eggs
5 tbsp. chicken fat, divided
salt and pepper to taste

Sauté chicken livers in 2 tbsp. of chicken fat until done. Remove from pan and sauté onions in same fat until transparent. Cool. Grind together the livers, onion, and hard-boiled eggs. Add remaining 3 tbsp. chicken fat and mix well. Add salt and pepper to taste. Keep refrigerated.

## PEPPERLOIN A LA CHASE-PARK PLAZA

1 whole beef tenderloin (about 4 lbs.)

MARINADE:

fresh crushed black pepper
rock salt
1 bay leaf
2 sliced onions
1 garlic clove, crushed
1/2 cup oil

Remove membrane and fat from side of the tenderloin. Rub black pepper and rock salt on both sides. Place in pan with remaining herbs and cover with oil. Marinate for 2 to 3 days in refrigerator. Turn once or twice.

Drain and then sear on both sides over hot fire. Finish cooking over slow heat about 25 minutes. Serve with Mustard Sauce (see recipe), baked potatoes, and salad. Serves 8 to 10.

MUSTARD SAUCE:

3 tbsp. chopped onion
2 shallots, chopped
1/2 garlic clove, crushed
2 oz. white wine
12 parsley stems
1 bay leaf
1 clove
1 tbsp. brown sugar
1 cup cider vinegar
3 tbsp. dry mustard
1/2 cup prepared mustard
pinch thyme and oregano
1 qt. demiglace or brown gravy

Sauté onions and shallots slightly. Add remaining ingredients and cook slowly for 30 minutes. Strain. Finish with a dash of Tabasco sauce.

## TENDERLOIN ROOM
## The Chase-Park Plaza Hotel
## St. Louis

*The Tenderloin Room is an excellent dining room, housed in one of the great hotels of the world. The hotel is internationally famous and hosts distinguished visitors from all over the world. It is a world of gracious service, handsome appointments, gourmet restaurants with the Tenderloin Room being its finest. There is a lush Victorian decor. Gold chandeliers shine with dozens of tiny lights, creating an effect of warmth and intimacy. Dining here is an unforgettable experience.*

## CHARCOAL BROILED TENDERLOIN

7- to 8-lb. tenderloin (weight before trimming)
imported olive oil (enough to cover tenderloin)
2 handfuls half-cracked black pepper
1 garlic clove, crushed
1 handful rock salt
3 or 4 bay leaves, crushed

Trim tenderloin. (Remove head, silver, and tail; tenderloin should then weigh about 4 to 5 lbs.) Place in stainless-steel container or crock and cover with olive oil. Let stand for 1 1/2 to 3 days. (It is possible to marinate several tenderloins in the same crock. It is also possible to reuse the olive-oil marinade over and over again until it begins to turn rancid.)

Prepare a mixture of the black pepper, garlic clove, rock salt, and bay leaves. These ingredients should be well mixed. Spread out evenly in a flat pan or tray. Without drying off the oil, roll tenderloin in the mixture of dry ingredients. Place entire tenderloin on hot charcoal broiler. Cook from 15 to 25 minutes depending upon the intensity of the heat and degree of doneness desired.

## CHEESE SOUP À LA CHASE

1 qt. béchamel sauce (see recipe)
1 qt. Cheez Whiz (available in any store)
1 cup white wine
1 medium green pepper, finely diced
2 medium pimentos, finely diced
salt, pepper, and nutmeg to taste
1 oz. butter

Bring béchamel sauce to boil; blend in the Cheez Whiz, stirring with wooden spoon, until mixture comes to a boil. Add wine and seasonings. Sauté green peppers in butter. Add pimentos and peppers just before serving. Serves 10.

## BÉCHAMEL
*(White Sauce)*

2 oz. butter
2 1/2 tbsp. flour
1 qt. warm milk
salt and pepper to taste

Melt butter; add flour and stir well. Pour milk into the roux, stirring constantly. Let simmer 5 minutes. Season to taste. Strain.

## ESCARGOTS AL SOAVE

6 snails
6 shells
6 tsp. snail butter (see recipe)
small amount white wine
1 tbsp. bread crumbs

SNAIL BUTTER:

1 lb. softened butter
2 cloves garlic, put through a press several times
1 shallot, finely chopped
salt and pepper to taste
1 tsp. chopped parsley
1 tsp. Worcestershire sauce
juice of 1/2 lemon
hot sauce to taste

Beat soft butter; add remaining ingredients. Taste for seasoning.

Place some Snail Butter in shells, replace snails, top with more Snail Butter, and sprinkle on bread crumbs. Put platter in 400° oven for 8 minutes. Before serving, sprinkle wine over snails. Makes one serving.

## ROUILLE TOPPING
*(soup or appetizer)*

**5 green peppers, boiled and drained**
**5 canned pimentos, drained and dried**
**10 garlic cloves**
**1 cup olive oil**
**Tabasco to taste**
**salt and pepper to taste**
**2 1/2 slices white bread, trimmed, soaked in water, and squeezed**

Place ingredients in blender. Add olive oil, Tabasco and seasoning. Spread on 1/2-inch thick toast rounds.

## ITALIAN FLAGS

**1 large package cream cheese softened with cream**
**2 slices whole wheat bread**
**1 slice rye bread**
**1 slice white bread**
**1 slice prosciutto**
**1 slice salami**
**1 slice pepperoni**
**red food coloring**

Soften cream cheese to spreading consistency with small quantity of cream. Color one-third of the mixture red, the second third green, and leave remaining third original color. Stack bread with whole wheat on top and bottom, and rye and white bread in center. Layer with colored cream cheeses and meats. Trim crusts. Cut into nine pieces, inserting toothpicks in each.

## PIGNOLATA

**4 eggs**
**1/2 tsp. salt**
**4 cups flour**
**shortening**

Add salt to eggs and blend. Add enough flour to mixture to make a stiff dough. Roll into pencil-thin strips. Cut into half-inch pieces; deep fry until golden brown. Drain well.

### TOPPING:

**1 1/4 cups honey**
**1 cup sugar**
**3 tbsp. crushed stick cinnamon**
**3 small Hershey bars, broken**
**3 cups almonds, toasted and chopped**

Cook sugar and honey together 5 minutes after bringing to boil. Pour half the cinnamon and half the nuts over fried dough. Stir until well blended and all pieces are well coated. Mount onto platter lined with Saran Wrap. Sprinkle with remaining cinnamon, nuts, and broken chocolate bits.

---

# KEMOLL'S
## St. Louis

*Kemoll's has become synonymous with fine dining in the Italian tradition. Established in 1927, it is now an institution in this great city on the Mississippi. The recipes were taught to Mrs. Kemoll by her mother who learned them in her native Italy. This restaurant is a winner of many awards of recognition.*

## GNOCCLI ALLA CREAMA

**2 cups milk**
**1/4 tsp. salt**
**1/8 stick butter**
**2 1/2 cups flour**
**4 eggs**
**1/8 tsp. nutmeg**
**1/4 cup grated Parmesan cheese**

Place milk, salt, and butter into a pot and bring to a boil. Add flour all at once and cook slowly until mixture comes away from pot. Remove from heat. Add eggs, one at a time, nutmeg, and Parmesan cheese.

Push through pastry tube into skillet with slightly salted water. Drain and place in casserole. Top with Mornay Sauce (see recipe) and grated cheese. Preheat before serving.

## MORNAY SAUCE

**1/2 stick butter**
**4 tbsp. flour**
**1 1/2 cup hot milk**
**1/2 cup cream**
**salt to taste**
**1 egg yolk**
**1/4 cup cream**
**1/2 cup Gruyère cheese**

Combine butter and flour and heat. Then add milk, 1/2 cup cream, and salt. Continue cooking slowly until thickened, stirring constantly. Remove from heat and add egg yolk, 1/4 cup cream, and Gruyère cheese. Stir until smooth and creamy.

## PASTA VERDE
*(Green Noodles)*

**1 11-oz. package frozen chopped spinach**
**1 egg**
**1 cup flour (semolina is best)**

**1/4 lb. butter**
**1/2 cup grated Parmesan cheese**
**1/4 cup whipping cream**

Prepare spinach according to directions. Drain well and squeeze dry. Grind two or three times, using fine blade of food chopper. Mix in flour and egg. Turn onto lightly floured surface. Knead with more flour. Roll and cut (or pass through pasta noodle machine).

## SPIEDINI ALLA GRIGLIA

**3 2-oz. pieces of veal**
**3 thin slices prosciutto**
**3 thin slices provolone cheese**
**olive oil**
**seasoned bread crumbs**
**bay leaf**
**2 slices onion**

Flatten veal. Cover each piece with a slice of prosciutto and provolone cheese. Roll and dip in olive oil and bread crumbs. Thread on skewer with bay leaf and slice of onion between each piece of veal. Broil about 15 minutes, turning once.

## STUFFED ARTICHOKES

### ITALIAN CRUMBS:

**1 cup bread crumbs**
**1/2 cup grated Parmesan cheese**
**1 garlic clove, chopped**
**1/2 medium onion, chopped**
**1/4 cup parsley, chopped**
**salt and pepper to taste**

**2 artichokes**
**4 anchovies**
**Italian Crumbs (see recipe)**
**1 egg**
**1/4 cup olive oil**
**salt**

Break about two layers of outer leaves off artichokes. Cut 1/2 inch off top. Cut the stem leaving 1/2 inch of it on. Pound artichokes on the table to spread leaves; then wash and drain. Cut anchovies into 1/2-inch pieces and place in bottom of leaves. Put about 1 tsp. Italian Crumbs in each leaf. Beat egg and pour half into skillet. Turn artichoke down on egg and keep turning until all of artichoke is coated with egg. Remove from skillet and place them upright close together in a small pot. Add water to within one-half inch of top of artichoke. Salt to taste (about 1/2 tsp.). Cook about 50 minutes until leaves can be pulled out easily. Serves two.

## VAN CLIBURN SALAD

1 clove garlic
2 or 3 anchovies
fresh ground pepper
dry mustard (Coleman's preferred)
1 oz. vegetable or olive oil
juice of 1 lemon
dash vinegar
2 tbsp. Durkee's Sauce (obtainable in
    all stores)
romaine lettuce
1 hard-cooked egg, grated

Break garlic clove into small bits in wooden salad bowl. Rub bits of garlic into bottom of bowl until they disappear—the garlic flavor will permeate the other ingredients. Put the anchovies in and blend them into a paste. Grind pepper over the paste and blend it all with a spoon, spreading it over the bottom of the bowl. Add two pinches of dry mustard, the salad oil, and a dash of vinegar. Add lemon juice and Durkee's Sauce. Blend all until it is a runny liquid with no chunks. Place torn pieces of romaine into the bowl and toss (romaine is strong and stands up well). Then sprinkle the egg on top of salad, tossing again. Serves 4.

## SOLE DE GLARE

This is a quick and easy dish that tastes as if it took all day to make.

1/4 lb. butter
1 onion, peeled and diced into small
    pieces
1 tomato, peeled and diced
fresh ground pepper
1 sprig parsley, peeled and diced
4 fillets of sole
2 oz. Sauterne wine

To peel tomato easily, first drop into boiling water for 30 seconds. Take it out and peel will slip off. Melt butter in frying pan. Add fillets, skin side up. When they turn white around the edges, turn them over and let cook in the butter, moving them around in pan so they will not stick. Spoon about 2 tbsp. onion and then 2 tbsp. diced tomato over each fillet. Let fish cook 3 or 4 minutes more. Pour some white wine over the fillets and grind pepper over that. Tilt the pan and

---

## BRETTON'S RESTAURANT
### Kansas City

*Bretton's is one of Kansas City's finest restaurants. Owner Joseph Duran is the prime reason for its success. His cuisine is only the best. Attractive decor and an exciting atmosphere.*

---

baste the fillets with the liquid in the bottom. When the sole is extremely white, it is done. Carefully remove from pan. (Getting it out in one piece is difficult.) When the sole is on the plates, spoon more butter sauce over the top and sprinkle parsley over each fillet. (Four three-ounce fillets will be appetizers for four people. If using as a main dish, double the recipe.)

## BEEF HALANE

This beef dish was named after two of owner Joseph Duran's friends, Jack Halper and S. Harvey Bud Laner, who first tested it. It is a combination of Beef Wellington and Beef Stroganoff.

1/4 lb. butter
1 12-oz. sirloin steak
1/3 cup beef consommé
1/3 tbsp. rosemary
1 tsp. sage
1/2 onion, diced
2 pinches dry mustard
2 or 3 tbsp. brandy
1 oz. cream
1 tsp. chopped parsley
2 tbsp. mushrooms

Remove fat from steak and slice almost all the way through the center, leaving a little piece connected on one side. Open it out so that the two halves form a butterfly shape. Melt butter in frying pan. Add rosemary, 1/2 tsp. of the sage, diced onion, and mustard. Pour in brandy (this will release the flavor of the spices). Light the sauce so it ignites, burning out the alcohol in the brandy.

---

Sauté steak in the sauce and cook to desired doneness. Remove steak and add mushrooms to the pan; then add cream and consommé and simmer until hot. Add remaining sage and pour sauce over the steak. Sprinkle parsley on top. Serves 1.

## CREPES SUZETTE

6 to 8 eggs
1/2 cup cooking oil
1/2 cup cream
1 to 1 1/2 cups sifted flour

Whip eggs, cooking oil, and cream together in a mixing bowl. Add flour and stir until batter is thickened but still runny. Preheat a pan on the stove and rub it with a cloth that has butter rubbed into it. Ladle the batter into the pan, tilting so the batter covers the whole bottom. Pour the loose batter that doesn't stick to the pan back into the bowl. What is left is the crepe, which should be cooked on only one side. To remove from pan, put a towel on the counter and tap the pan on the towel until the crepe falls out. This makes 16 to 18 crepes to be used in the sauce.

## SAUCE:

1/4 lb. butter
1/2 cup honey
2 oranges
1 lemon
6 sugar cubes
1 oz. Cointreau
1 oz. brandy

Melt butter in frying pan and add honey (used because it neutralizes the alcohol taste and won't burn as would sugar). Rub a sugar cube over the skin of an orange, breaking the buds of the skin. (This releases the citric acid into the sugar cube, turning it slightly orange.) Do this with four sugar cubes, add them to the pan, and then squeeze the oranges into the pan. Do the same thing with the lemon and the other two sugar cubes and squeeze the lemon into the pan. Stir the mixture so the sugar cubes are dissolved. Put the crepes in the sauce and roll them, holding them steady with a spoon as they are rolled.

## LOBSTER ALBANELLO

2 lb. fresh lobster meat
1 lb. sliced fresh mushrooms
butter
6 shallots, chopped
4 oz. fish stock
1 qt. heavy cream
8 oz. dry white wine

Sauté lobster meat and mushrooms in butter with the shallots. Add fish stock, cream, and wine and cook until sauce is well blended. Garnish with parsley. Serve with a chilled white wine and tossed green salad. Serves 4.

## PASTA CON PESCE

1 lb. pasta (preferably homemade)
5 oz. lobster meat
5 oz. crabmeat
5 oz. shrimp

## TONY'S
## St. Louis

*Most anyone in this great city will tell you that Tony's is the best restaurant in town. It prides itself on doing things just right, on cooking and serving food with a very special touch.*

2 oz. sliced fresh mushrooms
1 tomato, peeled and seeded
2 tbsp. chopped fresh parsley
1 tsp. chopped shallots
1 lb. butter
salt and pepper to taste

Cook pasta until not quite done. Drain. Add butter, tomatoes, mushrooms, and shallots. Stir until butter is creamy, then add the seafood and parsley. Season to taste. Stir until piping hot and serve on preheated plates.

## VEAL PIEMONTESE

24 very thin veal scallops (about 2 oz. each)
2 cups sliced artichoke bottoms
1/4 lb. butter
6 oz. white wine
6 oz. veal stock (or beef bouillon)
3 cups heavy cream
salt and pepper

Lightly flour and sauté the veal scallops and artichokes in butter. Pour off butter and add wine; reduce to half, then add cream and veal stock. Season to taste. Remove scallops from pan and arrange on platter. Reduce cream and stock to half, then pour over scallops. Serve with risotto or pasta with butter. Serves 4.

## RACK OF LAMB ORIENTAL

2 2-lb. single lamb racks, well trimmed
salt and pepper
Dijon mustard
2 shallots, finely chopped
1/2 garlic clove
olive oil
2 tbsp. finely chopped parsley
1 cup bread crumbs
2 tbsp. melted butter

Season racks with salt and pepper. Roast racks for 20 minutes in preheated 375-degree oven. Remove and brush tops with Dijon mustard. Make up a bread crumbs mixture by sautéing shallots and garlic in small amount of olive oil until soft. Then blend in the parsley and bread crumbs. Sprinkle tops of racks with mixture to cover completely. Dot top of mixture with melted butter (1 tbsp. for each rack). Return racks to oven until bread mixture is golden brown. Serves eight.

## SPINACH PIE

7 green onions, tops and all, chopped
3 tbsp. minced parsley
1/4 cup olive oil
1 pkg. frozen chopped spinach
2 cups cottage cheese
1 cup crumbled feta cheese
1/4 cup ground Parmesan cheese
2 eggs, lightly beaten
salt and white pepper to taste

Sauté onions and parsley in olive oil. Cook spinach according to directions and drain well. Add spinach to onion and parsley mixture. Mix remainder of ingredients in separate container. Mix thoroughly. Then combine the two mixtures together thoroughly and bake in a *covered* pie shell for approximately 30 minutes or until filling is firm.

## MEDITERRANEAN RICE DRESSING

2 tbsp. melted butter
1 small onion, finely chopped
8 oz. lean ground beef
4 fresh tomatoes, peeled, seeded, and chopped (or 1 cup canned tomatoes)
3 tbsp. raisins
3 tbsp. pine nuts (or chopped pecans)
1 tsp. ground cinnamon
1 bay leaf
1 1/2 cups uncooked rice
3 cups chicken stock (or water)
1 1/2 tsp. salt
pepper to taste
1 tbsp. butter

---

### THE LODGE OF THE FOUR SEASONS
### Lake Ozark

*This is Mid-America's finest spa and resort. It is located on the scenic Lake of the Ozarks. Friendliness and graciousness abound. A strikingly beautiful dining room serves the very finest American-style food.*

Melt butter in ovenproof casserole. Add onion and cook until transparent. Add beef and cook until brown. Add tomatoes, raisins, pine nuts, cinnamon, bayleaf, and rice and mix well. Add *boiling* stock, and salt and pepper. Cover tightly. Bring to boil and then place in 375-degree oven for 20 to 22 minutes. Pour rice onto hot platter, then toss with a long-tined fork, adding the butter as you toss. Serves 6.

## TOMATO FLORENTINE

6 medium-size fresh tomatoes
salt
1/2 cup light cream
1 egg yolk
16 oz. fresh spinach, cooked, chopped, and drained well
1 tbsp. butter
salt
butter
pimento or mushroom caps

Cut tops from tomatoes about 1/4 inch. Remove seeds and juice by gently pressing the cut side. Sprinkle with salt. In saucepan, combine cream and egg yolk. Add spinach and butter. Salt to taste. Heat and stir just to simmering stage. Fill tomatoes with spinach mixture. Dot with butter. Garnish tops with small round cutouts of pimento or mushroom caps. Cover and bake in 350-degree oven for 15 minutes. Serves 6.

## MARINATED MUSHROOMS TOLEDO ROOM

2 oz. shallots, finely chopped
1/2 cup olive oil
1/2 cup dry white wine
1/2 cup water
juice of 2 lemons
1/2 tsp. coriander
1/2 tsp. rosemary
2 parsley sprigs
1 bay leaf
12 peppercorns

---

2 lbs. mushrooms, washed and trimmed
parsley, lemon wedges, watercress for garnish

Sauté shallots in olive oil over medium heat. Add wine, water, and lemon juice. In cheesecloth bag, tie the coriander, rosemary, parsley, bay leaf, and peppercorns and add to mixture. Boil gently for 10 minutes. Add mushrooms, cover, and simmer for 10 minutes more. Let cool and refrigerate. Serve the mushrooms garnished with chopped parsley, lemon wedge, and small bunches of watercress. Serves 6.

## CHOCOLATE MOUSSE FOUR SEASONS

2 oz. sweet dark chocolate
1/4 cup water
2 oz. Curaçao
1/2 tsp. vanilla extract
1/2 cup powdered sugar
3 egg yolks
1 1/2 cups whipping cream
6 tbsp. sugar
3 egg whites

Melt chocolate in double boiler. Add water, Curaçao, vanilla, and sugar. Heat and stir until a smooth paste is formed. Add egg yolks. Stir until smooth. Remove from heat and let stand until quite cool. Whip cream until double in volume. At the last moment, add sugar and fold the whipped cream into the cool chocolate mixture. Beat egg whites until stiff and fold into mixture. Portion the mousse into champagne glasses. Chill. Before serving, garnish each with a rosette of whipped cream topped with chocolate shavings and then dust with powdered sugar. Serves 6.

## OZARK CARROT CAKE

2 cups sugar
1 1/2 cups vegetable oil
4 eggs, beaten well
2 cups cake flour
2 tsp. baking soda
1 tsp. salt
2 tsp. ground cinnamon
3 cups grated carrots
1 cup chopped pecans

Into mixing bowl put sugar, oil, and eggs and beat well. Sift together the cake flour, baking soda, salt, and cinnamon and add to mixture slowly while beating. When mixture is well blended, add carrots and pecans. Pour mixture into two 9- X 2-inch cake pans that have been lightly brushed with shortening and dusted with flour. Bake for 40 to 45 minutes in preheated 325-degree oven. Remove and cool before icing.

## WONDERFUL CATSUP HONEY DRESSING
*(For fruit plates, and fruit and vegetable salads)*

1 cup salad oil
1/2 cup catsup
1/3 cup vinegar
1/3 cup honey
1 tsp. salt
1 tsp. paprika
1 tsp. grated onion
1 garlic clove

In bowl or electric mixer bowl, place salad oil, catsup, vinegar, honey, salt, paprika, and grated onion. Beat thoroughly with rotary beater or with electric mixer on medium speed until well blended. Add garlic and let stand about 10 minutes or until ready to use. Beat again just before serving (this is important) and remove garlic when it has flavored the dressing. Store in refrigerator. (Beat mixture every time you use it.) Makes 2 1/2 cups. Serve with a fruit plate or with fruit salad.

## CHEESECAKE

1 lb. cream cheese
2 oz. butter
3 1/2 oz. granulated sugar
1/2 tsp. salt
3 eggs
1/2 oz. Drambuie

Blend cream cheese and butter together, then add other ingredients. Put filling in a 9-inch graham-cracker-lined pie pan and bake in 350-degree oven for 20 to 25 minutes. Cool cake thoroughly. Dust with nutmeg. Cover entire top with sweetened sour cream, garnish with fresh, small strawberries, and glaze with currant jelly.

## PLAZA INN
## Kansas City

*The Plaza Inn is one of Kansas City's and the nation's finest hotels. It is located on the Country Club Plaza. Its dining rooms serve the best cuisine. The decor and surroundings are unusually beautiful.*

### CHICKEN MARTINIQUE

1 large spring chicken, boiled (use breast only, boned and cut into 1-inch cubes)
1 small can sliced mushrooms (or 12 fresh mushrooms)
1 pt. chicken stock
1/2 pt. cream
2 oz. sherry
1 oz. Cointreau
2 fresh pineapples
toasted coconut
toasted almonds, blanched and sliced
3 oz. butter
3 oz. flour
8 oz. Major Gray's chutney
8 oz. steamed rice

Split pineapples in half lengthwise, then hollow out enough to leave 3/4 in shell. Score what remains in the shell and leave remaining meat in place in shell. Mince removed pineapple and use in chicken mixture. Boil chicken in covered pot in least amount of water possible so as to obtain a rich stock. Make a roux with butter and flour; add hot stock, minced pineapple, and cream. Simmer gently, then add remaining ingredients and cook until well blended. Place mixture in the hollowed pineapple halves and bake in moderate oven on rock salt until pineapple hulls are thoroughly heated. Sprinkle generously with toasted coconut and almonds. Remove to china platter, wrap all in amber-col-ored cellophane, and tie top with red ribbon. Serve with chutney and steamed rice. Serves 4.

### TURBOT BONNE FEMME

8- to 10-oz. filet of turbot
1 shallot, peeled and chopped
1 pinch chopped parsley
1 oz. minced mushrooms
2 oz. white wine
2 oz. reduced fish stock
salt and white pepper
1 oz. Hollandaise sauce
1 oz. fish velouté

Place vegetables in buttered pan. Place turbot on top. Add remaining ingredients and bake in hot oven. Baste frequently. When fish is done, remove from pan. Add velouté to pan and reduce slightly. Remove pan from heat. Add Hollandaise sauce and blend. Pour sauce over fish on platter and glaze quickly under broiler. Garnish with lemon slice and parsley sprigs.

### SALMON MOUSSE

4 1/2 lbs. cooked boned salmon
3/4 lb. softened butter
3 egg whites, whipped
3 cups whipping cream, whipped
salt and pepper to taste
6 tbsp. gelatin (well dissolved in stock from salmon)

Cook salmon with salt and pepper. Save stock to make aspic for coating. Leave salmon in refrigerator until well chilled. Remove all skin and bones. Add egg whites and cream, then turn into loaf mould to set. When set, turn loaf onto platter. Using head and tail pieces, shape into natural form. Decorate and then coat with clear, seasoned fish aspic. Use remaining mousse to cut into fancy shapes. Garnish and coat with aspic and place around the large mousse.

## ROCK CORNISH GAME HENS STUFFED WITH WILD RICE

4 Rock Cornish hens
1 cup cooked wild rice
1 cup cooked long-grain white rice
1/2 cup sliced fresh mushroom
2 tsp. sage
2 tbsp. chopped parsley
salt and pepper

Combine rices, mushroom, sage, and parsley in a deep bowl. Salt and pepper to taste. Wash game hens inside and out; sprinkle them lightly inside with salt and pepper. Stuff the body cavities of the birds with rice mixture and close the openings with skewers. Place the stuffed birds in a roasting pan and baste with the following liquid. In a saucepan place 1 cup clarified butter, 1/2 cup orange juice, and 1/4 cup dry vermouth. Heat slowly and blend together. Roast the birds in a 350° oven for 1 hour, basting often. When hens are fully cooked turn oven to 450° and brown for 5 to 7 minutes. Serve immediately.

## PEPPERED CHICKEN

2 chickens, cut in 4 pieces each and boned
3 cups white sauce
2 large bell peppers, sliced in thin rings
3 oz. diced pimento
1/2 cup soy sauce
1 tsp. white pepper

---

## FOXFIRE GOLF & COUNTRY CLUB
## Pinehurst

*The elegantly decorated dining room of this 2000-acre Shangri-la in the Carolina sandhills offers outstanding cuisine and service. It overlooks two beautiful lakes with a picturesque view of several greens and fairways.*

Combine all ingredients in a large casserole and add the boned chicken. Cover and bake in 325° oven for 45 minutes. Serve with rice pilaf.

## SAVORY SHRIMP FROMAGE

2 cups deveined, peeled salad shrimp
1/2 cup each onion and celery
1/2 cup clarified butter
3 1/2 cup Cheddar cheese sauce
1/2 tsp. each salt and white pepper
4 coconuts with tops cut off

Sauté onion and celery in clarified butter until they are soft. Add shrimp, cheese sauce, salt, and pepper and heat slowly. When hot, put mixture in coconut shells and place in 300° oven for 8 minutes. Serve immediately with hot white rice.

---

## COOL TOMATO–HORSERADISH DIP

1 cup drained, finely diced tomatoes
1 cup sour cream
1/3 cup drained horseradish
2 tbsp. chopped chives

Combine all ingredients and chill for 2 hours. Serve with your favorite chips or crackers.

## BEEF-KA-BOB

4 12-inch skewers
1 1/2 lb. tenderloin cut in 1-inch cubes
2 or 3 large onions, cut in 3/4-inch pieces
3 bell peppers, cut in 3/4-inch pieces
12 medium mushrooms
4 medium, firm tomatoes, cut in 4 wedges each

Skewer alternating pieces in the following order: Pepper, meat, mushroom, onion, until the skewer is filled. Let stand 4 hours in a mixture consisting of:

1/2 cup Worcestershire sauce
1/2 cup dry vermouth
1/4 cup finely chopped dill weed
2 cups water
2 cups salad oil

Bake in 350° oven or under broiler until meat is done to your taste.

## DESSERT ALMOND ROLL

In a saucepan, melt 1/4 lb. butter. Stir in 1 cup sugar, 1 cup grated almonds, 1/2 tsp. flour, and a little milk if the mixture looks too dry. Spoon the batter, about 1 tsp. at a time, on a cookie sheet, making sure to leave enough room so the cookies will not merge when they bake. Bake in a 350° oven until they flatten out and brown. Cool until the flat crepes can be lifted and formed, one at a time, into a tube shape around the index fingers. (If too warm, the crepes will wilt; if too cool, they will shatter and break in your hands.) Cover with plastic wrap and set aside. When ready to serve, fill each almond roll with chantilly whipped cream, and place a small rosette of chantilly on top of each. Serves 20 to 24.

## MEDALLIONS OF CALVES' LIVER IN MEUNIERE SAUCE WITH CAPERS AND AVOCADO SLICES

Salt and pepper 2 thinly sliced pieces of calves' liver. Dip them in flour and shake off all the excess flour. Sauté the liver in clarified butter over high heat. Remove the liver slices to a heated plate. Add to the sauté pan about 1 tsp. lemon juice and about 1 tsp. chopped capers. Boil down a moment, scraping up coagulated juices. Spoon the sauce over the liver slices and garnish the liver with 3 thin slices of avocado. Serves 1.

## SETH JONES HOUSE DRESSING

Put into a blender jar:

1 button garlic, peeled and sliced
1 rib celery, scraped and sliced
1/2 medium onion, peeled and sliced
2 oz. drained flat anchovies
1 tsp. black peppercorns
1/2 tsp. sugar
2 tbsp. Dijon mustard
1 tbsp. lemon juice
pinch curry powder

## SETH JONES 1847 RESTAURANT
## Raleigh

*This is certainly one of North Carolina's finest, and the nation's as well. Great emphasis is placed on serving excellent food in a gracious manner. The recipes here were created by chef Claude Cook.*

Blend 30 seconds, then add:

3 eggs

Blend again, then add:

2 cups salad oil

Blend in salad oil in a thin stream, at high speed. Refrigerate until well chilled. Serve tossed with Romaine lettuce leaves *only*, a few watercress sprigs, and an occasional sliver of turnip. Makes 1 quart.

## SEAFOOD THERMIDOR WRAPPED IN CREPES

16 crepes, thin and lightly browned

BATTER:

3 eggs
1 tbsp. flour
1 tsp. salt
1 cup flour
2 cups milk

Mix in a blender.

THERMIDOR FILLING:

4 cups boiled seafood (lobster, scallops, shrimp)

2 cups light cream
4 tbsp. butter
6 egg yolks
1 cup dry sherry
salt and cayenne pepper

Melt butter in large saucepan and add cream. Bring to boil and add all the seafood. When the pot comes to a boil the second time, add the well-beaten egg yolks that have had the sherry and 1 tbsp. of cornstarch beaten into them. Let thicken and season with salt and cayenne pepper. Lay two crepes on a plate and spoon some of the thermidor onto the middle of each. Fold the edges over the thermidor, spoon some of the sauce over both of them, sprinkle lightly with grated Swiss cheese, and slide the plate under the broiler until the cheese has melted and edges of crepes have started to brown. Garnish with a parsley sprig. Serves 8 to 10.

## CRABMEAT REMICK

3 eggs
1 tbsp. wine vinegar
1 tbsp. dry mustard
1 tsp. lemon juice
salt and pepper

Put ingredients in a large mixing bowl. Beat with a wire whisk until it thickens slightly; add oil in a thin stream, whisking constantly, until you achieve the mayonnaise consistency. Then add:

1/2 cup chili sauce
30 drops Tabasco sauce
10 shakes Worcestershire sauce

Whisk until all are blended thoroughly and smoothly. Cover and refrigerate. Spoon some of the sauce over chunks of crabmeat that have been placed on a half-shell. Slide the shell under the broiler. When the sauce on top begins to bubble and brown slightly, remove and sprinkle with parsley and serve immediately. One batch makes enough for 20 to 24 servings.

## PLANTERS CHICKEN

1 whole boneless breast of chicken
1 potato, baked or boiled
1/2 green pepper
3 mushrooms
1 slice cooked ham
1 small onion

Roast breast of chicken for 15 minutes or until done. Dice potato, green pepper, mushrooms, ham, and onion. Sauté in butter until pepper and onion are done. Place on warmed serving plate. Add breast of chicken and top one side with Hollandaise sauce and the other with mushroom sauce. Serves 1.

## MUD PIE

8 oz. chocolate Oreo cookies
1/4 cup melted butter
16 oz. coffee ice cream
4 oz. chocolate fudge

Crush Oreo cookies to very fine consistency. Add melted butter. Line 8-inch pie pan with mixture. Place in freezer for 20 minutes. Meanwhile let ice cream come to semisoft condition. Add this to pie shell and refreeze for 1 hour. Remove from freezer and top with fudge. Serve immediately.

## SHE CRAB SOUP

1 tbsp. butter
1 qt. milk
1/4 pt. cream (whipped)
few drops onion juice
1/8 tsp. mace

## BARBADOES RESTAURANT
## The Mills Hyatt House
## Charleston

*Swiss chef Peter Lindner, winner of many culinary awards, presides over this luxurious restaurant where lazily turning ceiling fans, candlelight, and gourmet cuisine recall Charleston's West Indian origins and the leisurely plantation life of the antebellum South.*

1/8 tsp. pepper
1/2 tsp. Worcestershire sauce
1 tsp. flour
2 cups white crabmeat and crab eggs (if crab eggs are not available substitute an equal amount of crumbled hard-boiled eggs)
1/2 tsp. salt
4 tbsp. dry sherry

Melt butter in top of double boiler and blend with flour until smooth. Add the milk gradually, stirring constantly. To this add crabmeat and eggs and all seasonings except sherry. Cook slowly over hot water for 20 minutes. To serve, place 1 tbsp. of warmed sherry in individual soup bowls, then add soup and top with whipped cream. Sprinkle with paprika or finely chopped parsley. Serves 4 to 6.

## CHICKEN SALAD IN A COCONUT

4 oz. boneless diced chicken breast
1 stalk celery, diced
mayonnaise to taste
curry to taste
4 pineapple chunks
4 pecans
pinch of salt
lime juice to taste

Cut a fresh coconut. Drain milk and place chicken salad in shell. Garnish with fresh fruits and shredded coconut. Serves 1.

## LOW COUNTRY PAELLA

A fascinating version of this famous dish, utilizing the abundant Low Country seafoods and served à la Russe.

1/4 pepper, diced
1 1/2 oz. diced tomato
1 1/2 oz. raw rice
1 oz. small shrimp
2 oz. fresh fish filet
1 oz. scallops
3 mussels or clams
3 slices carrot
1 bay leaf
1 chicken breast, boned and cut up
small clove garlic
pinch of saffron
2 cups chicken broth

Sauté pepper, tomato, rice, carrot, and seasoning in small amout of olive oil until tender. Add fish and chicken. Cover with broth and simmer for 35 minutes. Garnish with June peas and diced pimento. Serves 2.

## FRUIT DUMPLINGS

1 lb. flour
1 tbsp. sugar
1 tbsp. butter
1 cup milk
1 egg yolk
1 tbsp. baking powder
salt
1/2 lb. fresh pitted, skinned peaches or apricots
butter
cottage cheese

Add sugar and baking powder to 1/2 cup milk. In another bowl, combine flour, milk, butter, and egg yolk and mix until a thick dough is formed. Let stand 30 minutes. Then roll dough and cut into 4 pieces. Put fruit in middle of each piece and roll up. Cook dumplings in boiling salted water, covered, for 5 to 10 minutes. Remove. Dot with butter and cottage cheese. Serves 4.

## PORK ROLLS WITH CORNBREAD DRESSING

2 onions
3 tomatoes
1 stalk celery
3 tbsp. margarine
8 slices pork shoulder
salt and pepper to taste
1/2 tsp. crushed rosemary
1 cup beef stock
1 tbsp. soy sauce
2 cups cornbread dressing

Slice onions, tomatoes, and celery thinly. Place in skillet with margarine and sauté lightly. Sprinkle pork with salt, pepper, and rosemary. Place small amount of dressing atop each slice of pork. Roll up. Secure with toothpicks. Brown rolls in fat. Remove rolls from pan and place on vegetables in skillet. Add beef stock and soy sauce. Simmer 30 minutes. Garnish with parsley. Serves 4.

---

## THE ADVENTURE INN
## Hilton Head

*Hilton Head's oldest hotel, situated by the ocean, has a very decorative dining room. The menu is quite extensive and includes many Southern favorites, foreign specialties, and local seafood dishes.*

### CRAB SOUFFLE

1 1/2 cups scalded milk
1 cup soft bread crumbs
1/4 cup melted butter
1/2 cup grated cheese
1 cup fresh blue crabmeat
1 tbsp. minced onion
2 tbsp. minced green pepper
1 tbsp. minced pimento
4 eggs, separated

Combine milk, bread crumbs, butter, cheese, crabmeat, onion, green pepper, and pimento. Mix well. Beat egg yolks and stir into crab mixture. Fold in beaten egg whites. Turn into deep baking dish. Bake 1 hour in 350° oven. Serves 4.

### VEAL MEDALLIONS

8 small veal cutlets
salt
flour
2 eggs, beaten
oil for frying
bread crumbs
1 tbsp. butter
lemon wedges

Pound veal cutlets. Salt and dip both sides lightly in flour. Then dip both sides in beaten eggs. Then dip in bread crumbs. Fry in hot oil over medium heat until golden brown. Drain and dot with butter. Serve with lemon wedges. Serves 4.

---

## HUNGARIAN GOULASH

2 lbs. cubed beef shoulder
1 tbsp. lard
1 large onion, chopped
1 tsp. pepper
2 cups stock
1 large tomato, diced
1 green pepper, diced
1 tbsp. Hungarian paprika
1 tsp. marjoram
1 clove garlic
1 tbsp. salt
1 tbsp. flour

Sauté onion in lard. Add paprika and cubed meat and brown lightly. Add salt and other seasonings. Add 1 cup of stock and braise until meat is soft. Remove meat. Thicken juice with flour. Add small amount of stock, then add green pepper and tomato. Cook just until green pepper is soft. Put meat back in and bring to boil again. Serves 4.

## COUNTRY CAPTAIN

4 chicken legs, whole (thigh and leg in 1 piece)
seasoned flour
1/2 cup oil
1/4 cup diced onions
1/2 cup diced green pepper
1 clove garlic, minced
1 1/2 tsp. curry powder
1/2 tsp. thyme
2 cups stewed tomatoes
3 tbsp. currants
3 tbsp. toasted almonds

Coat chicken with seasoned flour and brown in oil. Remove and drain chicken and place in casserole dish. Simmer remaining drippings, onions, green pepper, garlic, curry powder, thyme and tomatoes until pan is deglazed. Pour this sauce over chicken and bake uncovered for 30 minutes. Add and mix in the currants. Garnish with almonds. Serves 4.

## SEAFOOD GUMBO

For 10 minutes simmer 3 lbs. of throats and fin bones from fresh, salt-water fish in water seasoned with onion, bay leaf, and a pinch of gumbo filé. Remove from fire and strain, reserving stock. Place throats and fin bones in shallow pan to cool. When cool, remove remaining meat. Prepare a mirepoix with 2 diced potatoes. Sauté until almost tender. Combine reserved stock, mirepoix, and fish. Season with 1 level tsp. thyme, a pinch dry mustard, Sauterne, and salt and pepper to taste. Simmer. Blanch 2 1/2 cups chopped okra in lemon juice and water. Strain and add to stock. Serve as an appetizer before a light meal.

## CRAB SAVANNAH

Blend 1 cup heavy béchamel sauce with 1/4 cup Sauterne. Season with a pinch thyme, dry mustard, and tarragon. Blend in 1/2 cup sliced mushrooms, 1 lb. drained, lump crabmeat and 1/4 cup diced pimento. Be careful not to stir or simmer crabmeat too long as it will break up and lose its delicate appearance. Glaze with Hollandaise. Place in broiler until golden brown. Serve an an entree on large scallop shell. Place mixture within a bordure of dutchess potatoes.

## SAUCE BÉCHAMEL AND CRABMEAT HILTON HEAD

Blend 1/2 cup Sauterne into 3 1/2 cups fish velouté. Season with salt, white pepper, 1 thyme leaf, and 1/8 tsp. dry mustard. If sauce is not creamy enough,

---

## AUDUBON ROOM
## Hilton Head Inn
## Hilton Head Island

*Located in magnificent Hilton Head Inn, the Audubon Room is one of South Carolina's, as well as the nation's, finest dining rooms. It is informal, yet elegant, and serves coastal South Carolina cuisine and Southern-style delights.*

---

tighten with pale roux. Simmer 20 minutes. Blend in 1/2 cup sliced mushrooms, 1/4 cup diced pimento, and 1 cup lump crabmeat. Once crabmeat has been added, do not stir sauce; rather, blend gently.

## POMPANO

Lightly salt and pepper 6 7-ounce filets of pompano. Dredge in flour and dip in heavy egg wash consisting of 70% egg and 30% milk. Place filets in heavy pan skin side up so that they will not curl during cooking. Sauté over medium heat in enough drawn butter to cover halfway. Turn only as filets become golden brown around the edges. Drain excess fat and garnish with grilled tomato half, artichoke bottom with Hollandaise sauce, and a bouquet of parsley and fresh lemon. Serve as an entree with Sauce Béchamel and Crabmeat Hilton Head.

## SHRIMP AMELIA

Place 36 large green shrimp in enough water to cover. Add 1/4 tsp. salt, 1/2 tsp. lemon juice, and boil until tender (approximately 4 minutes). Remove from fire. Peel and devein, reserving stock. Place stock on low fire. Check to see that there are at least 3 cups. Add 1/4 tbsp. horseradish, a pinch ground thyme, salt, and white pepper to taste. Into stock blend 1/2 cup espagnole sauce, 1/4 cup Sauterne, 1/4 cup light cream, and 1/4 cup ketchup. If sauce appears to be too thin, thicken with small amount pale roux. Simmer for 20 minutes. Place on large scallop shell within a bordure of dutchess potatoes, glaze with Hollandaise sauce, and place in broiler until golden brown. Garnish with bouquet of parsley and serve proudly as an entree.

## SHE CRAB SOUP

Prepare mirepoix of 1/2 cup each: finely chopped carrots, celery, onions, and green pepper. Sauté in butter and 1 heaping tbsp. tomato paste, being careful not to brown. Add a 6-oz. can crab roe, a 16-oz. can lump crabmeat, and 2 tbsp. pale roux. Remove from heat and blend in 1 pt. light cream. If soup is too thick, thin with additional milk. Season to taste with salt, white pepper, and ground thyme. Serve as an appetizer. Serves 12.

## RED SNAPPER BORA BORA

**6 to 8 oz. Gulf red snapper**
**3 tbsp. unsalted butter**
**1/2 fresh pineapple**
**1/2 cup béchamel sauce**
**1/4 cup grated Swiss cheese**

Trim skin of snapper close to flesh. Remove core of pineapple and slice meat into thin slices. Butter baking dish and place snapper filet skin down in dish. Butter top of filet and place 3 to 4 slices of pineapple on top. Bake at 400° for 15 to 20 minutes. Add juices from pineapple hull to béchamel. Using the fingers, scrape the sides of hull to release juices for sauce. After snapper has baked, bring from oven and pour sauce over filet. Sprinkle filet completely with cheese and broil 3 to 5 minutes or until cheese is golden brown. Serve with carrots and fresh pineapple slices.

## QUAIL WITH HONEY SAUCE

**2 small quail**
**1/4 oz. cognac**
**4 strips bacon**
**4 grape leaves**
**1/2 cup honey**
**1/2 cup cocktail sherry**
**1 cup small mushrooms**
**4 cherry tomatoes**

---

# THE ORANGERY
## Knoxville

*Here is a great award-winning restaurant featuring the very finest Continental cuisine amid delightful surroundings. The restaurant has several dining areas that are as formal or as relaxed as you might wish. The atmosphere is warm and leisurely. The food is the best to be had anywhere.*

---

**1 10-oz. carton heavy cream**
**1/4 tbsp. salt**

Clean and truss a pair of small quail. Wrap in bacon or pork fat. Salt slightly. Pour a few drops of cognac into the cavity of each quail. Place each bird on a grape leaf, breast down. Cover with another grape leaf. Use trussing string or baking twine to secure grape leaves. Bake in 400° oven 35 to 40 minutes. Bring quail from oven, discard leaves, and reserve drippings. Take out trussing string and stuff each quail with two cherry tomatoes. Bake again, breast up, 15 to 20 minutes or until breast is golden brown. While birds are in second baking, make sauce. Put drippings, cocktail sherry, mushrooms, and honey in sauté pan. Reduce to 1/4 cup. Add cream and stir until thick. Remove quail from oven. Remove tomatoes and add them to the sauce. Cut each quail in half. Serve on bed of long-grain rice. Pour sauce over quail.

## FILET DE SOLE EN CROUTE

**8 to 10 sole filets**
**1 lime**
**1/2 lb. pastry dough**
**1/2 cup mushroom duxelles**

Using fresh sole filet if possible, trim and remove cartilage. Make duxelles using as little cream as possible. Refrigerate. Make a semisweet pastry dough or use puff pastry. Roll dough into an 8 x 12-inch rectangle about 1/4 inch thick. Place half the sole filet in center of dough. Cover with mushroom duxelles. Squeeze the juice of 1/4 lime over the duxelles. Place the other half of sole filet on top of duxelles and squeeze juice of 1/4 lime over sole. Wrap the filet tight enough to hold juices but loose enough for expansion. Dough may be shaped in form of a fish for a more delightful presentation. Bake on buttered baking dish in 425° oven for 20 to 25 minutes. Serve with Belgium carrots.

## BAKED BROWN BREAD

1 cup Kellogg's All-Bran
1 cup buttermilk
1 cup flour
1/4 cup sugar
4 tbsp. dark molasses
1/2 cup raisins
1 tsp. soda
1/4 tsp. salt

Mix all ingredients together. Bake in a well-greased loaf pan at 325° for 1 hour. Much easier than a steamed brown bread and equally good.

## APRICOT NUT BREAD

1/2 cup diced dried apricots
1 egg
1 cup sugar
2 tbsp. melted butter
2 cups flour
1 cup sliced almonds
3 tsp. baking powder
1/4 tsp. soda
3/4 tsp. salt
1/2 cup orange juice
1/4 cup water

Soak apricots 1/2 hour. Drain. Grind. Beat egg until creamy. Stir in sugar and butter. Sift dry ingredients. Add alternately with orange juice and water. Add nuts and apricots. Mix well and bake at 350° about 1 1/2 hours. Very good with cream cheese filling and delicious with afternoon tea.

## BLUEBERRY MUFFINS

1 3/4 cup flour
3/4 tsp. salt
1/3 cup sugar
3/4 cup milk
3 tsp. baking powder
2 eggs, beaten
1/4 cup melted fat
1 cup floured blueberries

Sift dry ingredients. Beat eggs. Add milk and melted butter. Stir liquid into dry ingredients. Add blueberries. Stir as little as possible. Bake 15 to 25 minutes at 425° in greased muffin pans.

## SATSUMA TEA ROOM
### Nashville

*This delightful restaurant was started over fifty years ago by two young home economics teachers. Their idea was that they could serve excellent food in attractive surroundings at a reasonable cost. Over the years they have achieved their goal and taken pride in its accomplishment.*

## BACON MUFFINS

2 cups flour
4 tsp. baking powder
1/2 tsp. salt
2 tbsp. sugar
2 eggs, beaten
1 cup milk
4 tbsp. melted bacon fat
6 strips bacon, fried crisp and chopped

Mix and sift dry ingredients. Mix egg and milk and stir into dry ingredients. Stir in melted fat and chopped bacon. Bake in greased muffin tins at 425° for 20 to 25 minutes. Surprisingly good.

## RICE MUFFINS

2 eggs, beaten
1 cup cooked rice
1 1/4 cups milk
4 tbsp. melted fat
1 1/2 cups flour
1 tbsp. sugar
1/2 tsp. salt
3 tsp. baking powder

To beaten eggs add rice, milk, and melted fat. Sift dry ingredients. Combine dry ingredients into eggs and milk. Put batter in hot greased muffin pan. Bake in 425° oven for about 25 minutes.

## HOE CAKE OR CORN PONE

1 cup white, water-ground cornmeal
1 tsp. salt
2 tbsp. bacon fat or lard
1 1/2 to 2 cups boiling water

Mix cornmeal, salt, and fat in bowl. Pour on boiling water, enough to make a thick mush. Be sure water is boiling. Mix thoroughly and shape dough into pone cakes. Heat greased iron griddle and put pones on hot griddle. Bake in oven preheated to 450°. Correctly made, this is the very best of all the Southern corn breads. Making good corn bread is an art.

## RIZ BISCUITS

2 1/4 cups flour (more if needed)
1 tbsp. sugar
1 1/2 tsp. salt
1 tsp. baking powder
1/2 tsp. soda
3 tbsp. fat
1 yeast cake
1/2 cup warm water
3/4 cup buttermilk

Dissolve yeast in warm water. Mix dry ingredients. Cut in fat until mixture is mealy. Stir milk into yeast mixture and then add to flour mixture. Roll out 1/2 inch thick, and cut. Brush tops with melted butter. Let rise 1 hour or more. Bake at 375°. These biscuits can be baked a light brown and frozen until ready to use. This is an excellent roll that can be made in a hurry.

## BAKED GRITS WITH CHEESE

2 1/2 cups cooked grits (3/4 cup uncooked)
2 eggs, lightly beaten
1/2 cup grated sharp Cheddar cheese
1/2 stick butter or oleo
1/2 tbsp. dry mustard
2 tsp. onion juice

Cook grits. Add all ingredients to hot grits. Pour in greased casserole. Bake in 350° oven for 50 minutes. Delicious for a luncheon dish. Serves 4 to 6.

## HOMEMADE TAMALES

### MASA DOUGH:

19 oz. masa harina (corn flour)
1 oz. lard
20 oz. pork or beef stock
1 tsp. salt

Add salt, lard, and stock to masa flour, mixing thoroughly with spoon. Cover with a damp cloth and refrigerate until ready to use.

### FILLING FOR TAMALES:

5 lbs. boneless pork shoulder
5 lbs. boneless chuck
2 cups enchilada sauce

Place meat in sauce pot, cover with water, and boil until both meats are completely tender and literally fall apart. Chop into very small cubes. Place meat in sauce pan containing enchilada sauce and mix thoroughly.

### CORN HUSKS:

Open husks to insure they are completely clean; then soak them in hot water for about 1 hour so that they are completely pliable. (Failure to do this will make them break.) Keep damp until ready to use.

### ASSEMBLING TAMALES:

Lay corn husks out flat on table. Spread masa dough in center of husks so that it is an even ¼ inch thick. Add 3 to 4 ounces of the meat filling. Fold corn husks around meat filling so that they resemble "party snappers," tying both ends with a strip of corn husk. Tie the knot firmly in order that it will hold the filling tightly in place. Over a double boiler steam tamale for approximately 45 minutes or so until done. For service, slit body of tamale and push ends towards center in a manner similar to opening a baked potato so that tamale will "pop" open. Place generous portion of enchilada sauce inside tamale. Serve hot.

---

# EL SOMBRERO
## Arlington

*This restaurant brings a little bit of Old Mexico to Arlington, Virginia. Mexican artifacts, such as plates, tin masks, serapes, sombreros, and papier-mâché figurines, line the white stucco walls. The food is great at the* Holiday Award-winning El Sombrero.

### FLAN

2/3 cup sugar
1/2 cup water
4 whole eggs
4 egg yolks
1/3 cup sugar
1/8 tsp. salt
1 cup heavy cream
2 1/2 cups milk
vanilla

Over low heat stir 2/3 cup sugar until brown (caramelized). *Carefully* add 1/2 cup water; continue stirring until it becomes liquified and smooth. Pour mixture, which should have the texture of corn syrup, in equal proportions into eight 4-ounce molds. Scald 1 cup of heavy cream and 2 1/2 cups of milk. *Do not boil.* Beat together (but not until foaming) 4 eggs, 4 yolks, 1/3 cup of sugar, and 1/8 tsp. salt. Add beaten eggs to scalded milk and cream (remove skin from mixture first) and add vanilla flavor. Pour mixture equally divided into 8 4-ounce molds. Set molds into pan of boiling water and bake in preheated oven at 325° until set (about 45 minutes). When done, immediately set molds in cold water to cool quickly. Refrigerate until serving. Makes 1 quart. Serves 8.

### NACHOS

4 4-inch corn chips or tortillas
4 oz. grated cheese
1 oz. finely chopped jalapena peppers

On the corn chip or cooked tortilla, generously spread the grated cheese in even portions and top with thoroughly drained and dried jalapena pepper. Distribute evenly among the 4 corn chips. Place in hot oven for approximately 2 minutes to melt the cheese. Place nachos on plate and serve immediately.

### CARNE CON CHILE COLORADO

1 tbsp. lard
6 lbs. beef cubes
1 tbsp. flour
1 tbsp. garlic powder
1 small onion
24 oz. enchilada sauce
1 1/2 tbsp. salt

Trim all fat from beef, using a lean piece of meat such as round steak, and cut into 3/4-inch cubes. Chop onion very fine. Place lard in skillet and as soon as hot, add meat cubes. Thoroughly sear meat, stirring constantly. Add flour to meat and continue browning. Add garlic powder and minced onion, continuing to stir. Add enchilada sauce and stir in thoroughly, adding salt at same time. Simmer slowly on a low flame, stirring from time to time, until meat is completely tender. Serve approximately 8 oz. per casserole dish. Serves 12 to 15.

### BOTANAS
*(Mexican Pizza)*

6 3-inch diameter corn tortillas or corn chips
3 oz. refried beans
1 1/2 oz. grated cheese
1 1/2 oz. chorizo sausage
2 oz. guacamole
1 ripe olive

Finely cube chorizo sausage into bite-size pieces and sauté until all fat has been rendered from it. On the tortillas or chips, spread beans and sprinkle cheese on top, topping with the chorizo sausage. Place in a hot oven for approximately 2 minutes until cheese has melted. On an oval or round plate, place guacamole in center and surround it with the 6 botanas. Top guacamole with black olive.

## BROILED FRESH FISH

6 3/4-lb. fresh, cleaned trout or rockfish, with heads left on or cut off as you prefer
salt and freshly ground black pepper
9 tbsp. sweet butter
2 tbsp. fresh lemon juice
3 tbsp. Sauterne
1/3 cup chopped fresh parsley

Preheat oven to 450°. Sprinkle fish lightly with salt and pepper inside and out. Place 4 tbsp. of the butter in a baking dish large enough to hold the fish. Set the pan in the preheated oven. When the butter starts to bubble, place the fish side by side in the pan and bake for 2 to 3 minutes. Turn the fish over and turn the broiler on. When the skin starts to brown, turn the fish and broil the other side until the skin browns. (The total cooling time is about 10 minutes.) Remove the fish from the pan and arrange on a heated platter. Reserve pan juices. In a saucepan, melt the remaining 5 tbsp. of butter. Add the lemon juice, wine, parsley, and pan juices. Stir and heat the sauce. Pour the sauce over the fish and serve immediately. Serves 6.

## BORDELAISE SAUCE

5 tbsp. butter
4 tbsp. minced celery
4 tbsp. minced carrots
4 shallots, minced (or substitute 3 spring onions)
3 tbsp. parsley
3/4 cup dry red wine
2 1/4 cups rich beef stock
1 tsp. salt
1 tsp. freshly ground black pepper
1/2 tsp. whole thyme
3/4 tsp. rosemary leaves
1/2 tsp. crushed coriander seed
2/3 cup sautéed, sliced fresh mushrooms

Melt butter in a saucepan and sauté celery, carrots, shallots, and parsley for about 3 to 5 minutes. Add the wine and simmer until reduced by one-half. Add the remaining ingredients and simmer slowly for about 10 minutes. Serve hot with any type of beef. Serves 8.
NOTE: This sauce may be thickened if desired by addition of 1 1/2 tbsp. flour. It may be held in the refrigerator for up to 5 days.

## SAUTÉED CALVES' LIVER WITH MUSTARD SAUCE VIRION

6 slices calves' liver, at least 1/2 inch thick, with skin removed

---

## THE ROYAL STEWART
## The Tides Golf Lodge
## Irvington

*The Tides Golf Lodge is a luxurious resort with a view of Chesapeake Bay. The Royal Stewart dining room serves American gourmet cuisine.*

flour
salt and freshly ground black pepper
4 tbsp. sweet butter
2 tbsp. olive oil
1/4 cup brown stock or canned beef broth

Sprinkle the liver with some salt and pepper and lightly dredge in flour. Heat the butter and oil in a large skillet. When they are hot, but not burning, add the liver and sauté very quickly on both sides until nicely browned. Do not overcook, as meat should be of medium doneness. Total cooking time is 5 to 6 minutes depending on thickness of meat. When cooked, transfer meat to a heated platter. Have the sauce ready. Just before pouring the sauce over the liver, add the brown stock to the pan used for sautéing the liver. Bring to a fast simmer and add into the Mustard sauce. Be sure to taste for seasoning and pour over the liver. Serve immediately, garnished with crab apples and parsley.

## MUSTARD SAUCE:

1/2 cup brown stock or canned beef broth
1/2 cup dry white wine
3/4 cup heavy cream
2 tbsp. sweet butter
1 generous tbsp. Dijon mustard
salt and freshly ground black pepper

Simmer together the brown stock and wine until the liquid is reduced to approximately 1/2 to 2/3 cup. Slowly add the heavy cream and cook, stirring occasionally, until the sauce has thickened. Remove from the heat and whisk in the butter and mustard. Correct seasoning. Serves 6.

## CREAM OF POTATO AND LEEK SOUP

5 or 6 leeks (or, if necessary, substitute spring onions)
2/3 cup water
4 large potatoes, peeled and quartered

---

3 cups canned chicken broth
6 tbsp. butter
1/2 tsp. freshly ground black pepper
1/3 cup minced fresh parsley
1 cup milk
3 egg yolks
1 cup heavy cream
1 1/4 tsp. salt

Clean the leeks well, discarding the outside leaves and the roots. Drain and chop the leeks into small pieces. In a small covered saucepan, simmer the leeks in 2/3 cup water until they are tender and set aside. In a larger pot, cook the potatoes in boiling water until tender, approximately 20 minutes. Drain. Combine the potatoes, leeks, chicken broth, butter, and black pepper and simmer gently for 10 minutes. Let the mixture cool for 5 minutes, then puree it by putting through a blender. (It may take more than one operation to do this so as not to overload your blender.) Put the puree in a saucepan. Slowly add the milk, whisking constantly, then the parsley. Beat the egg yolks and heavy cream together. When ready to serve the soup, reheat it to a simmer and slowly add the cream and egg mixture. Taste for seasoning and add salt and pepper if necessary. Serve hot. Serves 8.

## POULET À LA MOUTARDE

2 tbsp. butter
2 tbsp. olive oil
pieces of chicken for serving of 6
salt
freshly ground black pepper
1 large onion, chopped (about 1/2 cup)
4 tbsp. flour
1/2 tsp. turmeric
1 1/4 cup milk
1/4 cup Sauterne
1 1/3 cups chicken stock (or 1 10 1/2-oz. can chicken broth)
3 generous tbsp. Dijon mustard
2/3 cup minced fresh parsley

Preheat oven to 350°. In large skillet, heat butter and oil and brown chicken; season with salt and pepper. Remove. In the remaining fat, cook onion until translucent. To onion add flour and turmeric. Cook gently, stirring for 2 to 3 minutes. Ever so slowly, add milk and then the wine to the onion mixture, stirring constantly, and cook until the sauce thickens. Place chicken in a casserole and pour sauce over it. Bake, covered, in a 350° oven for 1 hour. Remove the chicken to a warm serving platter. To sauce, add mustard and parsley, whisking to blend the mixture well. Pour sauce over chicken and serve. Serves 6.

## CHEESECAKE WITH CHERRY SAUCE

3 8-oz. pkgs. soft cream cheese
3/4 cup sugar
6 eggs
1/2 pt. sour cream
1/4 tsp. vanilla
1 cup graham cracker crumbs
1/2 cup sugar
1/4 cup melted butter

Blend cream cheese and sugar. Add eggs, one at a time, and beat until smooth. Add sour cream and vanilla. Set aside. Mix graham cracker crumbs, sugar, and butter. Line bottom of springform pan with crumb mixture. Pour cheese mixture in pan and bake at 350° for 10 minutes. Then lower heat to 325° and bake 50 to 60 minutes. Serve topped with cherry pie filling or other fresh fruits.

## CREAM OF PEANUT SOUP

1/4 cup butter
2 stalks celery, chopped
1 small onion, chopped
2 tbsp. flour
2 cups chicken broth
1 cup milk
1 cup light cream
1 cup peanut butter
salt and pepper
paprika

Brown celery and onions in butter. Add flour and chicken broth and bring to a boil. Add milk and cream. Strain. Add peanut butter and simmer for 5 minutes. Season to taste. Serves 6.

## HUGUENOT TORTE

2 eggs
1 1/2 cups sugar
1 1/4 cup sifted flour
2 1/2 tsp. baking powder
1/4 tsp. salt

## EVANS FARM INN
## McLean

*Evans Farm Inn is furnished with antiques that recall the time of George Washington. Primitive cooking utensils, enormous hand-hewn beams, old sconces, and early poetic samplers enhance the ambiance of this old inn.*

1 cup pared, sliced apples
1 cup chopped pecans
1 tsp. vanilla

Beat eggs and sugar until well blended. Sift dry ingredients and add to egg mixture. Fold in apples, nuts, and vanilla. Pour into paper-lined pan (8 X 8 X 2 inches) and bake at 350° for 45 minutes. Top with whipped cream. Serves 6 to 8.

## VIRGINIA WHISKEY CAKE

*(Adapted from the eighteenth century files of Helen Duprey Bullock, author of "The Williamsburg Cook Book")*

1 cup granulated sugar
1 cup firmly packed brown sugar
1 cup butter
3 eggs
3 cups sifted cake flour
1/2 tsp. baking powder
1/2 tsp. mace
1 cup 100-proof bourbon whiskey
2 cups broken pecan meats

Combine the sugars and cream with butter. Add well-beaten eggs. Sift flour and mace; add alternately with whiskey. Add nuts. Bake in well-greased or paper-lined tube pan at 250° for 2 1/2 to 3 hours. The cake should have a moist crumbly texture similar to a macaroon. Wrap in aluminum foil and store in cool place. (Do not freeze.) The cake cuts eas-ier when cold, but should be served at room temperature. It will keep for 2 weeks or longer. Slices about 1/2 inch thick are best. Save the crumbs for parfaits or sundae topping. For added flavor, add 1 tbsp. of Whiskey sauce (1/2 cup light corn syrup, 1 tbsp. rum, 2 tbsp. whiskey) to cake about half an hour before serving. Whipped cream topping is optional.

## BARBECUE SAUCE

1/4 lb. butter
1 cup ketchup
4 tsp. Worcestershire sauce
1 tsp. prepared mustard
1 tsp. prepared horseradish
1/2 cup vinegar
juice of 2 lemons
1 clove garlic, crushed
1/4 tsp. Tabasco sauce
1 tsp. pepper
4 tsp. brown sugar
3 tsp. paprika
2 tsp. celery salt
dash monosodium glutamate

Mix all ingredients and simmer for 30 minutes. Strain and refrigerate. Makes 1 quart.

## THE INNKEEPER'S SPOON BREAD

3 cups water
1/4 lb. butter or margarine
2 tbsp. sugar
1 tsp. salt
2 cups white cornmeal
3/4 cup bread flour
6 eggs, beaten
2 1/2 cups milk

Blend water, butter, sugar, and salt and bring to a boil. Add cornmeal and flour. Mix. Add beaten eggs and milk. Mix thoroughly. Pour into greased baking dish, preferably 8 X 6 inches. Bake at 350° until knife inserted in center comes out clean, approximately 45 minutes. Serves 8 to 12.

## WATERCRESS AND MUSHROOM SALAD

4 bunches watercress
2 lbs. sliced raw mushrooms
4 heads Boston lettuce

### DRESSING:

1 cup wine vinegar
1/2 cup olive oil
1 tbsp. sugar
1 clove garlic, finely chopped
freshly ground black pepper

Wash and pick over the watercress, mushrooms, and Boston lettuce. Drain well and wrap gently in a towel. Chill. Combine olive oil, wine vinegar, garlic, sugar, and season to taste with freshly ground black pepper and salt. Just before serving, place watercress, Boston lettuce, and mushrooms in a salad bowl. Add dressing and toss until every ingredient glistens. Serves 4 to 6.

## FILET BEEF À LA WELLINGTON

4 lbs. filet
6 tbsp. butter
4 mushrooms, finely chopped
1/2 large onion, finely chopped
2 oz. chopped regular or Smithfield ham
1 cup crumbled pâté de foie gras
salt
freshly ground black pepper
4 tbsp. dry sherry or Madeira
1 lb. flaky pastry

Sauté filets in butter for about 3 minutes on each side. Remove from pan and allow to cool. Sauté mushrooms and onion in the remaining butter until golden, add crumbled pâté de foie gras, ham, and sauté the mixture until lightly browned. Season to taste with salt and freshly ground black pepper. Add enough sherry or Madeira to bind the mixture. Spread the top filet thin with this mixture. Allow to cool. Wrap filet in rolled-out pastry. Paint pastry edges with lightly beaten egg white and press together firmly. Decorate pastry with pastry leaves, etc. and paint lightly with egg yolk. Bake in a moderately hot oven

(400°) for 35 to 45 minutes until the pastry is golden. Serves 6.

## HOTEL ROANOKE PEANUT SOUP

2 qts. chicken broth
1 small onion, diced
1/4 lb. butter
2 branches celery, diced
3 tbsp. flour
1 pt. peanut butter
1/2 cup ground peanuts
1 tsp. celery salt
1 tsp. lemon juice
1 tsp. salt

Melt butter in cooking vessel and add onion and celery. Sauté for 5 minutes, but do not brown. Add flour and mix well. Add hot chicken broth and cook for half an hour. Remove from stove, strain, and add peanut butter, celery salt, lemon juice, and salt. Sprinkle ground peanuts on soup just before serving. Serves 8.

## SPOON BREAD

1 1/2 cups cornmeal
1/8 lb. butter
1 tsp. sugar
1 1/3 tsp. salt
5 eggs
2 cups milk
1 1/2 cups boiling water
1 tbsp. baking powder

Mix cornmeal, salt, and sugar together. Scald with boiling water. Add melted butter. Beat eggs and add milk to eggs. Put the 2 mixtures together. Add

baking powder. Pour into baking pan and bake 30 to 40 minutes in oven at 350°. Serves 10.

## CLAMS CASINO

12 clams, open
1 cup bread crumbs
1/2 cup chopped bacon
1/4 cup finely chopped onion
1/2 fresh green pepper, chopped
1/2 cup butter
1/4 cup grated Parmesan cheese
1 tsp. garlic powder
few drops lemon juice
few drops Worcestershire sauce
salt and white pepper

Sauté onions and bacon in butter, to a golden brown. Add pimento, parsley, bread crumbs, lemon juice, Worcestershire, garlic powder, salt, and white pepper. Simmer slowly for 10 minutes. Allow to cool. Cover each clam. Bake in a hot oven (400°) for 10 to 15 minutes.

## BAKED SHRIMP CASABLANCA

20 large shrimp, peeled and cleaned
4 large mushrooms, finely chopped
4 shallots, finely chopped
1/2 lb. crumbled crabmeat
2 tbsp. cognac
1/2 cup finely chopped parsley
1 1/2 cup white wine
1/2 cup butter
2 tbsp. flour
1/2 cup lemon juice
1 cup sliced mushrooms
1 cup chopped onion
1/2 cup fish bouillon

Sauté mushrooms and shallots in butter until golden brown. Add crabmeat, cognac, parsley, flour, bread crumbs, 1/2 cup white wine, lemon juice, and fish bouillon. Simmer slowly for 20 minutes. Season to your taste with salt and white pepper. Allow to cool. Butterfly shrimp. Cover each with stuffing and add sliced mushroom, butter, white wine, and onion. Place in casserole. Bake for 20 minutes in a hot oven (400°). Serves 5 to 6.

## PEPPER DRESSING

1 qt. mayonnaise
1/2 cup water
1 tbsp. lemon juice
2 dashes Tabasco sauce
1 tsp. Worcestershire sauce
1 tsp. bottled steak sauce
1/2 tbsp. dry mustard
1/2 tbsp. sugar
1 tbsp. salt
1/2 tbsp. granulated garlic
1/4 cup Parmesan cheese
1/4 cup freshly crushed whole black
   pepper

Blend all ingredients together, whipping by hand. Refrigerate before serving. Makes 5 cups.

## CASCADES SCALLOPED OYSTERS

2 qts. fresh oysters
1 tsp. salt
1/2 tsp. pepper
1 tbsp. Worcestershire sauce
1 tbsp. lemon juice
1 lb. saltine crackers
2 tbsp. melted butter

Preheat oven to 375° F. Grease a 2-quart casserole. Season oysters with salt, pepper, Worcestershire sauce, and lemon juice. Coarsely crumble the crackers. Line bottom of casserole with a layer of crackers, then a layer of oysters, and repeat procedure, finishing with crackers. Sprinkle butter over top layer of crackers. Bake at 375° for 20 minutes. Serves 12.

## RATATOUILLE

1 1/2 lbs. zucchini squash
3 ribs celery
1 large onion
1 large green pepper
1 large eggplant
8 medium tomatoes
1/2 cup butter
3 cloves garlic, minced
1 tbsp. oregano
1 tbsp. basil
1 tbsp. salt
1 tsp. pepper
4 tbsp. grated Parmesan cheese

## THE CASCADES RESTAURANT
## Williamsburg

*This beautiful restaurant is set in a deeply wooded area overlooking the three-level waterfalls for which it was named. At the salad bar, the diner may concoct his own Chef's Salad. Rack of Lamb Perselle is carved and served at the table. The menu features pork, beef and seafood brochettes, delightful chicken dishes, and delicious Shrimp DeJonge. A Virginia seafood feast is sometimes offered in addition to the regular menu.*

Preheat oven to 350° F. Grease shallow earthenware or other casserole. Slice zucchini and celery; cut onion and green pepper into large squares; and cut eggplant into large cubes. Scald tomatoes in boiling water for 60 seconds, drain, remove skin, and cut in half. Squeeze out and discard the tomato juice and cut each half into 4 pieces. Reserve. Blanch separately in boiling salted water the zucchini, celery, green pepper, and eggplant. Reserve. In a large pan sauté onions in butter for 4 to 5 minutes. Add garlic, oregano, basil, salt, and pepper, and continue to sauté until onions are transparent. Combine all ingredients in prepared casserole and sprinkle with Parmesan cheese. Bake at 350° for 10 to 15 minutes. Serves 8 to 10.

## CASCADES BEEF BURGUNDY

1/4 cup vegetable oil
1 large onion, finely chopped
2 cloves garlic, minced
4 lbs. boneless chuck roast, cut in 1-inch cubes
3/4 cup all-purpose flour
1 1/2 qts. beef stock
1 1/2 cups tomato puree
1 tbsp. salt
1 cup red wine, divided
1 bay leaf

Heat oil in a heavy p[...] and sauté until tender. [...] beef, and sauté until [...] Sprinkle flour over the [...] and toss it together. Add [...] stir until smooth. Add the [...] salt, 1/2 cup of wine, and bay leaf, and bring to a boil. Simmer for 2 1/2 hours or until beef is tender. Add remaining wine, and adjust seasoning. Serves 8 to 10.

## CASCADES GRITS SOUFFLE

2 cups milk
1/2 cup instant grits
1/2 cup grated Cheddar cheese
2 tbsp. grated Parmesan cheese
1 tsp. salt
1/2 tsp. baking powder
2 tbsp. melted butter
1/2 tsp. sugar
3 eggs, separated

Preheat oven to 375° F. Grease a 1 1/2-quart casserole or 1 1/2-quart souffle dish. Scald milk, add grits, and cook until slightly thickened. Add Cheddar and Parmesan cheese and cook until thickened, stirring constantly. Remove from heat. Add salt, baking powder, butter, and sugar; mix well. Beat egg yolks and add to grits. Whip egg whites until they hold soft peaks; fold in. Pour into prepared dish. Bake at 375° for 30 minutes. Serve hot. Serves 6.

## HONEY DRESSING

1/2 cup vinegar
1/4 cup sugar
1/4 cup honey
1 tsp. dry mustard
1 tsp. paprika
1 tsp. celery seed
1 tsp. celery salt
1 tsp. onion juice
1 cup vegetable oil

Mix the vinegar, sugar, honey, mustard, and paprika together, boil 3 minutes, and cool. Add the celery seed and salt, onion juice, and vegetable oil and beat or shake vigorously. Serve with any fresh or frozen fruit salad. If kept under refrigeration, shake well before using. Makes 1 3/4 cups.

## PECAN TARTS

4 eggs
3/4 cup sugar
1/2 tsp. salt
1 1/2 cups light corn syrup
1 tbsp. melted butter
1 tsp. vanilla
1 cup pecan halves

Preheat oven to 400° F. Prepare tart shells. Beat eggs lightly and add sugar, salt, corn syrup, cooled butter, and vanilla; stir until mixed well. Spread pecan halves on bottom crust and cover with the filling. Place in oven and immediately reduce heat to 350°. Bake 40 to 50 minutes or until mixture is firm in center. Cool before serving. Serves 12.

## PASTRY CRUST MIX

3 cups all-purpose flour
1 tsp. salt
2 tsp. sugar
1 cup shortening
ice water

Mix dry ingredients together. Blend in shortening with knives or pastry blender until mixture is of pebbly consistency. Store in covered container in refrigerator. When needed, measure out these amounts:

|  | Single Crust | Double Crust |
|---|---|---|
| 8" pie | 1 to 1¼ cups | 2 to 2¼ cups |
| 9" pie | 1½ cups | 2½ cups |
| 10" pie | 1¾ cups | 2¾ cups |
| 12 tart shells | | |

Moisten pastry mix with enough ice water to hold dough together when pushed lightly with a fork. Roll out on lightly floured board or pastry cloth. When recipe calls for prebaked shell or shells, line pan with dough, prick well with a fork, and bake at 425° for 12 to 15 minutes or until golden brown. Makes 4 1/2 cups.

## APPLE PIE

1 1/4 to 1 1/2 cups sugar
1/8 tsp. salt
3/4 tsp. cinnamon

## CHOWNING'S TAVERN
## Williamsburg

*Josiah Chowning advertised in 1766 that "all who favour me with their Custom may depend upon the best of Entertainment for Themselves, Servants, and Horses...." Chowning's today offers good colonial fare. The garden is open in good weather, at which time one may get cool drinks and afternoon snacks. Dinner is served there also, if the evening weather is pleasant.*

1/2 tsp. nutmeg
2 tbsp. all-purpose flour
6 to 8 tart apples (2 to 2 1/2 lbs.), peeled and sliced
lemon juice (optional)
1/2 tsp. grated lemon rind
1 to 2 tbsp. butter

Preheat oven to 425° F. Roll pastry for bottom crust over rolling pin for ease in lining pan. Cover pastry for the top crust while filling the pie to keep it moist. Mix dry ingredients together in large bowl. Add sliced apples and mix to coat. Place apple slices in pan, laying slices first along the outside and then working toward the center until bottom of pastry is covered. Continue placing in same way until pan is filled. Sprinkle with lemon juice and rind and dot with butter. Moisten edge of bottom crust. Roll top crust around rolling pin, unroll over apple filling, and trim to 1/2-inch larger than pie pan. Press edges firmly together, flute, and slash vents in the center of the crust. Bake at 425° for 50 to 60 minutes until apples are done and crust is golden brown. Makes 1 9-inch pie.

## CHOWNING'S TAVERN
## BRUNSWICK STEW

1 stewing hen (6 lbs.), or 2 broiler-fryers, (3 lbs. each)

2 large onions, sliced
2 cups okra, cut (optional)
4 cups fresh or 2 cans (1 lb. each) tomatoes
2 cups lima beans
3 medium potatoes, diced
4 cups corn cut from cob or 2 cans (1 lb. each) corn
3 tsp. salt
1 tsp. pepper
1 tbsp. sugar

Cut chicken in pieces and simmer in 3 qts. water for a thin stew, or 2 qts. for a thick stew, until meat can easily be removed from bones, about 2 1/4 hours. Add raw vegetables to broth and simmer, uncovered, until beans and potatoes are tender. Stir occasionally to prevent scorching. Add chicken, boned and diced if desired, and the seasonings. If canned vegetables are used, include juices and reduce water to 2 qts. for a thin stew, 1 qt. for a thick stew. Brunswick Stew is one of those delectable things that benefit from long, slow cooking. It is a rule in some tidewater homes never to eat Brunswick Stew the same day it is made as its flavor improves if it is left to stand overnight and reheated. Serves 8 to 10.

## CHOWNING'S TAVERN WELSH RABBIT WITH BEER

1 tbsp. butter
1 lb. grated sharp Cheddar cheese
3/4 cup beer, divided
dash cayenne pepper or Tabasco sauce
1 tsp. dry mustard
1/2 tsp. salt
1/2 tsp. Worcestershire sauce
1 egg, slightly beaten

Melt butter in top part of double boiler. Add cheese and all except 1 tbsp. of beer. Cook over hot, not boiling water, until cheese melts. Combine seasonings with remaining tbsp. of beer and stir into cheese. Stir in slightly beaten egg. Serve immediately over toast or broiled tomato halves. Any cheese mixture that is left can be refrigerated and used as an excellent spread for crackers or toast. Serves 4.

## BURGUNDY ICE

3 qts. water
gratings (only) of 10 lemons
2 lbs. sugar
2 cups lemon juice
2 qts. Burgundy wine

Mix together and freeze until creamy; after frozen half through, add 6 egg whites and 12 oz. of sugar. Makes 2 gallons.

## HAMPTON CRAB IMPERIAL

1 lb. backfin crabmeat
1/2 tbsp. chopped pimento
1/2 tbsp. chopped green pepper
1 tbsp. butter
1 egg yolk
1/4 tsp. dry mustard
1 rounded tsp. drained capers
1 1/2 tsp. Worcestershire sauce
salt and white pepper to taste
1 cup mayonnaise, divided
paprika

### HEAVY CREAM SAUCE:

4 tbsp. butter
5 tbsp. all-purpose flour
1 cup milk
1/2 tsp. salt

Preheat oven to 375° 10 minutes before crab is ready to go in. Pick over crabmeat and discard any bits of shell or cartilage. Refrigerate. Sauté pimento and green pepper in butter. Make a heavy cream sauce by melting the butter in a heavy skillet over medium heat and stirring in the flour, milk, and salt. Continue stirring until mixture is smooth and thick. Combine sautéed vegetables, cream sauce, and other ingredients except crabmeat, mayonnaise, and paprika. Mix in 3/4 cup mayonnaise. Fold in crabmeat very gently so lumps will not break up. Spoon into shells or shallow baking dishes and spread remaining mayonnaise on top of each crab filling. Bake at 375° for 30 to 35 minutes or until golden brown. Sprinkle with paprika and serve at once. Serves 6.

## CHRISTIANA CAMPBELL'S TAVERN-MADE DISH OF SHRIMP AND LOBSTER

1 1/2 green peppers, quartered
3 medium tomatoes
2 6-oz. pkgs. long-grain and wild rice, mixed
1/2 lb. quartered fresh mushrooms

---

# CHRISTIANA CAMPBELL'S TAVERN
## Williamsburg

*This historic hostelry, operated as a tavern and coffeehouse by Christiana Campbell from 1771 until about 1780, has been reestablished as a distinctive eating place. This tavern offers a convivial atmosphere and fine food similar to that which the colonial burgesses and men of affairs enjoyed there over 200 years ago. There are five dining rooms and a taproom, plus a porch and dining courtyard. Seafood from Chesapeake Bay, steak, Virginia game pie, famous Southern spoon bread, Captain Rasmussen's Clam Chowder and much more are served.*

1/4 lb. butter, divided
3/4 lb. cooked and shelled lobster
1 lb. cooked and cleaned shrimp
1 15 1/2-oz. can pearl onions
3/4 cup dry sherry
1 tsp. lemon juice
Worcestershire sauce to taste
salt and white pepper to taste
parsley

Partially cook green pepper in boiling water, remove, and cut quarters in half. Reserve. Scald tomatoes in boiling water for 60 seconds, drain, remove skin, and cut in half. Squeeze out and discard the tomato juice and cut each half into 4 pieces. Reserve. Cook the rice according to the package instructions. Sauté mushrooms quickly in a small amount of butter and reserve. Cut the lobster into bite-size pieces. Melt remaining butter over medium heat and sauté lobster, shrimp, and onions. Add sherry, lemon juice, and seasonings. Add green pepper, tomato, and mushrooms and cook over low heat, stirring gently, until heated through. Arrange the seafood and vegetables in a heated serving dish with the rice. Sprinkle with a dash of sherry. Garnish with chopped parsley if desired. Serves 4 to 6.

## ALMOND BUTTER SAUCE

2 tbsp. slivered almonds
1/2 cup butter, divided
2 tbsp. finely chopped pimento

---

2 tsp. finely chopped parsley
2 tsp. lemon juice
1 tsp. salt

Sauté almonds in 2 tbsp. butter slowly until golden brown. Cool. Cream remaining butter and add almonds, pimento, parsley, lemon juice, and salt; mix thoroughly. Serve with fried or broiled seafoods. If fresh parsley is not available, 1 tsp. dried parsley leaves can be reconstituted in the lemon juice before adding to the butter mixture. This sauce can be stored in the refrigerator for 2 weeks.

## CHRISTIANA CAMPBELL'S TAVERN SPOON BREAD

1 1/3 tsp. sugar
1 tsp. salt
1 cup cornmeal
4 tbsp. butter
3 eggs
1 tbsp. baking powder
1 1/3 cups hot milk

Preheat oven to 350°. Grease 2-quart casserole. Mix sugar and salt with cornmeal and blend well. Add butter and pour in 1 1/3 cups boiling water, stirring constantly. Allow to cool. Beat eggs with baking powder until very light and fluffy; then add to cornmeal mixture. Stir in milk and pour into prepared casserole. Place casserole in shallow pan of hot water and bake at 350° for 35 to 40 minutes. Serve hot. Serves 8.

## CRABMEAT RAVIGOTE

1 lb. regular crabmeat
1/4 cup tarragon vinegar
3 tbsp. chopped pimento
2 tbsp. chopped chives
2 tbsp. sweet pickle relish
2/3 cup mayonnaise, divided
salt and pepper to taste
cleaned crab shells or lettuce
capers
pimento

Pick over crabmeat and discard any bits of shell or cartilage; marinate in vinegar 15 minutes. Drain crabmeat and add chopped pimento, chives, relish, 1/2 cup mayonnaise, salt and pepper to taste. Divide mixture evenly into 6 cleaned crab shells or crisp lettuce cups; shape into domes. Spread with thin coating of remaining mayonnaise. Sprinkle well-drained capers over top and garnish with pimento. Serve very cold. Serves 6.

## CORN PUDDING

Take 6 large, tender, milky ears of corn. Split the corn down the center of each row, cut off the top, and then scrape the cob well. Beat 2 eggs and stir them into the corn. Add 1/4 cup flour, 1 tsp. salt and 1/2 tsp. black pepper. Stir in 1 pt. fresh milk and mix all together thoroughly. Put into a cold buttered pan about 4 inches deep. Cover the top with 2 heaping tbsp. butter cut into small pieces. Bake in a moderately hot oven about 1 hour. Serve hot.

## SALLY LUNN

Put 1 yeast cake in 1 cup warm milk. Cream together 3 tbsp. shortening and 3 tbsp. sugar. Add 2 eggs and mix well. Sift in 3 1/2 cups flour to which 1 1/4 tsp. salt has been added, alternately with the milk and yeast. Beat well. Let rise in a warm place (about double bulk). Knead lightly. Put into well-greased Sally Lunn mold. A 3 1/2 X 10-inch ring mold or an Angel Food cake tin may be used. Let stand and rise again (double) and bake at 300° for 1 hour.

## CREAM OF PEANUT SOUP

Take 4 stalks celery and 1 onion, chop and braise in 1/4 lb. butter. Add 2 tbsp. flour and cook until well blended. Add 1 gallon chicken stock and bring to boil. Stir in until well blended 1 lb. peanut butter. Add 1 qt. cream and serve.

## PECAN PIE

6 eggs
1 1/2 cups dark corn syrup

---

## KING'S ARMS TAVERN
## Williamsburg

*This is an excellent eating place located on the site where Jane Vobe operated a tavern in 1770. The waiters, students from the College of William and Mary, wear colonial costumes and serve lamb chops, escalloped oysters, cream of peanut soup, Sally Lunn bread, Frosted Fruit Shrub, and greengage plum ice cream.*

1/2 cup maple syrup
1 cup sugar
2 tbsp. melted butter
vanilla, to taste
2 cups pecans
pastry for 10-inch pie

Beat eggs and sugar together. Add vanilla to butter, then add to egg/sugar mixture. Add syrups and pour over pecans. Bake at 300° for 45 minutes.

## PECAN CONFECTIONS

Beat 1 egg white to a stiff froth; add gradually 1 cup brown sugar, 1 pinch of salt, 1 level tbsp. flour. Stir in 1 cup chopped pecans, drop on greased tins by small spoonfuls far apart. Bake in a very slow oven 15 minutes. Remove from tin when partly cooled. Makes 2 dozen.

---

## SWEET POTATOES

Mix together scant 1/2 tsp. nutmeg, 1/4 tsp. cinnamon, 3/4 cup sugar, 1 scant tsp. salt. Add 2 1/2 lbs. dry pack sweet potatoes, 1/4 lb. butter and 2 cups milk. Bake in hot oven until glazed on top.

## GREENGAGE ICE CREAM
*(A very famous recipe)*

BASE:

18 egg yolks
1 1/2 lbs. sugar
2 qts. heavy cream
1 qt. milk

Beat the yolks with a small part of the sugar. Bring the cream and milk to a boil. Pour some of it over the yolks. Pour yolks into the boiling milk. Do not boil but cook until mixture coats the spoon. Cool and add the other ingredients. Freeze. Light cream may be used for less richness.

PLUM MIXTURE:

1 1/2 #10 cans Greengage Plums, drained (or equivalent in smaller cans)
1/2 #10 can of juice from plums
1/2 pt. concentrated lemon juice
2 lbs. sugar
1 tbsp. green coloring

Mix together the base and greengage mixtures and add one oz. of vanilla flavoring. Makes 4 1/2 gallons.

## CONIGLIO COI PEPERONI
### (Rabbit)

1 rabbit
1 1/2 bottles of red wine, Barbera preferred
3 cloves
2 bay leaves
3 stalks celery, chopped in large pieces
3 carrots, chopped in large pieces
1 large onion, sliced
pinch marjoram
pinch thyme
4 black peppercorns
1/4 cup pure olive oil
3 tbsp. butter
4 tbsp. bacon fat
1 square of bitter chocolate, grated
4 tsp. sugar
5 tbsp. cognac
1/2 can Mancini sweet roasted red peppers

You must first marinate the rabbit in a red wine for at least 24 hours. Cut rabbit into pieces; add wine, carrots, celery, marjoram, thyme, salt, peppercorns, and place aside for at least 24 hours. Heat oil and butter together; add bacon fat and cook onions in this until golden in color. Take out rabbit and place in the heated pan, turning each piece over until brown. This is done over high heat. When brown, add the rest of the marinade. Cover and allow to simmer for 2 1/2 to 3 hours. Add the roasted red peppers and sugar to the rabbit; then add cognac. Return to high flame. Serve at once. Serves 5.

## ANTIPASTI

1 cup butter
4 tbsp. olive oil
4 cloves garlic
8 anchovy filets, finely chopped
pinch salt

Heat butter and oil together and sauté garlic, being careful not to allow it to brown. Add anchovies and cook slowly over low flame until anchovies are dissolved into a paste. Add salt. Dip raw vegetables into this sauce.

## FUNGHI CRUDI

This is a northern Italian specialty using raw fresh mushrooms. Slice the mushrooms, add diced scallions, and mix with the following sauce:

1 tsp. salt
1/2 tsp. freshly ground black pepper
1/2 cup lemon juice
1/2 cup pure olive oil

Mix together until well blended.

---

# CANTINA D'ITALIA RISTORANTE
## Washington, D.C.

*This is the only restaurant to receive the coveted* Holiday *Award after only one year of operation; it has received the award every year since 1969. Exceptionally good are the regional dishes from the north of Italy—the Piemont, Val d'Aosta, and Liguria areas. The owner, Joseph Anthony Muran-de Assereto, remains on the premises as long as there is a single customer dining.*

## ZUPPA DI FONTINA

This is a bread and cheese soup. Slice 1 lb. of imported fontina cheese very thinly. Slice 1 loaf of long French bread into rounds and toast them. Then, in alternate layers of bread and cheese, place in individual soup bowls. Bring 8 to 10 cups of hot beef stock to boil and pour over the toast and cheese in bowls. Serve immediately.

## FETTUCCINE BEL PAESE

Add cooked fettucini egg ribbon noodles to a sauce made by combining the following:

1/2 cup table cream
1/2 lb. imported Bel Paese cheese
1 tbsp. unsalted butter

Heat the cream and butter together; add cheese and allow it to melt; add a pinch of salt. Toss together and serve at once. Do not add any other cheese to this dish since the tangy taste of Bel Paese would be lost by the addition of, say, Parmesan.

## FILETTI DI PESCE PERSICO

12 filets of perch
flour
2 eggs, beaten and lightly salted
bread crumbs, dried and finely seasoned with basil and grated Parmesan cheese
1 cup butter
1/4 cup pure olive oil
12 leaves sage
2 sprigs parsley, chopped

Make a marinade of 1/2 cup of oil, the juice of 1 lemon, 1 green onion finely chopped, salt, and pepper. Marinate the filets for 1 hour before cooking. Drain. Dip in flour, then in egg, then in bread crumbs. Heat butter and oil in shallow fish pan. Place filets and brown on both sides. Add sage leaves and parsley to cooking fat. Serve at once.

## SCALOPPE DI VITELLO SAVOIARDA

This dish can only be made with milk-fed veal. No other will do.

20 pieces veal, 1/4 inch thick
1/2 cup dry white wine
1/2 cup sweet butter
flour
salt and pepper
2 green onions, diced (including blades)
3 fresh mushrooms, thinly sliced

Place the scallops between sheets of wax paper and pound with flat side of meat cleaver until as thin as possible. Season with salt and pepper. Dust with flour. In a pan, melt butter and add mushrooms and scallions and cook for about 2 minutes. Remove and place aside. Now add veal, turning over each one as soon as meat turns from pale pink to white. Now add sauce and serve. Serves 4.

## GNOCCHI ALLA BAVA
### (Potato Dumplings With Fontina Cheese)

4 lbs. potatoes
4 cups all-purpose flour
salt
1/2 lb. imported fontina cheese (it is important to use only imported Italian fontina cheese; no other will do)
1/2 cup melted butter

First, wash and boil the potatoes until soft. Drain and allow to cool. Peel and mash until smooth. Add flour, a little salt, and work this mixture into a dough. Break off small pieces and shape them into sausagelike rolls the thickness of a finger. Press each piece with the thumb against a fork which will leave each *gnocchi* with ridges on it. Place *gnocchi* on a floured surface (preferably a marble slab) to keep them from sticking. Bring a large pot of water to boil. Add 1/2 tsp. salt. Drop the dumplings a few at a time. Remove them with a perforated spoon as soon as they rise to the top, usually 2 to 3 minutes. Then in a fireproof dish, alternate layers of cheese and dumplings. Sprinkle with melted butter. Cover and bake in moderate oven for 5 minutes. Serves 6.

## GOVERNOR'S CHICKEN

1 1/3 cups skinned, boned chicken, breast or thigh, cut into bite-size pieces
2 egg whites
1 1/2 tsp. cornstarch
cooking oil

Mix cornstarch and egg whites with fingers until blended. Coat chicken pieces with this mixture. Heat oil to warm (250°). ("Warm" is a Chinese cooking term and is hotter than we normally think of as warm.) Deep fry chicken until pale gold in color but still rare (3 to 4 minutes). Drain on paper towels and keep warm.

### SAUCE:

1 1/2 tbsp. sherry wine
1 tbsp. soy sauce
1/4 tsp. yuan-shai-chih (soy base paste)
1/4 tsp. hoisin (plum sauce)
1/2 tsp. sugar
4 tbsp. roasted peanuts, brown skins removed

Combine above ingredients and set aside. To complete sauce:

1 tbsp. oil
1/2 tsp. crushed red pepper (very hot)
3 scallions, split lengthwise, cut into 1-inch pieces
1/4 tsp. minced, peeled ginger

Heat oil over medium flame in heavy skillet. When very hot, increase heat and add scallions and ginger. Stir fry for 3 or 4 seconds; then add chicken. Add reserved mixture and stir until chicken is cooked through, about 1 minute. Serve at once. Serves 1.

## TUMBLEWEED BAMBOO
*(Mushrooms and Mustard Greens)*

2 cups peanut oil
1 1/2 cups finely cut broccoli leaves
1/2 cup bamboo shoots, cut into small triangular pieces

Heat oil to just below smoking (400°). Add broccoli and bamboo and cook just until leaves achieve stiffness. Remove vegetables with strainer or pierced spoon. Drain and serve immediately.

## COURT OF THE MANDARINS
## Washington, D.C.

*Aline Berman, the owner of Court of the Mandarins, believes that Peking cuisine has never been properly introduced to the American public. Master chef Wu creates delicate Chinese dishes.*

## BEEF AND SNOW PEAS

6-oz. flank steak, sliced against the grain 1/8 inch thick
1/2 egg white
1/2 tsp. cornstarch
1/2 cup plus 1 tsp. peanut or soybean oil
1/4 cup snow peas
1 clove garlic, crushed and chopped
1/3 tsp. salt
1 tsp. soy sauce
1 tsp. sherry
1/3 cup chicken broth blended with 1/2 tsp. cornstarch

Blend egg white and cornstarch and rub into the surface of the meat. Heat oil in heavy skillet to 300°. Cook meat until outside is sealed (about 30 seconds). Drain oil from skillet and clean thoroughly so that there are no bits of meat sticking to bottom. Barely cover bottom of skillet with oil and heat until just below smoking point. Add snow peas, garlic, and salt. Stir and cook for 2 minutes. Add sherry and soy sauce and stir to blend. Add chicken stock-cornstarch mixture and stir again until sauce becomes translucent (about 30 seconds). Serves 2.

## BUDDHIST VEGETABLES

1/2 cup thinly sliced carrot sticks
1/2 cup dried Chinese mushrooms
1/2 cup water chestnuts
1/2 cup snow peas
1/2 cup young tender broccoli
1 clove garlic, crushed, then chopped
1/8 cup peanut or soya oil
1/4 tsp. salt
1 tsp. soya sauce
2 tsp. dry sherry wine

Barely cover Chinese mushrooms with boiling water and soak for half an hour. Slice all the vegetables. Heat oil in heavy skillet, stirring to prevent burning. When oil reaches 350°, add vegetables and garlic to the skillet and stir over high heat for 2 to 3 minutes. Add salt, soya sauce, and sherry to skillet and stir briefly to blend. Serve over plain rice. Serves 2.

## HSIAO HSING FISH

6 oz. filet sole or flounder (dry on paper towel)
1/2 tsp. cornstarch
1/2 egg white
1/2 cup corn oil
1/2 cup chicken broth
1 rounded tsp. sugar
1/2 tsp. salt
1/4 cup Hsiao Hsing wine (obtain in Chinese grocery—this wine is made of rice but tastes like dry sherry)
1/4 tsp. cornstarch, blended with
2 tsp. water

Combine cornstarch and egg white and rub into fish. Heat oil in heavy skillet to 200° to 225°. Cook fish briefly in oil (about 20 seconds). Drain oil from fish and set aside. Add chicken broth, sugar, salt, and sherry to skillet. Bring mixture to boil. Add fish and cook for 2 minutes. Add cornstarch-water mixture to skillet and cook 20–30 seconds or until sauce becomes translucent. Serve with plain rice. Note: if canned chicken broth is used, place can in refrigerator for 2 hours before using. Open can and remove lumps of congealed fat.

## FISH IN VINEGAR SAUCE

1 1/4 lb. sea bass
3 tbsp. vinegar
3 tbsp. sugar
3 tbsp. soy sauce
1/3 cup water
1/3 cup defatted chicken stock
1 level tsp. cornstarch
1/2 tsp. sesame seed oil for flavoring

With knife blade pointing toward the fish's head, make several deep slashes crosswise every 2 inches. Poach fish in boiling water until cooked. (To test, insert knife into one of slashes. If meat is still adhering to bone, fish is not cooked sufficiently.) Once cooked, leave fish in pot while preparing sauce. Mix cornstarch in 1/3 of the water and set aside. Combine all other ingredients, stirring constantly over medium heat until boiling. Add cornstarch mixture and continue stirring until sauce is translucent. Add sesame seed oil. Pour sauce over fish. Garnish with narrow carrot strips, Chinese mushrooms, or anything colorful in thin strips. Serves 4.

## TOLTOTT KAPOSZTA
### (Stuffed Cabbage)

2 lbs. sauerkraut
12 large white cabbage leaves, unbroken
1 onion, chopped
1 lb. ground beef
1 lb. ground pork
1 cup steamed rice
2 eggs
1/2 tsp. salt
1/2 tsp. white pepper
1 tsp. cloves
3 bay leaves
1/4 lb. bacon
1 smoked pig's knuckle
2 tsp. paprika
sour cream

Steam cabbage leaves in hot water until slightly wilted. Drain and cool. Brown onion and bacon in small amount of oil. Meanwhile, in large bowl, mix ground meat with rice, eggs, salt, pepper, and paprika. Add brown onion and bacon and mix again. Divide meat mixture onto leaves, then roll and tuck in the ends. Wash sauerkraut and put half of it into a large kettle. Add the cabbage rolls and remainder of sauerkraut. Add allspice, bay leaves, cloves, paprika, and pig's knuckle. Add enough water to cover sauerkraut and cook for 2 hours or until done. Place 1 tsp. sour cream on each serving.

## RED CABBAGE

2 lbs. red cabbage
2 oz. drippings from roasted duckling
1 small onion, chopped
2 bay leaves
5 cloves
5 allspice
sugar, salt, pepper, and vinegar to taste
water

Cut and shred cabbage. Add drippings, onion, bay leaves, cloves, allspice, sugar, salt, pepper, vinegar, and water. Boil for 90 minutes or until tender.

## ROAST POTATOES

8 small potatoes, peeled
1 onion, sliced
2 tbsp. oil
salt, pepper, and paprika

## CZIKO'S HUNGARIAN RESTAURANT
## Washington, D.C.

*Cziko's is one of the finest Hungarian restaurants outside of Hungary. Many mouth-watering delights, from Transylvanian goulash to delicate desserts are served here.*

Boil potatoes in water with a pinch of salt, until tender. Sauté onion in oil until golden. Add cooked potatoes, salt, pepper, and a pinch of paprika.

## SULTKACSA
### (Roast Duckling)

2 4 to 5-lb. ducklings
1 tsp. rosemary leaves
salt and pepper

Wash ducklings. Rub with salt and pepper inside and out. Sprinkle rosemary leaves inside. Roast at 375° for 1 3/4 hours. Baste occasionally during last half hour of baking. Let duckling cool and cut in half lengthwise. Remove inside bones and cut again. Reheat for 10 minutes and serve with sauce, red cabbage, and roast potatoes.

### DUCKLING SAUCE:

2 cups chicken stock
2 tbsp. flour
1 cup water
salt and pepper

Boil the bones, which have been removed from the duckling, with 2 cups of chicken stock. Mix flour and water to a smooth paste and add to the leaves. Boil for 15 minutes and pass through a sieve.

## PALACSINTA
### (Crepes Stuffed with Apricot Jam or other fillings)

11 oz. flour
4 oz. milk
3 eggs
4 oz. soda water
dash salt

With wire whisk, beat eggs slightly. Add flour, soda water, milk, and salt and mix together well. Mixture should be smooth, not too thick. Pour small amount of mixture into a well-greased 6-inch skillet, enough to cover bottom. Tilt skillet back and forth to spread batter thinly and evenly. Cook each crepe over medium heat until light brown on bottom and firm to touch on top. Loosen edges with spatula. Turn and brown second side. Fill each crepe with jam (about 2 tsp.) and roll. Sprinkle with powdered sugar. Serve hot.

## CSIKOS TOKANY

2 lbs. pork shoulder
2 oz. bacon
2 oz. vegetable oil
2 red tomatoes, cut up
1 large green pepper, chopped
1 large onion, chopped
1 tsp. paprika
2 gills sour cream
2 cloves garlic

Cut meat into strips of 2-inch lengths. Cut bacon into strips and fry with onion, pepper, and garlic until onions are golden yellow. Add tomatoes, paprika, and a little water to keep paprika from burning. Place the meat into the casserole with salt, pepper, and a little more water if necessary. Simmer, covered, until tender. Stir from time to time. In separate bowl, mix 1 cup water with sour cream and a little flour. When meat is tender, add this to thicken the sauce.

## MARHAPORKOLT
### (Beef Goulash)

1 lb. beef shank
1 lb. chopped onion
1 green pepper, chopped
1 clove garlic, mashed
1 cup oil
1/2 cup tomato puree
1 tbsp. paprika
salt and black pepper to taste
beef stock or water

Cut the meat into 1-inch cubes. Chop green pepper and onion. Then fry pepper and onion along with the mashed garlic until yellow. Add paprika, salt, black pepper, and tomato puree. Add a little water and bring to boil; then add the meat. Simmer until tender. Onion should thicken the sauce.

## MEXICAN CORN BREAD

1/2 cup butter or margarine
1/4 cup sugar
2 eggs
2 cups creamed corn
1/3 cup chopped Italian sweet peppers
2 cups shredded Cheddar cheese
1 1/2 cups sifted flour
4 tsp. baking powder
1/4 tsp. salt
1 cup cornmeal

Cream together butter and sugar. Add eggs one at a time, beating well after each addition. Mix in corn, peppers, and cheese. Sift together flour, baking powder, and salt and mix with meal. Add dry ingredients to cheese mixture, mixing just enough to blend well. Turn into buttered 9 X 14-inch pan and bake in 325° oven about 40 minutes or until golden brown. Cut into 3 X 4-inch pieces. Serves 16.

## GUACAMOLE SALAD

4 large ripe avocados, mashed
1 tsp. garlic salt
1 large onion, chopped
2 large fresh tomatoes, chopped after peeling
1 tsp. hot jalapeno sauce

Mix mashed avocado with garlic salt, onion, and tomatoes. Stir in hot sauce. Serve with crisp corn tortillas or stuff soft tortillas with the mixture.

## TEXAS CHILI WITH BEANS

1 lb. ground beef
1 large onion, chopped
1 large sweet green pepper, chopped
1 tsp. salt
1 tsp. garlic powder
1 lb. cooked pinto beans (weighed before cooking)
1 dash oregano
1 tsp. chili powder
1 large can tomato sauce
2 cups water
hot jalapeno sauce to taste

Brown meat in heavy pan. Add onion, peppers, garlic powder, oregano, salt, chili powder, tomato sauce, hot sauce, and 2 cups of water. Cook 35 minutes over medium flame. Add and stir in cooked beans and continue to simmer another 30 minutes. Serve hot.

## DON PEDRO'S MEXICAN CANTINA
### Washington, D.C.

*Washington's most recommended Mexican restaurant is located in the downtown area of the city. It has two charmingly decorated dining rooms. The delicious cuisine is expertly prepared and served.*

### ENCHILADAS

8 corn tortillas (soft)
1 large onion, chopped
1 cup grated yellow cheese
2 tbsp. bread crumbs
1 tsp. garlic salt
1 tsp. red chili powder
1 dash black pepper
1 dash oregano
2 cups ground beef or chicken

Season meat with garlic salt. Sauté in small amount of oil until done. Mix chopped onions, meat, more garlic salt, chili powder, black pepper, oregano, cheese, and bread crumbs. Warm tortillas in cooking oil (only until warm). Stuff each tortilla with 2 or 3 tbsp. of mixture and roll them. Put tortillas in shallow pan, seam side down.

### SAUCE:

2 tbsp. flour
1 tsp. garlic salt or to taste
1 pinch red chili powder
1 pinch oregano

Dissolve flour in boiling water. Add garlic salt, chili powder, and oregano and cook 10 minutes over low heat. Pour sauce over rolled tortillas, top with grated cheese, and bake in 350° oven 30 minutes. Serves 4.

### CHILES RELLENOS
*(Stuffed Chili Peppers)*

4 green chili peppers, already stripped (canned may be used)
2 cups cooked ground beef or chicken meat
2 tbsp. grated New York yellow cheese

1 tsp. garlic salt
dash black pepper
2 tbsp. bread crumbs

Brown beef or chicken in small amount of oil. Season with garlic salt and black pepper and continue to cook. Cool meat, then add cheese and bread crumbs. Stuff peppers with this mixture. Put aside in a plate.

### FLOUR BATTER:

2 tbsp. flour
1 cup milk
1 egg

Beat all together until smooth.

### CHEESE SAUCE:

2 tbsp. grated New York yellow cheese
1 cup milk
2 tbsp. flour
1 pinch hot jalapeno sauce

Dissolve flour in milk; add cheese and hot sauce. Cook on medium heat, stirring until mixture thickens and is smooth. Pour flour batter over stuffed peppers and brown in cooking oil. Remove cooked peppers from skillet and pour cheese sauce over them. Serve warm. Serves 2.

### FLAN
*(Egg Custard)*

5 or 6 large eggs
1 can evaporated milk
1 1/2 cups sugar
1 tsp. vanilla flavoring

Beat eggs. Add sugar and beat well. Add milk and vanilla. Continue beating until thoroughly mixed. Let stand while caramel is being prepared. Prepare caramel by stirring 1/2 cup sugar in top of double boiler, stirring it constantly until brown. Avoid lumps. When completely melted and browned, turn off heat and pour in the flan mixture. Put double boiler in 325° oven for 1 hour. Test cooked mixture with a toothpick or clean knife. When either come out clean, take the hardened mixture from oven and chill thoroughly in refrigerator. Serves 10.

## ESCALLOPED TURKEY

3-lb. stewed or roasted turkey
2 1-lb. loaves of toasted, dried bread
3 chicken bouillon cubes dissolved in 3
   pts. boiling water or turkey broth
2 cups diced onion
2 cups diced celery and leaves
2 tsp. rubbed sage
1 tsp. salt
4 eggs, slightly beaten
1/2 cup melted margarine or butter

Break dry toast into small pieces in a mixing bowl. Add onions, celery, sage, and salt. Pour boiling liquid over mixture, stir, cover, and set aside for 10 minutes. Add eggs and stir gently. More liquid may be needed to make this a moist mixture. Layer this dressing in a baking dish, starting on the bottom with dressing and topping off your dish with dressing. Pour melted margarine or butter over the top of the last dressing layer. Cover and bake 45 minutes at 350°. Serve with a gravy made of turkey broth. Serves 6 to 8.

## HAM AND EGG CASSEROLE

12 eggs, scrambled
1/2 lb. diced ham
2 cups thin white sauce
1/4 lb. mild cheese
2 cups crumbled potato chips

Dissolve cheese in white sauce. Toss together scrambled eggs and ham. Pour into casserole. Ladle the white sauce and cheese mixture to cover the ham and eggs. Sprinkle potato chips over the top. Bake 35 minutes at 300°. Serves 6 to 8.

---

## WELLS INN
## Sistersville

*This is a beautiful and historic inn where visitors enjoy turn-of-the-century splendor. The restored main building has chandeliers that are originally from the Wells building and wall sconces from the Sistersville Opera House. The food is excellent.*

### BAKED STEAK

1/2 lb. cubed steak per serving

Dip steak in flour, coating it well. Sprinkle with salt and pepper. Brown steak in bacon fat, using as little fat as possible. Remove steak from fry pan to baking dish. Drain excess fat from fry pan. Make gravy in fry pan using 2 dissolved beef bouillon cubes in 3 cups water or beef broth. Bring to boil, stir in 1/4 cup cornstarch that has been dissolved in 1/2 cup warm water. Salt and pepper to taste. Ladle gravy over steak in casserole. Cover and bake 45 minutes at 350°. Sautéed onions may be added on top of the gravy to give an added flavor. Serves 6.

### SOUR CREAM AND BLUEBERRY PIE

1 pt. thick chilled dairy sour cream
1 pt. chilled canned blueberry pie filling
1 baked 9-inch pie crust

---

Scoop sour cream and blueberry [filling] filling alternately in mounds into the pie crust. Use a spatula or dinner knife and gently swirl the sour cream and blueberry pie filling so as to give it a gentle marbled effect. Chill several hours before serving.

## PEANUT BUTTER SAUCE

1/2 cup margarine or butter
3 tbsp. flour
1 2/3 cups water
2/3 cup peanut butter
3 cups powdered sugar
1/4 tsp. vanilla

Melt margarine, blend in flour, and add water. Bring to boil, stirring constantly. Add peanut butter; blend. Remove from heat. Add vanilla and powdered sugar. Beat until smooth. Makes approximately 1 quart. Note: The Peanut Butter Sundae is a specialty at The Wells Inn.

## SAUERKRAUT FOR REUBEN SANDWICHES

1 cup sauerkraut, squeeze juice out of kraut before measuring
1/2 cup thin slaw dressing
dash of Worcestershire sauce
1/4 cup grated Parmesan cheese

Mix all ingredients together well. Refrigerate for 24 hours. Note: The Wells Inn uses this for corned beef reubens.

## CUILLERE OU EN ...AUBE
*(...aised Beef)*

...oast, about 8 lbs.
1 cup ... wine
2 tbsp. vinegar
4 tbsp. peeled, chopped shallots
1 clove garlic, peeled, crushed, and chopped
4 tbsp. chopped fresh tarragon leaves
1 tsp. salt
1 tsp. pepper
2 tbsp. bacon fat
2 cups Sauce au Madere (recipe below)
6 strips bacon
1 cup all-purpose flour
1/2 cup water

Put beef in large crock or enamel kettle. Add wine, vinegar, shallots, garlic, parsley, and tarragon. Cover and marinate beef in mixture for 3 days. Remove meat from marinade. Reserve marinade. Season meat with salt and pepper. Heat bacon fat in large skillet and brown meat on all sides. Remove and set aside. Drain the fat from the skillet and add the reserved marinade. Bring to boil and reduce to half its volume. Add the Sauce au Madere and simmer for 10 minutes. Preheat oven to 325°. Grease a large Dutch oven and place the beef in the center of the pot. Place the bacon strips across the top. Pour sauce over the meat just to cover. Blend flour and water to a smooth paste. Seal the lid on pot by covering the seam generously with the paste. Bake at 325° for 6 hours. Serves 6.

### SAUCE AU MADERE
*(Madeira Wine Sauce)*

1 cup Madeira wine
1/2 cup peeled, chopped shallots
2 cups Sauce Demi-Glace (recipe below)
2 tbsp. butter

In a saucepan combine Madeira and shallots and cook over medium heat until wine is reduced to half its volume. Add Sauce Demi-Glace, bring mixture to boil, and simmer over low heat for 5 minutes. Strain sauce through fine sieve; add butter while sauce is still hot.

### SAUCE DEMI-GLACE
*(Brown Sauce. A basic sauce with many uses.)*

1/2 cup bacon fat
1/2 cup ham fat trimmings

---

### THE GREENBRIER
## White Sulphur Springs

*One of the very finest hotels in all the world would naturally have a dining room with food fit for kings. Eighteen presidents have been guests here and have enjoyed the excellent cuisine and gracious service. The famous cuisine is created under the aegis of internationally famous master of the culinary arts M. Hermann G. Rusch, who is a holder of the coveted Chef of the Golden Dozen Award, among others.*

1 large onion, peeled and chopped
3 carrots, scraped and chopped
4 stalks celery, chopped
2 leeks, cleaned and chopped
1 clove garlic, peeled and crushed
2 bay leaves
2 sprigs fresh parsley
1 tsp. dried thyme leaves
1/2 cup all-purpose flour
1/2 cup dry white wine
1/2 cup tomato puree
2 qts. Brown Stock (recipe below)
salt and pepper to taste

Preheat oven to 375°. Melt bacon fat with ham trimmings in skillet with ovenproof handle. Add onion, carrots, celery, leeks, garlic, bay leaves, parsley, and thyme. Cook over medium heat for 15 minutes or until vegetables are lightly browned. Add flour, mix well, and bake at 375° for a few minutes until flour is brown. Remove from oven and transfer mixture to a large kettle. Add wine, tomato puree, and brown stock. Cover and let simmer over low heat for 2 hours. Occasionally remove scum from top with spoon. Strain sauce through a cheesecloth and cool. Add salt and pepper to taste. Store in glass container in refrigerator.

### BROWN STOCK
*(Fond Brun)*

2 lbs. beef short ribs
2 lbs. veal knuckles or shank
4 lbs. beef bones
2 carrots, scraped
2 stalks celery

---

1 onion, peeled
10 peppercorns, crushed
1 bouquet garni (1 bay leaf, 2 sprigs fresh parsley, 1 sprig fresh thyme)
4 tomatoes
1 clove garlic, peeled
1 tbsp. salt

Preheat oven to 425°. Cut up ribs and veal knuckles in large pieces (or have butcher do this); spread them in large flat roasting pan with the beef bones, and roast at 425° for 15 minutes. Add carrots, celery, onion, and peppercorns; roast another 15 minutes. Transfer everything from the roasting pan to an 8-quart kettle. Add 6 qts. water, the bouquet garni, tomatoes, garlic, and salt. Bring very slowly to boil. Remove any scum from top. Cover and simmer, do not boil, over low heat for 4 hours. Cool. Skim fat from top and strain through a sieve and then through cheesecloth. Makes 4 quarts.

### GERMAN CARROT CAKE

4 cups almond flour
1 1/4 cups filbert flour
5 cups peeled, grated carrots
1/2 cup cornstarch
1 tsp. cinnamon
1/2 tsp. salt
1 grated lemon peel
11 egg yolks
1 1/3 cups sugar
11 egg whites
1 1/3 cups sugar
3/4 cup granulated or sliced almonds

Preheat oven to 300°. Put the almond and filbert flours, carrots, cornstarch, cinnamon, salt, and grated lemon peel into a large mixing bowl. Then set aside. In a small mixing bowl, whip yolks and sugar at high speed. Then mix into the dry ingredients. Beat egg whites and sugar until thick but not stiff. Then fold into base batter. Pour into 2 10-inch pans that have been greased heavily and coated with granulated or sliced almonds. Bake at 300° for about 1 hour.

### GRATIN DAUPHINOIS
*(Cheese Potatoes)*

6 medium-size potatoes
1/2 tsp. salt
1/2 tsp. pepper
1 tsp. dried thyme leaves
1 clove garlic, peeled and chopped

1 tbsp. butter
1 1/2 tbsp. grated Gruyere cheese
1 egg, slightly beaten
3/4 cup light cream

Preheat oven to 375°. Peel and slice potatoes very thin. Sprinkle with salt, pepper, thyme, and garlic; mix well. Butter a shallow 2-quart baking dish, and arrange potatoes in layers, sprinkling cheese on each layer. Mix egg with cream and pour mixture over potatoes. Bake uncovered at 375° for 40 minutes, or until potatoes are tender and top is brown. Serves 4.

## QUICHE LORRAINE

3 eggs, whipped
1 pt. light cream
1/2 cup grated Swiss cheese
salt, pepper, and cayenne to taste
1/2 cup chopped onions
1/2 cup diced ham
1/2 cup melted butter
1/2 cup crumbled crisp bacon
1/2 cup diced Swiss cheese
2 X 9-inch pastry shell

Mix eggs, cream, grated cheese and seasoning. Sauté onions and ham in butter. Add bacon and diced cheese and spread evenly on bottom of pastry shell (pie form or French tart). Pour egg mixture on top, filling to rim of shell. Bake in oven at 400° for approximately 40 minutes. Serves 8 for lunch. Serves 30 for cocktails.

## MULLIGATAWNY
*(The Greenbrier's own delectable interpretation of this East Indian curry soup.)*

1 cup cut onions
1 cup flour
1/2 cup curry powder
2 qt. broth
1/2 cup shredded coconut
2 apples (peelings and diced fruit)
1 cup cream
1/2 cup diced eggplant

Sauté onions until brown. Add flour. Simmer for 20 minutes. Add curry powder, mixing in well. Add broth and heat to boil. Add coconut and apple peelings and let simmer for 1 hour. Strain. Bring to a boil again and add the cream and diced apples. Add eggplant which has been sautéed in butter until soft. Season to taste.

---

## THE GREENBRIER
## White Sulphur Springs

### CERVELLO DI VITELLO, VILLA BETACCI
*(Calves' Brain in Egg Batter with Truffles and Artichokes)*

1 calves' brain
2 tsp. vinegar
1 onion wedge
1 bay leaf
2 cloves
1 egg
1 tsp. heavy cream
salt, pepper, and flour

Soak brain in water. Remove skin between crevices. Put brain in small casserole, cover with cold water. Add vinegar, onion wedge, bay leaf and cloves. Bring slowly to a boil. Simmer for 5 minutes, then remove from fire. When cool, take brain out and put it on a napkin. Cut brain in half. Season with salt and pepper and powder with flour. Then dip completely in egg batter (1 egg and 1 tsp. heavy cream beaten together). Put in clarified butter to brown on both sides. Serve with quartered artichokes sautéed in butter and slices of truffles.

### CHOPPED CHICKEN LIVERS

This is an excellent canapé spread on either Melba Toast or crackers.

3 onions, chopped
1/2 cup butter
1 lb. chicken livers
2/3 cup sherry wine
1 jigger (2 oz.) brandy
1 tsp. salt
freshly ground pepper

Chop onions and sauté in butter until golden. Add the chicken livers and the sherry and simmer with lid on for 1/2 hour, then set to cool. Add the brandy, salt and pepper. Grind up and press through a colander, or put all in a food blender. It is important to add the brandy and seasoning after the cooking. "Sherry to stew, brandy to finish" is the adage. The sherry and brandy combine to take some of the sharpness from the chicken liver. Serves 6.

### VICHYSSOISE

1 tbsp. butter
2 small leeks, finely sliced
1 onion, finely sliced
2 cups chicken broth

---

2 medium-sized potatoes
salt and pepper to taste
1 cup scalded milk
1 cup cream
chopped chives

Melt butter in saucepan. Add the leeks and onions and simmer gently on a slow fire for 10 to 15 minutes, stirring from time to time with wooden spoon until nearly cooked. This is very important in order to produce the proper flavor of the Vichyssoise. Add the chicken broth, potatoes, salt, and pepper and let simmer for another 15 minutes. Add milk, bring to boil. Correct the seasoning (it must be well seasoned). Then pass through a very fine sieve. Pour into a bowl and put in refrigerator. When soup is well chilled, stir in the cream. The consistency should be that of a heavy cream. Pour into cold cups. Sprinkle with chives and serve. Serves 6.

### CHOCOLATE SOUFFLE PUDDING

1 pt. milk
4 oz. butter
4 oz. flour
5 egg yolks
2 tbsp. melted sweet chocolate
5 egg whites
5 oz. granulated sugar

Boil milk. Mix and add flour and butter and continue stirring until the mixture is stiff; then, remove from fire and add egg yolks—one at a time. After all the egg yolks are in, add melted chocolate and mix thoroughly. Beat egg whites and sugar to meringue and fold into chocolate mixture. Pour mixture into a buttered and sugared dish or mold and bake at 350° for approximately 30 minutes. To prevent burning, place dish of souffle in pan of water while baking. Serve with Sabayon or Vanilla sauce. Serves 8.

### SOUFFLE AU KIRSCH

1/2 cup powdered sugar
1/2 cup flour
1 pt. milk
4 eggs
3 tbsp. Kirsch liqueur
1 tbsp. sweet butter

Mix sugar and flour with 1 egg and the yolks of the other 3 eggs. Dilute with the boiling milk; then cook for 2 minutes, stirring constantly. Remove from fire and add sweet butter. When cool, add the Kirsch and the 3 egg whites, whisked to a very stiff froth. Bake in a buttered baking dish, cook in a moderate oven for about 40 minutes. Remove from oven and serve at once.

The Tropics

## CREPES

1 lb. flour
1 pt. milk
6 oz. sugar
6 oz. butter
5 eggs

Put sugar in large bowl, add eggs one at a time, and whip. Gradually add flour, then fold in the milk. Add melted butter, then orange and lemon peel. Cook crepes individually.

### FILLING:

Form almond paste (frangipane) by mixing 4 oz. powdered almond, 4 oz. sugar, and 4 oz. creamy butter. Whip together until it becomes white, then add 4 eggs, one at a time. Add orange juice, lemon juice, and Grand Marnier. Spread almond paste over crepes, then roll into cigar shape. Mix some icing sugar with egg white and streak it lightly on top of crepes. Put in 300° oven and bake until golden brown, about 10 minutes. Sprinkle Grand Marnier around the plate, *not* over the crepes. Set aflame and serve quickly. Serves 8.

### CONCH SOUP OR CHOWDER

2 lbs. diced conch
2 lbs. diced potatoes
8 oz. diced onion
4 oz. diced white leeks
4 oz. diced celery
4 oz. diced green pepper
fresh tomatoes, diced
4 oz. diced carrot
4 oz. chopped bacon

Fry bacon, onion, leeks, celery, and carrots together. Cook over medium flame until vegetables are wilted. Add conch, potatoes, tomatoes, and then add consommé or cold water. Season with salt, pepper, bay leaves, thyme, and a drop of Angostura. If soup is not thick enough, add a little cornstarch diluted in 1 cup sherry wine. Serves 10.

---

### RIB ROOM
### King's Inn & Golf Club
### Freeport

*This dining room in the Bahamas has the atmosphere of an old English inn. The ambiance is created by furnishings such as pewter plates and booths made of rough-hewn beams.*

### SCAMPI FLAMBE WHISKY

6 scampi
1 tsp. chopped parsley
1 tbsp. chopped onion
1 piece garlic, chopped
salt and pepper
2 oz. whisky
rice
1 egg yolk
1 tsp. butter
3 tbsp. olive oil

Put 1 tsp. butter and oil in pan and heat. Add onion, parsley, garlic, and brown. Add scampi and salt and pepper. Cover and cook for 4 minutes. Remove pan from heat and add whisky. Set aflame. Add egg yolk, mix well, and serve at once on top of rice pilaf. Serves 1.

### CREPE OF CRAB

2 lbs. crabmeat
2 pts. fish stock
white wine
béchamel sauce
1/2 pt. Hollandaise sauce
juice of 1 lemon
salt and pepper to taste
fresh cream
16 crepes

Prepare 16 very thin crepes. Sweat 2 lbs. crabmeat in a saucepan until all the water has evaporated from the crab. Mix with Poisson Creme sauce (recipe below).

### SAUCE:

Reduce 2 pints fish stock in white wine. Add béchamel sauce and reduce some more. Finish the sauce with cream and Hollandaise sauce. Add seasoning to taste with juice of 1 lemon, salt, and pepper. To serve, garnish the crepes with the crab mixture and form a cigar shape or simply fold the crepes. Put on serving plate, cover with sauce, and glaze under broiler for a few minutes. Serves 8.

### BAHAMIAN LOBSTER CREOLE

lobster
8 oz. sliced onions
4 oz. sliced sweet green pepper
fresh tomatoes, peeled

Cook lobster in boiling water, then cut into fairly large pieces. Fry in plenty of butter with seasoning. In another pan, slowly sauté the onion until cooked thoroughly. Add green pepper and tomatoes and cook a little longer. Put lobster and vegetables together and add hot pepper sauce to taste. Cover and simmer gently for 10 minutes. Serve with white rice or peas and rice. Serves 4.

### SORBET OR SHERBET AU CHAMPAGNE

2 lbs. sugar
3/4 pt. water
juice of 3 lemons
1 bottle dry champagne
1 cup Grand Marnier

Mix all ingredients well and freeze. Sherbet must have the appearance of being white and light. Serve in sherbet glasses. Serves 10.

## WELSH RAREBIT, EUROPEAN STYLE

3 oz. fresh butter
1/2 lb. grated Canadian Red cheese (or other type if unavailable)
paprika, salt, and pepper
Worcestershire sauce
1 egg yolk
1 egg

Cream together the butter and cheese. Season with paprika, salt, pepper, and Worcestershire. Thoroughly mix in 1 egg yolk plus 1 egg. Spread this mixture 1 inch thick on toast, place in a baking pan, cover with melted butter, and allow to rise for 15 minutes in a medium oven. As a variation, bacon and freshly sliced tomato can be spread on the toast *before* adding the cheese mixture. It is quite practical to make a quantity of this mixture and keep it in a jar in the refrigerator so that it is ready for use when required. It can also be used to make cheese croutons or cocktail bits.

## PEAS AND RICE

1/4 lb. butter
1/4 lb. bacon
3 medium onions, chopped
1 celery stalk, chopped
5 oz. tomato paste
2 fresh tomatoes, chopped
1 cup pigeon peas (if unavailable substitute canned garbanzo beans)
3 cups uncooked rice
4/5 qt. water
2 sprigs fresh thyme
salt and black pepper

Put butter and bacon in saucepan and cook bacon until crisp. Add onions and celery until soft, then add tomato paste and fresh tomatoes. Cook for 15 minutes, then add pigeon peas, water, rice, and seasoning. Cover. Bring to boil, then reduce heat to simmer and cook for 45 minutes. Serves 8.

## FRENCH SALAD DRESSING

4 parts olive oil to 1 part vinegar
salt and pepper
dash Worcestershire sauce or mustard
a few drops of onion juice, if desired
garlic, as desired

Mix 4 parts olive oil to 1 part vinegar (we use wine vinegar). Season with salt and freshly ground pepper, adding a dash of Worcestershire sauce or mustard. Add onion juice as desired. For those who like garlic, rub the inside of the bowl with a piece of garlic before

---

## THE BUENA VISTA
## Nassau

*This is one of the finest restaurants in the Bahamas and the Caribbean. Its name appears in the colony's records of 1788. It is housed in one of Nassau's finest old homes. The food prepared by master chefs is typical of that of the region.*

adding the lettuce. We always add chopped chives, parsley, or tarragon when in season.

## BRAISED LETTUCE

2 large lettuce heads, quartered
boiling salted water
thinly sliced raw onions
a little butter
salt and pepper
Campbell's consommé

Quarter lettuce heads and put in boiling salted water for 3 minutes. Remove, drain, press out well, and arrange the lettuce in a buttered, fireproof dish. Cover with a layer of thinly sliced raw onions, dot with a few knobs of butter, and season with salt and pepper. Finally, add sufficient undiluted Campbell's consommé so as to not quite cover the lettuce. Bake in moderate oven for 1 hour. Serves 4.

## RICE TRAUTMANNDORF

1/4 lb. raw rice
3 pts. milk
1 inch fresh vanilla bean
grated lemon rind
a few raisins
sugar to taste
1 qt. stiffly whipped cream

Parboil rice in well-salted water. Drain and then finish off in 3 pints of milk seasoned with 1 inch of fresh vanilla bean. Add grated lemon rind, a few raisins, and sugar to taste. Allow rice to cool thoroughly. Finally fold in stiffly whipped cream, put into glass dishes, and chill in refrigerator. Serve with raspberry syrup, known in Germany as Himbeersaft.

---

## APPLE SOUFFLE

3 green cooking apples
sugar
fresh lemon peel, grated
lemon or lime juice
5 eggs, separated

Cook apples with plenty of sugar; pass through a sieve. Season to taste with grated fresh lemon peel and lemon or lime juice. Always remember that in baking a souffle, the flavoring has to be strong. Separate 5 eggs and put the egg whites into the refrigerator to keep cool. Beat 4 of the yolks and add them to the apple puree. Stiffly whip the 5 egg whites and fold them carefully into the apple puree 30 minutes before you are ready to serve the souffle. Pour mixture into a buttered souffle dish or any deep-sided, fireproof pie dish. Fill nearly to the brim. Stand dish in a baking pan half full of warm water and put in 450° oven that has been preheated. The souffle is done when the top is brown and firm to the touch. It should bake 30 minutes. If a darker top is preferred, leave in oven another 5 minutes—but remember, the longer you leave it in the oven the firmer will be the consistency of the souffle. If you put the souffle in the oven when you start to serve your main course, it should be just ready at the proper time.

## TENDERLOIN OF BEEF HENRY IVth WITH BEARNAISE SAUCE

Trim a 6-lb. tenderloin of beef, removing all the tissue and skin covering the filet. Roast with butter in a moderate oven for 25 minutes. Make a gravy with hot beef stock or hot pheasant consommé, a dash of cornstarch, and the juice from the pan. Serve sliced with Bearnaise sauce.

## BEARNAISE SAUCE:

1/2 cup white wine vinegar
1 tbsp. tarragon leaves
2 tbsp. finely chopped shallots
1 sprig chopped thyme
2 sprigs parsley, finely chopped
5 egg yolks
1 1/2 lbs. melted butter
salt, white pepper, and lemon juice

Combine vinegar, tarragon, shallots, thyme, and parsley. Cook over hot fire until reduced to half of its original volume. Add egg yolks, stirring constantly for 4 to 5 minutes, then remove from heat. Add slowly the melted butter, whipping vigorously until it has the consistency of whipped heavy cream. Season to taste with salt, white pepper, monosodium glutamate, and the juice of a lemon.

## FISH CHOWDER

1 1/2 lbs. boneless fish, diced in 1-inch
    cubes
1 cup diced potatoes
1/2 cup diced sweet green pepper
1/2 cup diced celery
1/2 #2 can whole tomatoes, chopped
5 cups water
1/2 cup diced onion
3 oz. salt pork or bacon
8 crackers, crushed
4 tbsp. lemon juice
salt and pepper

Place fish cubes in lemon juice for 30 minutes. Place salt pork in large pot and cook until almost brown, then add onions and cook until tender. Add water, potatoes, celery, green pepper, and tomatoes and cook over medium heat until vegetables are tender. Add fish and cook another 15 minutes. Add crackers, pepper, lemon juice, and salt. Remove from heat and let stand 30 minutes before serving.

## BOILED FISH

2 lbs. fish (cut in thick pieces)
1/2 lb. diced potatoes
1 medium onion, cut into rings
2 oz. diced salt pork
3 cups water
3 tbsp. lemon juice
1 hot pepper or hot sauce as desired
salt to taste

Cut fish into large pieces and score crosswise. Marinate with a small amount of lemon juice, hot sauce, and salt. Let sit for 30 minutes. Place in large pot: fish, potatoes, onion, and salt pork. Cover. Cook over medium heat for 5 minutes, then add water, lemon juice, and hot pepper, and cook until potatoes are well done. Remove potatoes first. Handle fish gently to keep from falling apart.

## SPANISH ISLE RESORT
### Spanish Wells

*Many claim that the Spanish Isle Resort has the finest food in the Bahamas. American and Bahamian specialties are served here in splendid surroundings.*

## FISH CREAM SOUP

1 large onion
1 lb. tomatoes
1 large carrot
1 medium sweet green pepper
1 large potato
2 stalks celery
1 lb. boneless fish
1/4 stick butter
salt and pepper to taste

Dice all ingredients and cook in 2 qts. of water until tender. Strain through metal strainer, pounding ingredients to make sure a fair amount of them are well sifted through the strainer. Do this several times. Place back on low heat, add 1 tsp. Lea & Perrins. Mix 2 tbsp. cornstarch with a little cold water to make a paste and add to soup. Cook 20 to 30 minutes, stirring frequently. Add salt and pepper last.

## CONCH FRITTERS

1 cup ground raw conch
1 medium onion, ground
1 celery stalk, ground
3 tbsp. Lea & Perrins
1 heaping tbsp. tomato paste
1 tbsp. hot pepper sauce
1 cup flour
1 heaping tsp. baking powder
1 egg
salt to taste

Put raw conch through meat grinder. Grind onion and celery. Using a large mixing bowl, combine all ingredients except water and mix with heavy spoon. Add seasoned water, a little at a time, until batter is semistiff. Pour a little vegetable oil in pan and heat over medium flame. Using a spoon, dip out batter and drop into hot fat and cook until brown. Serve with cocktail sauce.

## CONCH CHOWDER

2 cups ground, cooked conch
2 cups diced potatoes
1/2 cup chopped celery
1/2 cup chopped carrots
1/3 cup chopped sweet green pepper
1/2 cup chopped mushrooms
1 #2 can tomatoes, chopped
1/2 cup diced ham
2 oz. diced salt pork or bacon
1 oz. cooking oil
1/2 cup diced onion
1 tbsp. tomato paste
1/4 tsp. fresh thyme leaves
salt and pepper to taste
2 tbsp. Lea & Perrins
6 soda crackers, crushed

Pound conch to tenderize. Cook in water until tender, then grind. In large pot, add potatoes, celery, carrots, green pepper, mushrooms, tomatoes, and ham. Cover with 2 qts. water and cook over medium flame. Fry bacon or salt pork until brown. Remove from pan and sauté onions in same fat until tender. Add onions to other mixture and cook until all are tender. Add conch and cook 30 minutes more. Add Lea & Perrins and crackers last. Serve quickly.

## PORK CHOPS DOMINICAN STYLE

1/2 lb. pork chops
1 1/2 oz. onion
1 1/2 oz. tomato
1 oz. sweet bell pepper
1 1/2 oz. tomato sauce
1 cup chicken broth
1/2 can chick-peas

Season meat with salt and pepper. Sauté over low heat. When three-fourths done, add onion, tomato, and sweet pepper. Fry lightly a few minutes, then add tomato sauce, chicken broth, and chick-peas. Cook over low heat for 5 minutes or so. Serve with fried green plantain bananas and rice. Decorate with lettuce leaf, parsley, green and black olives, and slices of orange and tomato. Serves 1.

### COCONUT FLAVORED KID IN RUM

1/2 lb. kid (young goat)
1 oz. chopped onion
1 oz. chopped tomato
1 oz. chopped sweet bell pepper
olive oil
salt and pepper
a little oregano
1 oz. tomato sauce
1 tsp. vinegar
1/4 liter coconut milk

Sprinkle kid with olive oil. Then sauté in heavy pan, adding salt, pepper, and oregano to taste. After three-fourths cooked, add tomato, onion, and sweet pepper. Fry lightly a few minutes, then add tomato sauce, vinegar, coconut milk, and more salt and pepper as required. When meat is tender and gravy is thick, remove from flame and serve quickly with rice, yautia, and slices of ripe fried bananas. Decorate with lettuce

---

## EL EMBAJADOR
## Santo Domingo

*Great Caribbean foods are prepared at the El Embajador, which is said by many to be the finest hotel and dining facility in the Dominican Republic.*

leaf, parsley, green and black olives, sweet red pepper, and orange and tomato slices. Serves 1.

### DOMINICAN MANGU

2 green plantain bananas
small amount olive oil
2 eggs
a little chopped onion
2 slices avocado
1 slice tomato

Boil bananas until soft, then mash. Fry eggs and place on top of mashed bananas. Sprinkle with onion. Place a slice of avocado on each side and a tomato slice on top. Decorate with lettuce leaves, 1 sprig parsley, 1 green olive, 1 black olive, 2 slices of orange, 1 slice of fresh tomato, and 1/2 red pepper on top of all. Serves 1.

### CHICKEN CIBAO STYLE

1/2 lb. chicken, cut in large pieces
1 1/2 oz. chopped onion
1 1/2 oz. chopped tomato
1 oz. chopped sweet bell pepper
2 oz. olives
2 oz. capers

---

1 oz. tomato sauce
1 cup chicken broth

Serve with:

2 oz. spaghetti
1 1/2 oz. yautia
1 1/2 oz. yucca

Season chicken pieces with salt and pepper. Sauté over low flame in olive oil. When half done, add onion, tomato, pepper, olives, capers, and tomato sauce. Fry lightly, then add chicken broth. Let cook for 10 minutes. Serve with spaghetti, yautia, and yucca. Decorate with 2 slices of sweet green pepper, 1 black olive, and half of a hard-boiled egg.

### SAMANA
(*Dominican-style Fish*)

1/2 lb. sliced fish
1 1/2 oz. chopped onion
1 1/2 oz. chopped tomato
1 oz. chopped sweet bell pepper
1/4 liter coconut milk
1 oz. tomato sauce
salt and pepper to taste
lemon juice

Season fish slices with salt and pepper. Sauté in butter at very low heat. When half cooked, add onion, tomato, and peppers. Continue cooking until vegetables are tender. Add tomato sauce and a little lemon juice. Add salt and pepper to taste. Last, add coconut milk and let simmer for 10 minutes. Serve with boiled potatoes. When serving, garnish with lettuce leaves, fresh parsley, green and black olives, 1/2 of red pepper, 2 slices of orange, and 1 slice of tomato.

## CHOCOLATE VOODOO CAKE

Prepare 3 9-inch round layer cake pans. Prepare 1 1/2 cups coffee beverage and combine in double boiler with 6 oz. unsweetened, grated chocolate. Cook over simmering water, stirring constantly, until chocolate is melted and mixture thickens. Set aside to cool. Sift together and set aside:

**4 cups sifted cake flour**
**1 1/2 tsp. baking soda**
**1 tsp. baking powder**
**1 tsp. salt**

Cream together until soft:

**1 cup butter**
**2 1/2 tsp. vanilla extract**

Add gradually, creaming until fluffy after each addition, 3 cups firmly packed brown sugar. Then add in thirds, beating thoroughly after each addition, 4 well-beaten eggs. Measure 2/3 cup sour milk. Beating only until smooth after each addition, alternately add dry ingredients in fourths and milk in thirds to creamed mixture. Stir in chocolate mixture. Finally, beat only until batter is smooth and turn batter into pans. Bake at 375°, 30 to 35 minutes or until cake is done. Spread chocolate layers with creamy vanilla filling and swirl chocolate frosting around and over the cake.

## SHRIMP À LA PAULINE

**1 1/2 lbs. fresh or frozen large shrimp with shells**

Drop shrimp into a boiling mixture of:

**1 1/2 pts. water**
**3 tbsp. lemon juice**
**1 tbsp. salt**
**1 tsp. monosodium glutamate**
**3 or 4 sprigs parsley**
**1 clove garlic, peeled and split**
**1 bay leaf**
**small piece celery with leaves**

Cover tightly. Simmer 5 minutes or only until shrimp are pink and tender. Drain and cover with cold water to chill. Strain shrimp again. Remove tiny legs and peel shells from shrimp. Cut a slit to just below surface along back of shrimp to expose black vein. With knife point, remove vein in one piece. Quickly rinse

shrimp in cold water, drain, put into casserole and set aside.

For casserole mixture, heat 1/4 cup butter in skillet. Add 1 cup diced celery, 2/3 cup chopped onion, and 1/2 cup finely chopped green pepper and cook slowly until onion is tender, stirring occasionally. Thoroughly blend in 1 cup water, 3/4 cup tomato paste, 1 tbsp. minced parsley, and 4 or 5 drops Tabasco. Add 1/2 tsp. salt and 1/4 tsp. monosodium glutamate. Pour mixture into casserole. Mix gently to distribute shrimp evenly. Heat in 350° oven 30 minutes. When shrimp mixture is heated thoroughly, serve over hot rice. Serves 6.

## EGGS HABITATION

Lightly grease a 1 1/2-qt. casserole. Prepare 6 hard-cooked eggs. While eggs are cooking, set aside 1 can (4 oz.) sliced mushrooms (about 1/2 cup mushrooms) to drain, reserving liquid. Clean and chop 1 medium green pepper (1/2 cup), 1 medium onion (1/2 cup), and 1 stalk celery. Heat in skillet over low heat 1/4 cup butter. Add chopped vegetables and cook over medium heat, stirring occasionally, until onion is tender. Add mushrooms and continue cooking until mushrooms are lightly browned, stirring occasionally. Add gradually, stirring constantly, 2 cups sieved, cooked tomatoes. Simmer 5 minutes, stirring occasionally. Meanwhile, melt in a saucepan over low heat, 3 to 4 tbsp. butter. Blend in a mixture of 6 tbsp. all-purpose flour, 1/4 tsp. salt, 1/4 tsp. monosodium glutamate, and a few grains pepper. Cook over medium heat, stirring constantly, until mixture bubbles. Remove from heat and gradually add tomato/vegetable mixture, while stirring con-

stantly. Return mixture to heat and bring rapidly to boil, continuing to stir. Cook 1 to 2 minutes longer. Add to the reserved mushroom liquid enough cold milk to make 1 cup liquid. Pour into a bowl. Stirring constantly, gradually add the hot tomato/vegetable mixture to the milk mixture. Slice the hard-cooked eggs into the casserole, forming layers. Pour some of the tomato/milk mixture over each layer of eggs. Finally pour remaining tomato/milk mixture over sliced eggs. Sprinkle 1 cup buttered soft bread crumbs over top. Bake at 350° 15 to 20 minutes or until crumbs are lightly browned and mixture is heated through. Serves 6 to 8.

## BOUILLABAISE LECLERC

Set out a deep 10-inch heavy skillet with a tight-fitting cover. (Skillet should be large enough to allow fish filets to lie only one layer deep.) Set out 1 lb. red snapper filets and 1 lb. redfish filets. Thoroughly rub into fish filets a mixture of 2 tsp. minced parsley, 1 tsp. salt, 3/4 tsp. thyme, 1/2 tsp. allspice, 1/8 tsp. pepper, 2 finely crushed bay leaves, and 1 finely minced clove garlic. Clean and chop 1 large onion (3/4 cup). Heat in skillet over low heat 2 tbsp. olive oil. Add chopped onion and filets. Cover and cook over low heat 10 minutes, turning filets once. Meanwhile, wash 3 large ripe tomatoes. Dip into boiling water for about 1 minute to loosen skins. Peel tomatoes, cut out, and discard stem ends. Cut tomatoes into 1/4-inch slices and set aside. Remove filets from skillet, set aside, and keep warm. Pour 1 cup white wine into the skillet, stirring well. Add tomato slices and bring mixture to boil. Add 3 or 4 lemon slices, 1 cup hot fish stock or hot water, 3/4 tsp. salt, 1/8 tsp. pepper, and dash cayenne pepper. Simmer about 25 minutes, or until liquid is reduced almost one-half. Add the fish filets to skillet and continue cooking 5 minutes longer. Meanwhile, blend several tbsp. of the liquid in which the fish is cooking with a pinch of saffron. When fish has cooked 5 minutes, spread saffron mixture over filets. Remove filets from sauce and place on 6 slices buttered toasted bread. Pour sauce over fish. Serves 6.

## CURRIED GOAT OR LAMB

2 lbs. goat or lamb
2 tbsp. cooking fat
1 tbsp. curry powder
1/2 lb. diced potatoes
1 tsp. salt
1 onion
2 sweet peppers, diced
1 tsp. black pepper
1 1/2 cups water

Trim, wipe, and cut meat into 1-inch pieces. Season well with salt, pepper, and onions. Rub in curry well. Let stand 1 hour. Heat fat in skillet. Add meat and sauté. Then add water. Cover tightly and allow to cook on low flame until meat is tender. Add potatoes and cook until very soft and gravy is somewhat thickened. Serve hot in a ring of fluffy rice. Garnish with chutney.

## BEEF AND PEPPER CASSEROLE

12 oz. top round steak
1 lb. chopped ham
6 oz. chopped onion
6 oz. chopped sweet bell pepper
1 jar olives
1 oz. garlic
1 dash oregano
2 bay leaves
a little thyme
1 bottle red wine
8 oz. chopped onion
8 oz. chopped carrot
6 oz. chopped scallions
1 lb. tomatoes
3 oz. tomato paste
4 oz. corn oil

Cut steak in half. Open each half of steak so that inside of meat can be stuffed. Make stuffing by mixing chopped ham, onion, olives, garlic, sweet pepper, and spices. Stuff meat and roll each piece of meat back to its normal shape. Tie tightly with string. Brown meat in pan. When brown, remove from

---

### JAMAICA HILTON
### Arawak

*This is one of the greatest hotels in the West Indies and the world. The dining room has an international menu and features West Indian delicacies. Gerd Schwarz is the manager.*

---

pan and to same pan add onions, carrots, and scallions, then the tomatoes and tomato paste. Stir well, then add flour. When slightly browned, add wine and stock. Put meat back into pan and cook until tender. Serve with fried rice and braised eggplant.

## BANANA BREAD

4 or 5 ripe bananas
4 oz. sugar
pinch salt
1/2 tsp. baking soda
3 eggs
2 tbsp. corn oil
4 oz. sour cream
5 oz. flour

Mix bananas, sugar, salt, soda, and eggs. Add oil slowly, then add flour. Add sour cream last and bake in 325° oven until done.

## BAKED BANANA PUDDING

4 oz. bread crumbs
4 ripe bananas
2 eggs
1 pt. milk
4 tbsp. sugar
nutmeg
rose water

Mash bananas and add to them 2 tbsp. sugar and a squeeze of lime (some like more than a squeeze). Add a little nutmeg and rose water. Place this mixture into a very well buttered pie dish. Cover mixture with breadcrumbs. Make a custard with 2 beaten eggs and 1 pint milk plus 2 tbsp. sugar. Pour custard over bread crumbs and bake until golden.

## ARAWAK ARROW

4 oz. tenderloin
2 oz. lobster meat
3 oz. pineapple
1/2 oz. peanuts
1/2 oz. mango chutney
1/4 oz. white rum
2 oz. espagnole
1 oz. butter
1 oz. oil
salt and pepper
parsley

Cut beef into 4 pieces. Cut lobster into 2 pieces. Cut pineapple into 3 pieces. Arrange all on skewer. Sprinkle with salt and pepper. Sauté peanuts and mango chutney in butter; add rum and espagnole. Grill skewer in broiler or over hot coals, brushing with sauce now and then. Serve on bed of saffron rice topped with sauce. Garnish with grilled tomato and parsley.

## MANGO BOWL
*(Nonalcoholic)*

12 ripe mangoes
2 cloves
3 qts. water
sugar

Grate mangoes. Add water and cloves and bring to boil. Remove from heat and allow to cool. Strain. Sweeten to taste. Serve with crushed ice. Rum may be added for extra flavor.

### SANTEN
*(Coconut Milk)*

Santen is used in several of the recipes of Bali Floating Restaurant.

**1 coconut, grated**
**1 1/4 cups boiling water**

Pour boiling water over grated coconut. Let cool. Squeeze the coconut meat in the water for 2 minutes. Strain. Heavy liquid on top is santen.

### PISANG GORENG
*(Fried Bananas)*

Peel ripe bananas, cut in half, and then slice lengthwise. Make a good frying batter and dip banana slices in batter. Then fry in hot oil until light brown. Pisang Goreng can also be prepared without batter. Simply slice banana and fry in hot oil.

### ATJAR NANAS
*(Pickled Pineapple)*

**pineapple juice**
**pineapple slices**
**1/2 tbsp. grated onion**
**1 tbsp. vinegar**
**1/2 tbsp. turmeric**
**1/2 tbsp. ground long red hot pepper**
**cloves**

Make a sauce of the spices, vinegar, cloves, and pineapple juice. Add sliced pineapple and cook gently about 10 minutes.

### REMPAH
*(Small Meatballs)*

**1/2 lb. minced beef and pork**
**1 egg**
**salt and pepper**
**nutmeg**
**coriander**
**cumin seed**
**1 small onion, minced**
**4 oz. grated coconut**

Mix together; make into small balls and fry in oil until brown.

### GADO GADO
*(Mixed Vegetables with Peanut Sauce)*

**cauliflower**
**endive**
**bean sprouts**
**white cabbage**
**French green beans**

---

## BALI FLOATING RESTAURANT
## Oranjestad, Aruba

*Hosts Karl and Ron Schmand welcome you aboard this delightful floating restaurant. The architecture of the restaurant commemorates the great Battle of the Buffaloes. The high-peaked Minangkabau roofs are formed in the shape of buffalo horns. The food has an island flavor and is delicious.*

**cucumber**
**lettuce**
**hard-boiled eggs**

Wash vegetables and cook a short time; they should remain crisp. Make a peanut sauce (see below) but omit soy sauce. Pour the *warm* sauce over the *cold* vegetables that have been arranged on serving dish. Garnish with lettuce, sliced cucumber, and sliced boiled eggs.

### PINDA SAUCE
*(Peanut Soy Sauce)*

**1 tbsp. peanut butter**
**a little coriander**
**a little cumin seed**
**a little shrimp paste**
**a little fresh lemon juice**
**1 tbsp. finely chopped onion**
**1 tbsp. soy sauce**
**coconut milk**

Heat oil in pan and sauté onion with the spices; add peanut butter and make a smooth paste. Add soy sauce, lemon juice, coconut milk, and salt. Cook over low heat until mixture is not too thick.

### NASSI POETI
*(White Rice)*

**1 lb. rice**
**water to cook**

Wash rice thoroughly 3 or 4 times until water is clear. In order to obtain a very even temperature, a thick saucepan should be used. Add water to the rice to exactly one finger-joint above the rice. Bring to a full boil, then reduce heat and simmer gently until water is nearly absorbed. Cover tightly at this stage and continue cooking on very low flame for another 20 minutes.

### SAMBAL TELOR
*(Hard-boiled Eggs in Seasoned Sauce)*

**1 hard-boiled egg per person**
**2 tbsp. grated onion**
**1 clove garlic, crushed**
**1/2 tbsp. shrimp paste**
**1/2 tbsp. brown sugar**
**a little tamarind**
**1 tsp. laos (if available)**
**1 tbsp. ground long red hot pepper**
**1 1/2 cups fresh santen (coconut milk)**
**1 bay leaf**

Mix spices well and fry them in a little oil. Then add the Santen and bay leaf and let simmer and thicken, stirring now and then. Take out the bay leaf and pour sauce over halved hard-boiled eggs. Serve at once.

### FRICADEL DAGING
*(Indonesian Meatballs in special sauce)*

**1/2 lb. minced pork**
**1/4 tsp. cumin seed**
**1/4 tsp. pepper**
**1/4 tsp. ground nutmeg**
**1 small ground long red hot pepper**
**1 egg**
**1 onion, finely chopped**
**small amount shrimp paste**
**santen (coconut milk)**
**salt to taste**

Fry shrimp paste lightly in a little oil. Mix spices and minced meat, add an egg, and mix again. Make oval meatballs and fry lightly. Add coconut milk slowly and simmer gently until done.

### SAJOR LEMENG
*(Soup Indonesian Style)*

**white cabbage**
**string beans, cut**
**carrots, diced**
**1 clove garlic, diced**
**1 onion, diced**
**small amount turmeric**
**1 tsp. coriander**
**a little shrimp paste**
**santen (coconut milk)**
**1 oz. cut shrimp**
**1/2 lb. cubed beef or chicken**

Make a good stock of the beef or chicken. Fry shrimp paste and other spices in a little oil, then add vegetables. Pour in beef or chicken stock; add meat cubes, shrimp, and santen. Boil slowly only until vegetables are cooked. Vegetables should not be overcooked.

## RED SNAPPER CURACAO STYLE

2 lbs. filet of red snapper
1 large onion, chopped or sliced
1 medium green pepper, sliced
2 cloves garlic, chopped
4 tomatoes, peeled and chopped
salt and pepper to taste

MARINADE:

1/2 cup lime juice
2 scallions, finely chopped
1 clove garlic, minced
salt and pepper to taste

Rub the fish with the marinade for at least 1 hour. Cut the filets into serving pieces and coat them with flour and fry in hot butter quickly until nicely brown and crisp. Place in baking dish and keep hot. In the fish drippings, sauté the onion, green pepper, garlic, tomatoes, salt and pepper until the onion is transparent. Simmer for about 15 minutes. The creole sauce should be rich and thick. Just before serving, place the red snapper pieces in the sauce and heat thoroughly.

## FROG LEGS SAUTÉED À LA PROVENÇALE

12 frog legs
salt, pepper, lemon juice, and Worcestershire sauce as desired
flour
butter or oil
crushed garlic, as desired
chopped parsley

Season frog legs with salt, pepper, lemon juice, and Worcestershire. Sprinkle with flour. Sauté in butter or oil. At the last moment, add a little fine crushed garlic and chopped parsley. Heap on a platter and serve very hot. Serves 4.

---

# PENTHOUSE RESTAURANT
## Hotel Inter-Continental Curacao
## Willemstad, Curacao

*This great restaurant is perched atop a fine hotel in the beautiful city of Willemstad. It has a view for miles in every direction. The food is excellent.*

---

## VICHYSOISSE

4 medium-size leeks, white part only
1 oz. butter
3 medium potatoes, quartered and cut into slices the thickness of a quarter
1 pt. white consommé
salt
1 pt. boiled milk
1 1/2 oz. butter
12 slices French dinner rolls, very thinly sliced
heavy cream if serving cold

Finely mince white part of leeks. Put into pot with butter and sauté gently for 15 minutes. Add potatoes, moisten with white consommé, add salt to taste, and cook gently until potatoes are done. Finish the soup with the boiled milk and butter, pour into soup tureens, and add sliced rolls cut as thinly as possible. Creme Gauloise is made by adding cream and chilling.

## SOLE MURAT

1 medium potato, diced
2 raw artichoke bottoms, diced

1 sole
5 slices tomato
lemon juice
fresh parsley, chopped
butter, slightly browned

Sauté potato and diced artichoke in butter. Prepare the sole à la Meuniere and surround it with the potato and artichoke mixture. Lay on the sole tomato slices one-half inch thick that have been seasoned, dredged in flour, and sautéed in very hot oil until golden. Sprinkle on a few drops of pale melted meat glaze, a little lemon juice, and a pinch of chopped parsley. Cover all with slightly browned butter.

## DEMIDOFF CHICKEN SAUTÉ

1 chicken, cut up
vegetables as desired (carrots, turnips, potatoes, onions, etc.)
2 oz. truffles
3 tbsp. good veal stock

Brown chicken pieces in butter; add vegetables and bake until done. About 10 minutes before done, add truffles that have been cut to shape of crescents. Add veal stock. Simmer a few minutes longer. Serve chicken covered with the sauce.

## CHERRIES JUBILEE

fresh cherries, pitted
sugar and water syrup
cornstarch or arrowroot
cold water
1 tsp. Kirsch, heated for each serving

Poach pitted cherries in syrup just until tender and until syrup is reduced and thick. Thicken with a little cornstarch that has been diluted in cold water. Allow 1 tbsp. of thickening per half pint of syrup. Put cherries in small silver timbales. Pour thickened syrup over, then pour 1 tsp. of heated Kirsch into each timbale. Flame when serving.

## COURTBOUILLON

2 qts. water
2 tbsp. butter
6 whole black peppercorns
2 whole cloves
1 bay leaf
2 tbsp. vinegar
2 sprigs parsley
1 large onion, chopped
1 large carrot, chopped
3 stalks celery, chopped

Peel and chop vegetables. Melt butter in deep saucepan over medium flame. Add chopped vegetables. Sauté 5 minutes, or until golden brown. Add water, peppercorns, cloves, bay leaf, vinegar and parsley, cover tightly, and simmer 30 minutes. Strain and set aside for use in boiling shellfish.

## TURTLE BOURGEOISE

2 lbs. snapping turtle meat
1 onion, minced
1 tbsp. butter
1 tbsp. flour
1 bay leaf
1/2 cup sherry wine
1 clove garlic, minced
1 sprig thyme, minced
1 cup water
salt and pepper
6 slices buttered toast

Have turtle meat cut into 1-inch cubes. Melt butter in saucepan over medium flame. Add onion and sauté 3 minutes, or until golden brown. Gradually stir in flour. When smooth, add garlic, thyme, water, and bay leaf. Blend well. Add turtle meat and sherry wine, salt and pepper to taste, and cover to simmer gently over medium flame 1/2 hour, or until turtle meat is tender. Serve piping hot over buttered toast placed on preheated individual plates.

### VARIATION:

Any variety freshwater turtle may be prepared in same manner. Cook until tender. Serves 4 to 6.

## SMOKED MULLET WITH SPICED BUTTER

1 large smoked mullet (1 1/2 lbs.)
1 bunch watercress
1 tsp. chopped chives
1 lemon, sliced
1/4 lb. butter
1/8 tsp. pepper
1/8 tsp. dill
1/8 tsp. paprika

## GOURMET RESTAURANT
### St. Maarten

*Mullet Bay Beach Hotel's finest dining room was the site of the 1974 meeting of the* Chaine des Rotisseurs *Gourmet Society. It is a truly excellent dining room located on this half-French, half-Dutch tropical island.*

Arrange smoked mullet in shallow baking dish; place in preheated moderate oven (350°). Bake 10 minutes or until mullet is thoroughly heated. Meanwhile, melt butter in small saucepan over medium flame, brown carefully but do not allow to smoke, and add pepper, paprika, and dill to taste. Place hot mullet on preheated platter, quickly split fish open, pour spiced butter over fish, sprinkle lightly with chopped chives, and garnish with watercress and lemon slices. Serve immediately. To serve, cut through backbone and skin with very sharp knife.

### VARIATION:

Any soft-smoked whole fish, such as trout and whitefish, may be prepared in same manner. If preferred, chives may be omitted. Serves 4.

## DILL SAUCE LAUTERBRUNNEN*

1/2 tbsp. chopped dill
2 oz. butter
2 tbsp. potato flour
1 cup fish stock
1/4 tsp. salt
1/8 tsp. pepper

Melt butter in top section of double boiler placed in lower section halfway filled with boiling water. Gradually add flour, stirring constantly. Add fish stock, stirring constantly until sauce begins to thicken. (If thinner sauce is preferred, use more fish stock.) Add salt, pepper, and dill, blend well, and simmer gently 20 minutes. Serve piping hot over baked, pan-fried, or boiled fish. Serves 4.

*Lauterbrunnen is the name of the picturesque Swiss village situated in the Valley of Lauterbrunnen in the Bernese Oberland.

## MUSSELS FISHERMAN'S STYLE

4 doz. mussels, in shells
1 small onion, chopped
1 bay leaf, crumbled
2 tbsp. minced parsley
pinch of cayenne

1/2 cup dry Sauterne
1/4 tsp. thyme
1/8 tsp. dill
2 oz. butter
salt and pepper

Select large, fresh mussels with shells closed. Scrub well, rinse under running water, and place in large saucepan. Add onion, bay leaf, parsley, cayenne, Sauterne wine, thyme, and dill. Cover tightly, steam actively 2 minutes or until shells open, remove, and drain. Strain broth through fine sieve and reserve. Take meats from shells, remove dark, hairy beard, set meats aside. Pour broth into small saucepan and simmer 2 minutes. Add butter, season with salt and pepper to taste. Add mussels, and heat to boiling point but do not boil. Place small bowl of sauce in center of preheated plate, arrange mussel meats around bowl. Dip mussels into sauce and eat.

### VARIATION:

Soft-shell clams may be prepared in same manner. Allow 1 or 2 dozen for each serving. Serves 4.

## MULLET CHOWDER

3 mullet heads
2 slices diced bacon
2 1/2 cups water
1 small onion, chopped
2 stalks celery, chopped
1/2 cup chopped mushrooms
2 sprigs parsley
2 medium potatoes, diced
2 tbsp. butter
2 tbsp. flour
1/8 tsp. pepper
2 tsp. salt
2 cups milk
paprika

Purchase freshwater mullet heads. Remove gills and wash heads thoroughly in salted water. Pour 2 1/2 cups water into deep pot; add salt, parsley, celery, and mullet heads. Cover and simmer 15 minutes. Strain. Save fish stock. Place bacon in large skillet. Brown over low flame 5 minutes. Add onions and mushrooms, sauté 5 minutes or until onions are light brown. Meanwhile, pour fish stock into deep pot and add potatoes. Boil 10 minutes or until potatoes are tender. Add sautéed onion, mushrooms, and bacon from skillet. Melt butter in separate pot, gradually stirring in flour and pepper. When smooth, slowly add milk, stirring constantly. Cook 5 minutes or until slightly thick. Combine milk mixture with fish stock mixture and bring to boiling point, stirring constantly. Serve piping hot in preheated bowls. Garnish with paprika, chopped parsley, or favorite green herbs. Serves 6 to 8.

## LOBSTER DANDIES IN WHISKEY
### (Shrimp)

1/4 cup butter
3 tbsp. oil
1 clove garlic
1/2 medium onion, chopped
1/2 large sweet green pepper, finely chopped
3 lemon peels, finely chopped
1 lb. deveined, peeled shrimp
1/3 cup cognac
1/3 cup whiskey
4 cups heavy cream
dash paprika
salt

Heat oil and butter in heavy pan. Add garlic, onion, green pepper, and lemon peel. Sauté until vegetables are tender, then add shrimp. Toss well, flame with cognac and whiskey, then stir in heavy cream, paprika, and salt. Cook until thick. Serve with rice.

## PORK TENDERLOIN SU CASA

2 4-oz. pork filets
ground black pepper
salt
flour
1/2 glass dry sherry
4 tbsp. heavy cream
a little light brown gravy (canned or fresh)
2 oz. fresh crabmeat
Hollandaise sauce

Season pork with pepper and salt, then roll in flour. Sauté in heavy skillet until lightly browned. Add sherry, gravy, and heavy cream to make a smooth consistency. To serve, place filet on serving plate with 1 oz. of crabmeat on top, then cover with Hollandaise. Glaze lightly under broiler. Serve with asparagus and Parisienne potatoes. Serves 2.

## SHRIMP OBREGAN

2 lbs. deveined, peeled shrimp
3 cloves garlic
peel of 1 lemon
1/2 small juice glass Pernod
1 qt. heavy cream
1 tsp. lemon juice
salt and butter to taste

Place sufficient butter in skillet and sauté shrimp to light brown color. Add Pernod gradually. Simmer until cooked down, then add garlic, lemon peel, salt, and heavy cream. Boil gently until thick, then add lemon juice just before serving. Serve hot. Serves 6.

---

### SU CASA
### Dorado Beach Hotel
### Dorado Beach

*Situated on 1,500 palm-dotted acres about twenty miles west of San Juan, this magnificent hotel was built by Laurance Rockefeller. Haute cuisine prepared by executive chef Alfred Fahndrich is served in this fine dining room.*

---

## MOROTA
### (Spoon Bread)

1 pt. milk
1/2 oz. sugar
1/4 oz. salt
2 oz. butter
6 oz. white cornmeal
1/4 oz. baking powder
3 eggs
1 tsp. vanilla extract

Heat milk until simmering, then add sugar, salt, and butter. Stir and bring to boil. Add white cornmeal to boiling milk. Stir for 3 to 5 minutes until very creamy. Remove from heat and let cool, then add eggs and baking powder. Mix well. Pour into baking pan and bake over pan filled with water for 1 hour in 400° oven. Serves 4.

## COLD BANANA SOUP WITH CINNAMON CROUTONS

Combine approximately equal amounts of peeled and sliced bananas, milk, and light cream and blend thoroughly in a blender. Add a dash of cinnamon, a dash of ginger, 1 tbsp. lemon juice, and blend the mixture again. Chill and serve with cinnamon croutons.

### CINNAMON CROUTONS:

Cut slices 1/2 inch thick from a loaf of bread. Remove the crust and cut the slices into small cubes. Brush the cubes with melted butter and bake them on a baking sheet in a hot oven until they are golden. While still hot, sprinkle them lightly with ground cinnamon.

## ARROZ CON COCO
### (Rice and Coconut Pudding)

1 cup rice
2 large coconuts or enough to make 6 cups coconut milk

---

1 piece ginger, mashed
6 cinnamon sticks
1 1/4 tsp. salt
1 cup sugar
1 cup seeded raisins

Soak rice in 1 qt. of water for 2 hours; drain thoroughly. Set aside 1 cup coconut milk and combine other 5 cups in a kettle with rice, ginger, cinnamon, and salt. Cook slowly without stirring for 30 minutes, then add sugar, raisins, and reserved cup of coconut milk. Mix well and cook another 40 minutes, removing rice gently from pan sides toward center every 10 minutes to prevent sticking. Pour into serving dishes and sprinkle with cinnamon if desired.

## LA BARQUILLA DE PINA NEPTUNE
### (Pineapple Boats stuffed with Shrimp, Prawns, and Mushrooms in a Rum and Sherry sauce)

2 lbs. prawns
2 lbs. red scampi
1 lb. fresh mushrooms
1 wine glass Puerto Rican rum
1/2 wine glass dry sherry
1 qt. heavy cream
1 tsp. lemon juice
6 medium-sized fresh pineapples scooped out to make boats
salt
butter
Hollandaise sauce

Place sufficient butter in skillet and sauté the mushrooms, prawns, and scampi until brown. Add rum and sherry gradually. Simmer until cooked down, then add cream and salt to taste. Boil gently until thick, then add lemon juice last. Pour into pineapple boats and top with Hollandaise sauce. Glaze under broiler until browned. Serve with Plantains in Almibar.

## PLANTAINS IN ALMIBAR

6 ripe bananas
1/4 lb. butter
1 cup sugar
3 tsp. cinnamon
1/2 to 1 cup Log Cabin syrup

Bananas should be large and blackish in color. Carefully split peels lengthwise and peel off. Cut off ends of bananas. Brown all sides of bananas in a large skillet containing the butter. Sprinkle the sugar, cinnamon, and syrup over the bananas. Cook very gently, watching constantly, until mixture caramelizes. Serves 6.

## SOPA DE FRIJOLES NEGRAS
*(Black Bean Soup À La Puro)*

3 lbs. black beans
12 qts. water
2 ham hocks
3 onions
9 green peppers
1 1/2 #2 cans pimentos
3 cups olive oil
3 platanos (plantains)
3 dashes mill-ground black pepper
salt to taste

### GARNITURE:

1 tbsp. steamed whole-grain white rice
1 tbsp. finely diced raw onion

Soak 3 lbs. of habichuelas negras (black beans) in cold water overnight. Put to boil in 12 qts. of water with 2 ham hocks. Then simmer over low heat for 1 1/2 hours. (Season with salt and pepper.) Add sofrito (finely chopped or ground onions, green peppers, and pimentos, sautéed in 3 cups of olive oil until soft). Then add 3 platanos (plantains) cut in fine slices. Continue to simmer the potage till beans are almost pureed, approximately another 1 1/2 hours. Remove bones from pot when desired thickness has been obtained. Serve with garniture of cooked whole grain white rice and finely diced raw onion. Serves 20.

## TEMBLEQUE
*(Coconut Pudding)*

1 qt. milk
8 oz. Coco Lopez (cream of coconut)
2 oz. cornstarch
1/2 tsp. vanilla extract

Mix 1 pint of milk, 8 oz. of Coco Lopez, and 1/2 tsp. vanilla extract. Bring this mixture to a boil. Blend 1 pint of milk with 2 oz. of cornstarch until dissolved, and add to mixture. Pour mixture into a champagne cup and chill to set. Serve cold with a generous sprinkle of cinnamon on top. Serves 12.

---

# SOVEREIGN'S COURT
## El Conquistador Hotel
## Las Croabas

*This magnificent hotel bills itself as "a hillside of miracles." There are 380 acres of tropical paradise here on the east coast of Puerto Rico where one has a dazzling view of the Virgin Islands, the Caribbean, and the Atlantic. One of several great dining rooms, Sovereign's Court offers gourmet meals served in a luxurious atmosphere.*

---

## EL YUNQUE BANANA CREAM PIE

4 eggs
1/4 cup sugar
pinch salt
1/4 tsp. nutmeg
1 tsp. lemon juice
1 1/2 cups milk
3 bananas

Beat 4 eggs lightly. Add 1/4 cup sugar, a pinch of salt, 1/4 tsp. nutmeg, 1 tsp. lemon juice, 1 1/2 cups milk, and 3 bananas, mashed and pressed through a fine sieve. Turn into a pastry-lined pie plate and bake in a hot oven (450°) for 10 minutes. Reduce the temperature to 325° and bake about 35 minutes, or until the custard is set. Serve cool with whipped cream. Decorate with sliced bananas. Serves 10.

## CHEF ALICEA'S STUFFED SHRIMP

1 1/2 loaves white bread
1/2 lb. chopped, cooked shrimp
1/4 lb. chopped, cooked lobster
3/4 lb. king crabmeat
2 cups mayonnaise
1/2 cup minced onions
1/2 cup minced green pepper
1/4 lb. butter
2 tsp. dry mustard
1 tbsp. Tabasco sauce
1/4 bottle Worcestershire sauce
3 eggs
salt, pepper, and Accent to taste
30 large raw shrimp (scampi size)
2 tbsp. paprika

Sauté onions and green pepper in 1/4 lb. butter until vegetables are soft. Take crust off bread, crumble into crumbs, and mix well with all ingredients except 30 raw shrimp. Combine mixture with onions, green pepper, and butter. Split shrimp up the middle, taking care not to cut completely through. Remove vein and lay in pan or casserole. Divide mixture into 30 equal balls and press gently into open shrimp. Put stuffed shrimp in 350° oven for half an hour. Serve 3 shrimp per person with grilled or baked tomato halves and a green vegetable. Serves 10.

## CARNE ENCEBOLLADA
*(Steak with Smothered Onions Puerto Rican Style)*

3 lbs. lean round steak (1/2 inch thick)
2 large onions
1 1/2 cups olive oil
1 tbsp. wine vinegar
1 bay leaf
1 clove garlic
2 tsp. salt
1/2 tsp. mill-ground black pepper
2 tsp. finely chopped parsley

Cut 3 lbs. lean round steak 1/2 inch thick in 8 pieces. Pound to 1/4 inch thickness. Prepare marinade with 2 large onions sliced thinly, 1 1/2 cups of olive oil, 1 tbsp. of wine vinegar, 1 bay leaf, and 1 clove of garlic finely chopped. Season with 2 tsp. of salt, 1/2 tsp. of black mill-ground pepper, and let marinate overnight in refrigerator. Sauté meat over high flame until brown on both sides. Remove and place on hot platter. Sauté marinated onion slices in same skillet until soft and lightly colored. Cover meat with onions. Sprinkle with fresh finely chopped parsley. Serve with a garniture, per person, of one fried banana (whole banana peeled and deep fried to a golden brown) and steamed whole-grain rice. Serves 8.

## VIANDA CON BACALAO

1 lb. pumpkin
1 lb. ñame (yams)
1 lb. yautia (malanga)
1 lb. sweet potatoes
2 green bananas
1 lb. bacon
1 lb. onions
2 lbs. clean codfish
2 tbsp. capers
2 tbsp. olives
2 cloves garlic
1 cup oil

Boil cod and place in cold water to remove skin and bones. Cut cod into small pieces. Fry bacon, chopped onions, garlic, and cod for 5 minutes before serving. Boil yam, yautia, and green bananas for 10 minutes in a separate container. Add pumpkin and sweet potato and return to fire until reaching a soft texture. Serve these vegetables to complement cod. Serves 10.

## ZARZUELA DE MARISCOS COSTA AZUL

*(fish chowder)*

1 lb. halibut
1 lb. red mullet
1 lb. sole
1 lb. jumbo shrimp
1 lb. scallops
8 oz. carrots
8 oz. onions
4 oz. leeks
4 fresh tomatoes
1 lb. potatoes
4 oz. finely chopped garlic
6 egg yolks
12 oz. olive oil
1 tsp. saffron
5 oz. tomato paste
4 oz. white wine

Cut seafood into small pieces and marinate for 4 hours in white wine, saffron, salt, and pepper. A fish stock made from fish bones should be prepared to be used later in the recipe. Mix chopped garlic and egg yolks, whipping constantly while pouring in olive oil until mixture thickens like a mayonnaise. (The blend obtained is called "Aioli.") Cut vegetables into small pieces. Sauté diced vegetables (except potatoes and tomatoes) in olive oil for a few minutes. Then add tomato paste and fresh tomatoes and moisten with fish stock. Simmer until vegetables become soft. Then add shrimp, scallops, diced potatoes, and marinade (just the liquid) into mixture. Let simmer for 10 minutes.

---

### SALON PONCIANA
### Hotel Inter-Continental
### Ponce
### Ponce

*Gourmet American, Continental, and native cuisines are served to the tempo of smooth latin rhythms in this famous dining room.*

Then add halibut, sole, and red mullet and simmer for 5 minutes. Just before serving, thicken fish chowder with "aioli." Serve with rice pilaf as side dish. Serves 12.

## PIÑON

12 ripe plantains
2 lbs. green beans
5 lbs. ground meat (1/2 beef, 1/2 pork)
2 lbs. onions
2 cloves garlic
8 oz. tomato sauce
8 oz. peanut oil
8 oz. pitless olives
1/2 lb. green peppers
2 oz. capers
12 eggs

Sauté in peanut oil the onion, garlic, green peppers, olives, and capers for 5 minutes. Add ground meat and tomato sauce. Simmer for 15 minutes and season to taste. Cut plantains into thin slices lengthwise. Place on a greased baking sheet. Bake in oven for 3 minutes and allow to cool. Use greased baking pan, approximately 8 to 10 inches long. Place alternate layers of sliced plantains, green beans, and meat sauce. Brush with beaten eggs. Repeat layers until it reaches a height of 2 inches. Cover with a last layer of plantains and beaten eggs. Place in oven at 250° for 40 minutes. To serve, cut into 2 X 3-inch squares. Accompany with a beef gravy and rice and beans. Serves 10.

## STUFFED DOUBLE LOIN OF LAMB ASPISI

6 lbs. boneless lamb loin
2 oz. Italian seasoning
6 oz. finely chopped onions
2 oz. chopped garlic
2 bunches fresh parsley

6 oz. butter
1 pt. fresh bread crumbs

Take boneless lamb loin and season with Italian seasoning, salt, and pepper. Sauté in butter the finely chopped garlic, onions, and parsley. Add fresh bread crumbs until all butter is absorbed. Also season this stuffing with Italian seasoning, salt, and pepper. Fold double lamb loin to form a cylinder. Sew ends together and stuff center with the spicy stuffing. Place in 250° oven for 45 minutes. When ready to serve make an aromatic gravy with Italian seasoning. Serve with roast potatoes, boiled tomatoes, and braised lettuce as side dishes. Serves 12.

## TEMBLEQUE

24 oz. milk
6 oz. sugar
3 oz. baking powder
2 oz. water
1 lemon
1 pinch salt
1/2 oz. cinnamon
1/2 oz. ginger
1 coconut milk (from 1 coconut)

Boil milk with sugar. Mix in separate container coconut milk, lemon, cinnamon, and ginger. Add mixture to boiled milk and sugar. Thicken with baking powder dissolved in the cold water. Add pinch of salt and cook for 3 minutes, stirring constantly. Pour in parfait glasses. Chill and sprinkle with cinnamon. Serve chilled. Serves 10.

## GUANIMOS DE MAIZ

1 lb. cornmeal
18 oz. chicken stock
4 oz. butter
12 ea. 8 X 8-inch pieces of plantain leaves (aluminum foil can substitute for plantain leaves, if not available)

Combine chicken stock, butter, salt, and pepper and bring to a boil. Remove from fire and add cornmeal slowly, mixing it with a wooden spatula or a mixer until smooth. Return to fire for 3 minutes. Place mixture on plantain leaves in 4 X 4-inch squares, 1/2 inch thick. Fold leaf to enclose mixture and secure with fine string. Place in boiling water for 20 minutes or steam for 10 minutes. Serve in leaf while still hot. Serves 10.

## FRESH CHICKEN LIVERS SAUTÉ AU PORTO

25 to 30 oz. fresh chicken livers, cut in small pieces
1 medium onion, chopped
4 oz. sliced mushrooms (fresh or canned)
2 oz. butter or vegetable oil
chopped parsley for decoration
2 cups beef gravy (from braised beef)
salt, pepper, and a little rosemary to taste
2 oz. port wine (dry sherry)

Quickly sauté chicken liver in hot frying pan. Remove liver to warm plate. Add some butter to the pan, then add onions, mushrooms, meat gravy, and wine and let simmer for 5 minutes. Return livers to this gravy and quickly warm up. Season with salt, pepper, and rosemary. Arrange on platter and decorate with parsley. Serve with omelette or as a main course with rice, noodles, or potatoes. Serves 6.

### ST. MORITZ SCHNITZEL

Cut 2 2-oz. cutlets from lean veal leg. Flatten carefully very thin, cover 1 cutlet with a slice of lean Danish ham and a slice of Swiss cheese (Borden's processed Swiss Cheese), and cover with the second cutlet. Season with salt and pepper, turn in flour, beaten egg, and bread crumbs. Fry the stuffed veal cutlet in sweet butter to a golden brown over low heat so that the cheese inside melts. Serve the St. Moritz schnitzel with a

---

# SWISS CHALET
## San Juan

*The tables and chairs in this restaurant were made by Swiss wood-carvers and Puerto Rican cabinetmakers. A group of Swiss chefs prepare the finest gourmet foods.*

---

wedge of lemon, a little brown gravy, and a garniture of vegetable.

### COQ AU VIN À LA GENEVOISE

3 2 1/2-lb chickens, disjointed
2 cups cooking oil
2 onions, chopped
1 clove garlic, chopped
2 bay leaves
rosemary, salt, pepper, and flour
3 cups red wine (Chambertin)
1 cup tomato puree
3 cups chicken stock (consommé)

Fry disjointed chicken that has been prepared with salt, pepper, and flour in hot oil until brown. Add diced vegetable, bay leaves, rosemary, tomato puree, and sprinkle with flour. Add wine and chicken stock, mix well, and cook on small fire, covered, for about 20 minutes. Remove chicken, strain sauce when thick enough, add some sautéed fresh mushrooms and some pearl onions.

---

Serve in casserole very hot with buttered rice on the side. Serves 6.

### OLD-FASHIONED BASLER SAUERBRATEN

4 1/2 lbs. bottom round of beef
1/2 cup cooking oil
2 large carrots, diced
2 large onions, peeled and diced
1 clove garlic, chopped
1 stalk celery, diced
2 cups red wine
1/2 cup red wine vinegar
2 tsp. sugar
salt
3 tbsp. flour
8 cups beef stock (consommé)
1 tbsp. tomato paste
bay leaves, rosemary

Wipe meat well with damp cloth and place in a deep mixing bowl. Add cut vegetables, vinegar, spices, and red wine until meat is covered. Leave meat in marinade for at least 4 days in cool place. Remove meat from the marinade, dry, then brown well on all sides in hot oil. Sprinkle with flour and tomato paste and let brown with some sugar. Add vegetables and liquid in which meat has been marinated, add some red wine and beef stock, mix well, and cook covered until meat is tender (2 to 3 hours). Remove meat and strain sauce. Cook the sauce until slightly reduced. Slice the meat in thin slices and serve covered with the sauce (add some dry raisins to the sauce). The sauerbraten is served with buttered Spaetzle and braised red cabbage. Serves 6.

## ESCARGOT STUFFED MUSHROOMS PROVENCALE

fresh mushroom caps
canned snails
dry white wine
fresh tomatoes (3 for every 2 doz. snails)
butter (1/4 lb. per 2 doz. snails)
salt and pepper
2 cloves garlic for every 2 doz. snails
fresh parsley, chopped (1 tbsp. per doz. snails)

Drain snails, place in saucepan, and cover with wine. Bring to boil; simmer 10 minutes, drain but reserve liquid. Peel tomato skins and put tomatoes in pot with butter. Add finely chopped garlic and parsley. Pour in remaining wine liquid and simmer until thickened (at least 1 hour). Sauté mushroom caps briefly in garlic butter and remove to baking sheet open side up. Sauté snails briefly in the same garlic butter. Then stuff 1 snail in each mushroom cap. Before serving, heat mushroom-snails through in a moderate oven; place several on each plate, cover with sauce, and serve.

## QUICHE LORRAINE

pastry for 2 9-inch 1-crust pies
8 slices bacon
1/4 lb. smoked ham, cut into small cubes
1 onion
1 lb. finely grated Gruyere cheese
1 lb. finely grated Emmenthaler (Swiss) cheese
2 cups cream
4 eggs, lightly beaten
1/2 tsp. nutmeg
salt and pepper

Preheat oven to 450°. Line 2 9-inch pie plates with pastry and bake 5 minutes. Cook bacon until crisp and remove from skillet. Pour off all but 2 tbsp. of fat. Sauté finely chopped onion until transparent and add pieces of ham. Crumble bacon and sprinkle, with onion and ham mixture, over bottom of pie plates. Fill each pie to within 1/4 of an inch from the top of the pie plate with the combined grated cheeses. In blender, combine eggs, cream, nutmeg, salt, and pepper. Pour over cheese, lightly stirring to fill any air spaces (the finer the cheese is grated, the less this should be a problem). Bake 15 minutes at 450°, then lower temperature to 350° and continue baking for 20 minutes to a half hour or until lightly browned on top and a knife inserted into the center comes out clean.

---

## CANE BAY PLANTATION
## St. Croix

*At this great resort guests enjoy the epicurean delicacies created by Maria Dublin, a famous chef known all over the West Indies for her Key Lime Pie and other specialties. Weather permitting, these delights are served to guests on the beautiful dining terrace.*

## GAZPACHO

2 cloves garlic
1 medium onion, sliced
1 cucumber, sliced
4 tomatoes (very ripe), peeled
1 green pepper, seeded
salt and pepper
1/4 cup wine vinegar
1/4 cup olive oil
2 cups tomato juice
Tabasco sauce to taste

Finely chop the first 5 ingredients. Rub bowl with another clove of garlic. Combine chopped vegetables with the vinegar, oil, tomato juice, and a dash of Tabasco sauce (to taste); place in bowl and refrigerate. (It's actually better if made at least 8 hours prior to serving.)

### GARNISH:

minced hard-boiled egg
croutons
1 cucumber
1 onion
1 green pepper

Each garnish should be also finely chopped and served on the side of the soup from individual dishes.

## CANE BAY'S VEAL ROLLATINI

6 large veal scallops
1/2 lb. sliced smoked ham
1/2 lb. sliced Emmenthaler or domestic Swiss cheese
1 pkg. frozen chopped spinach
1/4 cup flour
1 stick or 1/2 cup butter
2 cups beef broth
salt and pepper
1/4 to 1/2 cup red wine
oregano

Pound the veal scallops with a mallet until they are thin. On each piece of veal lay a thin slice of ham and a thin slice of cheese. Divide half a package of chopped spinach, thawed, into 6 parts and put 1 part on each scallop. Roll up the scallops and fasten with wooden toothpicks. Dredge the rolls in the flour, reserving the remainder. In a skillet brown rolls on all sides in the butter. Transfer the rolls to a shallow baking dish. With a wire whisk stir the reserved flour as smoothly as possible into the butter remaining in the skillet. Add 2 cups of beef broth, salt, and freshly ground black pepper to taste, and simmer the sauce stirring constantly, for about 10 minutes or until smooth and thickened. Remove the sauce from the heat and stir in the red wine. Strain the sauce over the veal rolls; sprinkle the dish with a little oregano and bake in a moderate oven (350°) for 30 minutes. Remove the wooden picks and serve.

## ROAST DUCKLING WITH BLACK CHERRY SAUCE

1 4 to 5-lb. thawed duckling
salt and pepper
1 cup pineapple juice
1 #2 can black pitted cherries
1/3 cup Cherry Heering brandy
1 tbsp. cornstarch

Heat oven to 420°. Remove giblets, wash, drain, and pat duckling dry. Season cavity and outside of duck with salt and pepper. Place duckling on a rack and roast for 30 minutes. Drain fat and reduce heat to 375°. Roast an additional hour, draining fat at the end of each 30-minute period. Pour the cup of pineapple juice over the duck and roast an additional 30 minutes basting with juice several times. Remove duck from pan, skim off the remaining fat, and reserve liquid. Quarter duck, discarding the backbone.

### SAUCE:

Drain the can of cherries. Combine the cherry juice with the strained reserved drippings from the pan. Bring to a boil, add cornstarch, and stir until smooth and thickened. Add cherries and Cherry Heering and heat through on a low fire. Just prior to serving, place cut pieces of duckling under the broiler for 5 to 10 minutes to crisp (most important!). Place crisped pieces of duck on heated platter, pour sauce over the fowl, and serve immediately.

## ESCARGOTS GRAPEVINE

24 escargots
1/3 lb. butter
3 cloves garlic, finely chopped
1 tbsp. parsley, finely chopped
1 tsp. shallots, finely chopped
2 tsp. finely chopped blanched almonds
1/4 tsp. curry powder
1 tsp. Worcestershire sauce
1/2 tsp. paprika
1/2 tsp. powdered thyme
1/2 cup cognac or white wine
salt and pepper to taste

Mix all ingredients with the butter, except cognac or white wine. Put a little of the butter mixture in each of 24 shells; put an escargot in each shell, and a little of the butter mixture to cover the top. Just before baking in a hot oven, pour over the white wine, or flambe with cognac after cooking. Serve immediately, with garlic bread.

## CONCH CHOWDER

2 lbs. chopped conch meat
2 onions, finely chopped
5 tomatoes, peeled and diced
1 bunch celery, finely chopped
5 green peppers, finely chopped
3 leeks, finely chopped
2 tbsp. butter
4 qts. fish stock or fish bouillon
5 carrots, diced
1 small green papaya, diced
1/2 cup sherry
saffron (a pinch)
Tabasco sauce to taste
bouquet garni (bay leaf, 1 sprig fresh thyme, 3 cloves, 5 sprigs parsley)

In a large saucepan sauté onions, leeks, tomatoes, celery, and green pepper in the butter. Add the conch meat, saffron, and 4 qts. of fish stock. Bring to boil gently, adding the bouquet garni. Season with salt and pepper to taste. When the conch meat is tender, add the carrots and papaya and cook until the carrots are tender. Remove the bouquet garni, and season to taste with Tabasco. Add the sherry just before serving. Serve with finger-shaped pieces of toast, rubbed with garlic and buttered.

## POMPANO GRAPETREE

2 lbs. filet of pompano fish
2 tbsp. butter

---

## GRAPETREE BEACH HOTEL
## Christiansted, St. Croix

*The Rotunda dining room of the Beach Hotel overlooks the hotel's pool and long, beautiful beach. French West Indian cuisine is expertly prepared and served to guests as they dine leisurely by candlelight.*

5 shallot cloves, chopped finely
1 sprig parsley, chopped finely
2 tomatoes, peeled and diced
5 large mushrooms, sliced
1 tsp. ground thyme
1 tbsp. Worcestershire sauce
1 tsp. paprika
1 tsp. curry powder
salt and pepper to taste
1 1/2 cups dry white wine

Butter a baking dish, using half of the butter. Utilize half of the shallots, parsley, tomatoes, mushrooms, thyme, Worcestershire sauce, paprika, and curry powder to form a bed in the dish on which to lay the filet of pompano. Then sprinkle over the fish salt and pepper, white wine, and the remaining shallots, parsley, tomatoes, mushrooms, thyme, Worcestershire sauce, paprika, and curry powder. Let it marinate for 1 hour. Before baking in 350° oven, put tips of remaining butter on the filet of pompano and cover with aluminum foil. No need to prepare a butter sauce—serve with the natural juices and wedges of lemon. Serves 3.

## CREPE DE FRUITS DE MER GUIGNOL

1/4 cup butter
2 tbsp. finely chopped shallots
1 tbsp. finely chopped parsley
1 tsp. finely chopped chervil
12 fresh mushrooms, sliced
4 1/2 oz. shrimp
4 1/2 oz. sea scallops
4 1/2 oz. lobster
4 1/2 oz. crabmeat
4 cups fish stock
pinch paprika
1 cup heavy cream
2 cups Hollandaise sauce
4 light crepes

---

Melt the butter in a pan; add the shallots, chervil, mushrooms, salt, and pepper. Add the shrimp, sea scallops, lobster, and crabmeat. Taste now and then for seasoning, and add paprika and parsley. Deglaze with champagne and fish stock. Let it simmer to reduce, then add the heavy cream. In the meantime prepare the Hollandaise sauce. Mix half the Hollandaise with the seafood, reserving the balance for broiling. Spread a little fish sauce in a gratin dish. Divide the seafood mixture between the 4 crepes, wrap them, and lay in the dish. Pour rest of Hollandaise sauce over the crepes, sprinkle lightly with paprika, and glaze quickly under the broiler. Serves 4.

## STUFFED CUCUMBERS

3 cucumbers
3 tbsp. butter
3 onions, finely chopped
4 tomatoes, peeled and chopped
8 mushroom caps, sliced
1 bay leaf
1 tsp. powdered thyme
salt and pepper to taste
bread crumbs
6 tbsp. grated Parmesan cheese

Cut peeled cucumbers in half and scoop out the seeds; parboil in boiling water for 5 minutes; drain very thoroughly, and allow to dry. Melt the butter in a skillet, add the onion, and cook slowly until brown. Add tomatoes, bay leaf, and sliced mushrooms; sprinkle with thyme and salt and pepper to taste, and cook gently until tender. Discard the bay leaf and divide the mixture among the 6 cucumber halves. Sprinkle with bread crumbs and Parmesan cheese, and run the stuffed cucumbers under the broiler. Serve in a hot dish.

## PLANTAIN FLAMBE CRUZAN RUM

4 ripe plantains
2 cups vegetable oil
2 tbsp. sugar
6 tbsp. Cruzan rum (gold)

Peel and split lengthwise 4 ripe plantains. Fry them in hot oil until golden brown; drain on absorbent paper. Arrange the plantains on a serving dish, sprinkle with the sugar, and pour over 6 tbsp. of warmed Cruzan gold rum. Ignite the spirit and serve flaming. Serves 4.

## SHRIMP TEMPURA

32 jumbo shrimp, cleaned, deveined,
   and butterflied
3 eggs
1 pt. milk
1/2 lb. flour
4 tsp. baking powder
1 tsp. salt

Beat eggs, add milk, then slowly add flour until smooth batter forms. Add baking powder and salt. Heat oil in deep fryer until 350° is reached. Cover each shrimp completely in batter. Slowly drop into oil until golden brown. Serve with French fries. Serves 8.

## CRUZAN FISH CHOWDER

1 1/2 qts. fish stock
2 lbs. diced fish
1 lb. diced onion
1/2 lb. diced green pepper
1/4 lb. diced leeks
1/4 lb. diced tomato
2 tsp. Worcestershire sauce
3 drops Tabasco sauce
3 tsp. salt
1/2 cup tomato paste
2 tsp. pepper
1 tsp. garlic salt

Sauté fish with diced vegetables until tender. Add tomato paste slowly, then add fish stock. Cook over medium heat for 1 hour. Add seasoning and cook for 15 minutes more. Serve immediately. Serves 8.

## ONION SOUP

2 lbs. onions
2 qts. beef consommé or stock

## GUTHRIE'S
## Christiansted, St. Croix

*This is one of the finest restaurants in the Caribbean. Located in Christiansted, it has a view of the lovely surroundings that are typical of this magnificent area of the world. The food is superbly prepared and graciously served.*

3 tsp. salt
2 tsp. pepper
2 oz. white wine
1/2 lb. butter
1 bay leaf
1 oz. monosodium glutamate
6 1/2-oz. slices Swiss cheese
1 cup croutons

Slice onions very fine. Melt butter, add onion, and sauté until brown. Add consommé or stock. Simmer for 30 minutes. Add remaining ingredients and simmer another 30 minutes. Place soup in au gratin bowls. Drop croutons on top and cover with a slice of cheese. Put under broiler to melt the cheese. Serve immediately. Serves 6.

## MUSHROOM CAPS STUFFED WITH ESCARGOTS

48 escargots
48 large button mushroom caps
1 lb. garlic butter
1 lb. butter
1 oz. chopped garlic
1 oz. chopped onion
1 oz. chopped celery

1 oz. chopped parsley
1 oz. cognac
1 oz. white wine
1 tsp. salt
1 tsp. pepper
1 oz. Worcestershire sauce

Soften butter and add above ingredients and mix well. Stuff caps with small amount of mixture. Place escargots inside caps. Cover with remaining mixture. Put into preheated 450° oven until butter is completely melted. Can be cooked in uncovered baking pan or escargot plates. Serve with garlic bread and salad. Serves 8.

## CONCH CREOLE

3 lbs. cleaned conch meat
1 lb. diced sweet green peppers
1/2 lb. diced onions
1/2 lb. diced tomatoes
2 cups tomato paste
2 tsp. thyme
2 bay leaves
1 tsp. poultry seasoning
4 tsp. salt
1/2 lb. green papaya

Put conch meat to boil with the papaya. Papaya helps tenderize conch meat, which is quite tough and rubbery. Boil until fork can penetrate conch easily. Drain juice and save. Sauté vegetables until tender, then add tomato paste. Combine conch stock and vegetables. Simmer for 1/2 hour. If sauce becomes too thin, add a little flour to thicken. Add conch meat and simmer for 10 minutes. Add seasoning and simmer another 5 minutes, then serve with rice. Conch Creole can be made and stored in refrigerator and simply heated when ready to serve. Serves 8.

## STUFFED BAKED KINGFISH

Bone a 10 to 12 lb. kingfish without destroying the whole fish. Sprinkle the inside with lemon juice, white wine, and a little salt.

### STUFFING:

2 lbs. crabmeat
1/2 lb. broken shrimp
2 cloves garlic, finely chopped
1 bundle parsley, finely chopped
1 stalk celery, finely chopped
1 large onion, finely chopped
2 bay leaves, finely chopped

Bind stuffing with 2 cups bread crumbs and 5 eggs. Finish seasoning with a dash of Tabasco sauce, marjoram, salt, and white pepper.

Place the stuffing in the middle of the fish. Fold over the other half of the fish so that it looks like a whole kingfish again. Now wrap the fish in cheesecloth and tie with string. Place it in a large pan of boiling water that has been seasoned with salt, whole black pepper, lime juice, and bay leaves. Simmer for approximately 15 minutes. Remove fish from water and place it on a rack to cool. When it is cool, unwrap it, place it in a baking pan and place in the oven and bake for another 20 minutes at 300°. Remove from oven, garnish with fresh limes and parsley. Cut the fish, retaining shape if possible. Serves 8.

## SAUTÉED KINGFISH CANEEL BAY

4 10-oz. fresh kingfish filets
2 limes
1 tsp. Worcestershire sauce
3 tomatoes, diced and peeled
2 fresh avocados, diced

Sauté kingfish filets in butter. Remove from pan. Add lime juice, Worcestershire sauce, tomatoes, and fresh avocados. Simmer for about 3 minutes. Pour over filets and serve with parsley potatoes. Serves 4.

## LOBSTER BROCHETTE VIRGIN ISLE

### LOBSTER BROCHETTE:

2 lbs. fresh lobster
3/4 fresh pineapple

---

## CANEEL BAY PLANTATION
## St. John

*This magnificent resort has three open-air dining rooms. Facing the main beach, one has two levels and a great view of St. Thomas as well. At night, diners can listen to the surf and see the sparkling lights of the neighboring island through the trees.*

2 limes
1 1/2 oz. rum
4 oz. cream of coconut
1 tbsp. cornstarch
salt, pepper, paprika

Cut lobster and pineapple into 1-inch cubes and put on a skewer. Season with fresh lime juice, salt, and paprika. Put in a shallow pan and bake for 20 minutes at 375°. Remove from pan and place on Caribbean Rice. To baking pan add rum and cream of coconut, bring to boil, and thicken with cornstarch. Pour over brochette, garnish with fresh lime and parsley, and serve. Serves 4.

### CARIBBEAN RICE:

1/2 lb. rice
2 oz. diced ham
1/4 fresh pineapple, diced
2 stalks celery, diced
4 oz. raisins
3 oz. butter
1 qt. chicken stock

Sauté diced pineapple, celery, ham, raisins, and rice in butter. Add chicken stock, bring to boil, and simmer 20 minutes. Serve.

### SHRIMP CREOLE

1/2 onion
2 green peppers
2 tomatoes
2 cloves garlic
1 bay leaf
1/2 oz. tomato ketchup
1 oz. tomato paste
dash Worcestershire sauce
dash Tabasco sauce
salt and pepper

---

2 oz. V-8 juice
20 shrimp

Sauté the vegetables in butter; first onions and garlic, then the green pepper, tomato ketchup, tomato paste, spices, and V-8 juice and let simmer. Boil the shrimp separately and add them to the sauce. Add Worcestershire and Tabasco sauces. Serve on pilaf rice. Serves 4.

## STUFFED CORNISH GAME HEN ANNABERG STYLE

4 1 lb. Cornish game hens

### STUFFING:

1/2 fresh pineapple
3 oz. shredded coconut
3 oz. raisins
2 oz. white bread crumbs
1/2 oz. rum
2 eggs

Combine shredded coconut, crushed pineapple, raisins, white bread crumbs, eggs, and rum. Mix well. Stuff hens with this mixture and roast for 25 minutes in 375° oven.

### SAUCE:

1/2 fresh pineapple, diced
1 oz. rum
1/2 tsp. ginger
1 bay leaf
3 cups brown chicken stock
1 tbsp. cornstarch
salt and white pepper

Brown diced pineapple. Add rum, chicken stock, and bay leaf. Bring to boil and simmer for 15 minutes. Thicken with cornstarch. Season to taste with salt, ginger, and white pepper. Serve hens on wild rice. Pour sauce over and serve. Serves 4.

## PINA COLADA FRAPPE

1/2 fresh pineapple, crushed
4 oz. cream of coconut
1 1/2 oz. rum

Blend pineapple and cream of coconut, add rum, and serve chilled. Serves 4.

## GINGERED SATI BABI

3 lbs. trimmed pork tenderloin
3/4 tsp. salt
1/8 tsp. ground black pepper
1 tbsp. ground coriander
1 tbsp. cumin seed
1/2 tsp. vegetable oil
1/2 cup sliced onions
1 tbsp. brown sugar
1/4 cup soy sauce
1 tsp. monosodium glutamate
1/4 tsp. powdered ginger
lime juice

Cut meat into 1 1/4-inch cubes. Combine all ingredients in a bowl, add meat, and marinate for at least 3 hours. Thread meat on skewers. Broil or cook in 350° oven for 15 minutes, basting frequently and turning often. Serve on bed of rice, using pork drippings for gravy. Serves 6.

## BAKED GROUPER WITH SHRIMP AND CRABMEAT DRESSING

Use 8 oz. grouper filets. Season with salt, pepper, Accent, and lemon juice. Place on buttered baking sheet and cover filets with white wine. Place in moderate oven and cook gently. Remove from oven, place fish on oven-proof dinner plate. Spread with 4 oz. dressing, sprinkle with Parmesan cheese, and place under broiler until golden brown. Garnish with lemon and parsley.

## DRESSING:

1/2 lb. finely chopped king crab
1/2 lb. finely chopped broken shrimp
1/2 cup finely chopped onion
1/2 cup finely chopped celery
3 cloves garlic, crushed
1/4 lb. butter
1/4 lb. flour
1 pt. milk
salt, pepper, and monosodium glutamate to taste

Place butter in heavy skillet and melt over medium heat, then add flour to make a roux. Add milk slowly until a

---

thick white sauce has been obtained. Add seasonings to taste. Fold in minced ingredients and cook for 5 to 10 minutes over slow fire. Dressing is ready to spread over grouper filets.

## HAM AND SHRIMP JAMBALAYA

2 cups water
2 tsp. salt
1 cup uncooked white rice
2 lb. uncooked medium shrimp (16 to 20 per lb.)
6 tbsp. butter
1 1/2 cups finely chopped onion
2 cloves garlic, finely chopped
1/3 medium can whole peeled tomatoes, finely chopped, including juice
3 tbsp. tomato paste
1/2 cup finely chopped celery
1/4 cup finely chopped sweet green pepper
1 tbsp. finely chopped parsley
3 cloves, crushed
1/2 tsp. crumbled dried thyme
1/2 tsp. cayenne pepper
1 lb. cooked lean smoked ham, trimmed of fat, cut into 1/2-inch cubes

---

Bring water and 1 tsp. salt to boil. Add rice, stir, and cover. Reduce heat to low and simmer for 20 minutes or until rice is tender and has absorbed all the liquid. Fluff rice with fork, cover, and set aside. Wash shrimp under cold water. Drop into enough boiling salted water to cover completely and cook briskly for 4 to 5 minutes or until shrimp are pink and firm. With a slotted spoon, transfer to bowl and set aside. In heavy skillet, melt butter over moderate heat. Add onions and garlic, stirring frequently. Cook 5 minutes or until soft and translucent but not brown. Add tomatoes, tomato liquid, and tomato paste. Stir over moderate heat for 5 minutes. Add celery, green peppers, parsley, cloves, thyme, cayenne, black pepper, and the remaining tsp. of salt. Stirring frequently, cook uncovered over moderate heat until vegetables are tender and mixture is thick enough to hold its shape in a spoon. Add ham and cook 5 more minutes. Stir in shrimp, then rice. Serves 10.

## CURRIED CHICKEN CHARLOTTE AMALIE

2 1/2 lb. deboned chicken, cut into 2-inch squares
2 cups diced onion
2 cups diced celery
2 cups diced potatoes
4 cloves garlic, crushed
4 tsp. curry powder
2 tbsp. Jamaica relish (or chutney)
2 apples, diced and peeled
2 oz. raisins
1/4 lb. butter
1 lb. rice
2 tsp. monosodium glutamate
2 cups chicken stock

Melt butter in heavy skillet over medium heat. When heated, place garlic in skillet and sauté until lightly browned. Add curry and stir 2 to 3 minutes. Add stock and all ingredients except potatoes. Cover and simmer until chicken is half cooked. Add potatoes and cook for 20 minutes, stirring until potatoes break down and thicken the mixture. Serve on bed of rice. Garnish with shredded coconut, sliced banana, and mango chutney.

## PINEAPPLE SANGRIA

6 or 7 ice cubes
9 oz. red Burgundy wine
3 oz. pineapple juice
1 oz. lime juice
1 oz. soda

Place ingredients in a large pitcher. Stir well and serve.

## PINEAPPLE FRENCH DRESSING

1 cup olive or salad oil
1/2 cup unsweetened pineapple juice
1/2 tsp. salt
few grains cayenne
1/4 tsp. white pepper
1 tbsp. honey
2 tbsp. chopped parsley

Place all ingredients in jar and shake well. Keep refrigerated.

## PINEAPPLE RUM PUNCH

1 1/2 oz. light rum
1 oz. pineapple juice
1 oz. orange juice
1/4 oz. grenadine

Combine ingredients in a shaker. Add ice cubes, shake well, and pour into tall glass. Garnish side of glass with pineapple wedge and cherry on toothpick.

## PINEAPPLE DONKEY KICK

2 oz. dark or light rum
1/4 oz. orange liqueur
1 oz. pineapple juice
1/4 oz. lime juice
1/4 oz. sugar

Combine ingredients in a bar glass. Add ice cubes, shake, and pour in a tall glass. Garnish edge of glass with pineapple wedge.

## PINEAPPLE DAIQUIRI

1 1/2 oz. dark or light rum
1/4 oz. orange liqueur
1 1/2 oz. pineapple juice
2 pineapple rings
1/4 oz. lime juice
1/4 oz. simple sugar syrup

Put ingredients in a blender cup. Blend slowly and add ice slowly until a frothlike mixture is made. Serve in a wine glass or Old Fashioned glass and try to fill it over the edge. Add cherry on top. Serve with short straw.

---

# PINEAPPLE BEACH RESORT
## St. Thomas

*This magnificent resort serves excellent cuisine and fascinating, exotic drinks. Delicious Continental and American foods are served in an open-air dining pavilion overlooking a beautiful pool and fountain.*

## PINEAPPLE CUSTARD PIE OR TARTS

3/4 cup sugar
2 tbsp. cornstarch
1/8 tsp. salt
1 cup milk
3 eggs, separated
1 cup drained, crushed pineapple

Mix sugar, cornstarch, salt, and milk in top of double boiler. Add 3 beaten egg yolks and cook until thickened. Remove from heat, add drained, crushed pineapple and 3 stiffly beaten egg whites. Cool. Pour into baked pastry shell.

## PINEAPPLE MARMALADE

1/4 cup dark brown sugar
1 cup canned crushed pineapple

Mix together and cook over medium heat, stirring constantly, until thick. Serve hot or cold.

## PINEAPPLE BAKED BEANS

2 16-oz. cans baked beans
4 oz. ketchup
3 oz. pineapple juice
4 slices canned pineapple, cut in small chunks
4 all-beef frankfurters, sliced into 1/4-inch pieces
1 tbsp. brown sugar
pinch monosodium glutamate
pinch ground cloves

Place all in a deep pan and mix carefully. Then place in deep casserole. Top with 1 or 2 pineapple rings. Place in 250° oven for 30 minutes.

## PINEAPPLE CHICKEN

2 2 1/2-lb. chickens, cut into small pieces
salt, pepper, bay leaves, oregano
garlic
lemon juice
1 onion, cut coarsely
1 cup sliced pineapple, cut coarsely
1 cup whole tomatoes, cut coarsely
1/2 lb. seedless raisins
2 tbsp. tomato paste

Season chicken with salt, pepper, garlic, and lemon juice. Let stand for 1 hour. Prepare a sauce with the onion, pineapple, tomatoes, raisins, and tomato paste. Sauté onion, pineapple, and tomatoes coarsely. Sauté onions with butter in a saucepan until lightly browned. Add the pineapple, tomatoes, raisins, and the juices from tomatoes and pineapple. Add the tomato paste and 1 cup pineapple juice, 2 bay leaves, pinch of oregano, salt and pepper to taste. Simmer for 30 minutes. Brown chicken in frying pan, and finish cooking in oven at 375° for 25 minutes. To serve, place chicken on a bed of rice, pour sauce over, and garnish with grated coconut. For a special treat, serve in an upright full pineapple shell after the inside has been removed.

## PINA COLADA

1 1/2 oz. light rum
1 1/2 oz. pineapple juice
2 pineapple rings
2 oz. cream of coconut
1/4 oz. lime juice
1/4 oz. orange liqueur

Place ingredients in a blender cup. Add ice and blend together until a creamy mixture is made. Pour into tall glass, add straw, and serve.

## PINEAPPLE SWEET POTATOES WITH RUM

4 cups hot, mashed sweet potatoes
1/4 cup butter
1/3 cup milk
1/2 tsp. cinnamon
1/2 tsp. salt
1/4 cup dark rum
1 cup pineapple chunks
1/2 cup pineapple juice
1/2 cup miniature marshmallows
butter
grated orange rind

Combine sweet potatoes, butter, milk, cinnamon, and salt. Combine rum, pineapple chunks, pineapple juice, and marshmallows and fold into sweet potato mixture. Mix until light and fluffy. Turn into buttered casserole. Dot with butter. Sprinkle with grated orange rind. Bake in 400° oven for 30 to 40 minutes. Serves 4.

## VEAL COTELETTES AMANDINE

4 veal steaks, 1/2 inch thick (or veal
    cutlets)
salt and pepper
2 tbsp. butter
4 tbsp. slivered almonds
2 tbsp. fresh lime juice

Pound veal with flat side of heavy knife until somewhat thinner. Dust with salt and pepper. Sauté in butter until lightly browned and tender. Remove from pan and keep warm. In same butter, quickly brown almonds, stir in lime juice, and cook 1 minute. Pour almonds and butter over cotelettes. Garnish with parsley. Serves 4.

## LOBSTER ANEGADA

4 large lobster tails (frozen rock lobster
    tails are similar to those of the
    Caribbean)
8 oz. tomato sauce
2 tbsp. sherry wine
2 tbsp. rum
1/2 tsp. pepper
1/2 tsp. prepared mustard
1/4 cup Hollandaise sauce (or mayon-
    naise)
grated coconut for topping

Cook lobster. Remove the meat and dice in large pieces. Save shells. Combine meat with tomato sauce, sherry, rum, pepper, mustard, and mix well. Simmer for 5 minutes. Fill lobster shells with mixture, cover with Hollandaise or mayonnaise, sprinkle with grated coconut. Place under hot broiler until bubbly. Serves 4.

## HOMEMADE PEACH CHUTNEY

2  cups crushed fresh or frozen
    peaches, (if available, substitute the
    pulp of 2 fresh, ripe mangoes)
1 tbsp. fresh lime juice
1 tsp. sugar
1/8 tsp. powdered ginger
1 tsp. chopped fresh mint or 1/2 tsp.
    dried mint leaves

---

## LITTLE DIX BAY
## Virgin Gorda

*Continental cuisine and Caribbean delicacies are served in the dramatic central pavilion of this magnificent resort. It has an excellent view of Little Dix Bay.*

Blend together the mashed fruit, lime juice, sugar, ginger, and mint. Serve immediately on toast or use as chutney.

## LITTLE DIX CONCH OR SHRIMP COCKTAIL

3 cups minced raw conch (conch is a
    Caribbean shellfish available in
    some supermarkets; if not avail-
    able, substitute 2 lbs. shelled, de-
    veined, and cooked shrimp)
1  medium sweet green pepper,
    chopped
1 medium sweet red pepper, chopped
1 heart of celery, chopped
3 scallions, chopped
6 tbsp. fresh lime juice
salt and pepper to taste
hot red pepper sauce to taste
6 sweet pepper shells, red or green,
    hollowed out

Mix together the chopped red and green peppers, celery, scallions, lime juice, salt, pepper, and red pepper sauce. Allow mixture to rest for at least 30 minutes. Spoon into hollowed out pepper shells. Serve chilled on lettuce leaves.

## LITTLE DIX COCONUT PIE

1 1/2 cups grated coconut
1/2 cup milk
3 eggs, well beaten
1 cup light brown sugar
1/2 tsp. cinnamon
1/2 tsp. apple pie spice

---

9-inch unbaked pastry shell
3 egg whites
1 tsp. fresh lime juice
3 tbsp. superfine sugar

Mix together the coconut, milk, well-beaten eggs, brown sugar, cinnamon, and apple pie spice, and turn into the pastry shell. Bake in a hot oven (400°) for 15 minutes. Remove. Cool slightly. Make meringue by beating the egg whites until stiff, adding 1 tsp. lime juice and the superfine sugar. Spread over the pie and replace in oven (still at 400°) and glaze for 5 minutes, or until meringue peaks are tinged with gold.

## FROZEN RUM SOUFFLE

3 eggs, separated
1/2 cup sugar
8 oz. whipping cream
12 pieces sponge cake, cut in 1-inch
    squares 1/4 inch thick
rum to taste, enough to soak the cake
grated sweet chocolate for topping

In a pan, add 1/4 cup sugar (4 tbsp.) to the 3 egg yolks and beat over hot-water bath until foamy. Then set pan on ice and keep beating until cold. Beat the 3 egg whites until stiff, add the remaining 1/4 cup sugar, and fold this into the egg yolk mixture. Whip the heavy cream and fold this into the mixture very lightly. Butter the inside, around the top, of a 1 1/2 or 2-quart souffle dish, so as to hold a paper band. Make a band of stiff paper about 2 1/2 inches wide to fit all around the inside rim of the souffle dish, arranged so that 1 1/2 inches extends above the top of the dish. Spoon some of the souffle mix over the bottom of the dish and arrange sponge cake pieces soaked in rum on top; then another layer of mix and sponge cake, continuing until the dish is filled to the top of the paper rim. Place in freezer. When frozen, sprinkle top with grated sweet chocolate. Remove the paper band and defrost to eating consistency. When served, it has the appearance of a hot souffle. Serves 6.

## ROAST DUCK À LA CLUB CARIBEE

4 1/2 to 5-lb. Long Island duck
1/2 medium onion, chopped fine
2 cloves garlic, chopped fine
1/2 tsp. salt
fresh black pepper
2 tbsp. soy sauce
2 oz. dry sherry
2 tbsp. liquid smoke mixed with another 2 tbsp. soy sauce

Wash duck and thoroughly dry inside and out. Fold excess neck skin to back and secure with skewer. Lace wings back tight. Stand duck upright at 45 degree angle and salt and pepper inside. Add onions, garlic, soy sauce, and sherry. Close and sew up or skewer opening and secure legs. Gently rotate duck so mixture coats all of insides. Place on rack in baking pan and brush on liquid smoke and soy sauce mixture. Cook for 2 hours in 300° oven. After first hour, prick skin all over every 15 minutes to let out grease and make skin nice and crisp. Cut in quarters to serve.

## LOBSTER TAILS IN RUM BUTTER

4 lobster tails
4 cloves garlic, chopped fine
1 tbsp. oil
2 tbsp. butter or margarine
1/2 cup dark rum
fresh ground black pepper

Remove shell from lobster tails by cutting tails in half lengthwise and removing both sections of meat, discarding back vein. Put oil and butter in skillet and add garlic. Bring to medium heat, then add lobster tail halves. Turn and stir until lobster turns white and is cooked, but do not overcook. When lobsters are done, add a little black pepper. Pour rum over to flame. As flame burns, keep tossing and turning. Serve at once as flame dies out. This is a colorful dish to do at the table over a burner.

---

## CLUB CARIBEE
## Hawksbill, Antigua

*Club Caribee covers thirty-eight acres of an old sugar plantation and has a full mile of shoreline with four private beaches, and a great dining room that serves island delicacies second to none.*

### PUMPKIN SOUP
*(As a puree first course or with beef and dumplings as an entree)*

### PUREE OF PUMPKIN SOUP:

4 medium onions
4 medium potatoes
equal amount fresh pumpkin or Hubbard squash
2 tsp. chicken base
salt and pepper to taste

Quarter onions and potatoes and cut peeled pumpkin in equal-sized pieces. Place all in saucepan and cover with cold water to 1 inch above. Add chicken base, salt, and pepper and boil until soft and tender. Remove potatoes, onions, and pumpkin to blender. Add enough water from pan to blend to puree stage. Season again to taste and return to pan to heat and serve.

### PUMPKIN SOUP WITH BEEF AND DUMPLINGS:

Make puree of pumpkin soup above and set aside. Meanwhile cut 2 lbs. beef chuck or pot roast that has some fat into 1-inch cubes and boil in small amount of water until very tender and water cooks down to about 1 cup. Add puree of pumpkin soup and bring to boil. Drop in dumplings (your favorite recipe), cover, and cook until done. We use a hard dumpling in the West Indies but some people prefer a lighter dumpling using more baking powder.

---

## CHICKEN WEST INDIAN

1 2 1/2 to 3-lb. chicken, cut into serving pieces
2 medium onions, sliced
1 medium green pepper, cut lengthwise in 1/4-inch strips
4 small garlic buds, chopped fine
3 whole cloves
1/4 tsp. ground thyme
1/2 small can tomato paste
3 tbsp. oil
salt and pepper to taste
2 limes
1 1/2 cups water

Dry chicken well and spread out on flat surface, skin side down. Squeeze juice of 2 limes over chicken, add salt and pepper to taste, and let stand. Heat oil to medium in skillet and sauté onions, peppers, and garlic until not quite done. Remove to platter leaving as much oil in skillet as possible. Place chicken in skillet skin side up and lightly brown, then turn to skin side down. Cover chicken with onions, peppers, and garlic from platter. Sprinkle thyme over all. Mix tomato paste with water and 1/2 tsp. salt and pour over chicken. Drop in three cloves, cover, and bring to boil. Reduce heat and simmer 30 minutes or until chicken is done. Serve with rice with a spoonful of sauce including onions and peppers over the rice.

## HOT COLD FISH
*(A spicy appetizer)*

4 medium onions, peeled and sliced thin
2 medium green peppers, sliced long and thin
2 carrots, cut round and very thin
1/2 tsp. crushed thyme
1 tsp. salt
1/4 tsp. black pepper
4 small hot chili peppers, seeded and quartered
1/2 cup fresh lime juice
1/2 cup cold water

1 cup dry white wine (Chablis preferred)
1 cup seasoned flour
1/2 cup olive oil
2 lbs. firm white fish

Combine first 10 items in saucepan and bring to boil. Reduce heat and simmer, covered, for 5 minutes. Remove from heat and let stand. Season flour with salt and pepper and place in shallow pan or plastic bag to coat fish. Select firm fish. Kingfish steaks are best but red snapper or halibut or any firm, white fish filets will do. Dust fish with seasoned flour. Add olive oil to skillet and fry fish over high heat quickly until both sides are brown (about 3 minutes each side). Remove fish immediately to shallow heat-proof dish. Pour mixture from saucepan over fish, spreading the vegetables evenly across top of fish. Let set to cool, then refrigerate for 24 hours. Remove from refrigerator 1 hour before serving. Serves 8 as appetizer; serves 4 as main dish. Just be sure your guests enjoy a hot spicy taste.

## BEEF PELAU

1/2 can pigeon or black-eyed peas
2 lbs. boiling beef, cut in 1-inch cubes
1 medium onion, cut in 1/2-inch pieces
1 medium green pepper, cut in 1/2-inch pieces
2 cloves garlic, chopped fine
2 tbsp. oil
1/2 tsp. thyme
1 can beef consommé
salt and pepper to taste
1 cup rice

Add oil to saucepan and sauté onion, pepper, and garlic until onions are golden. Drain. Remove from pan. Add beef and lightly brown all sides. Add consommé and enough water to cover 1 inch above meat. Bring to boil, then reduce heat, and simmer until tender. Drain off stock and add enough water to make 2 cups. Sprinkle thyme over meat and cover with onions and peppers. Add

## CLUB CARIBEE
## Hawksbill, Antigua

1 cup rice over this. Season stock with salt and pepper and pour over meat mixture. Add peas. Bring to boil, then cover, and reduce heat to very low. Cook for 30 minutes or until rice is done.

## WEST INDIAN SUNDAY BREAKFAST

A famous, standard West Indian Sunday breakfast can be a brunch delight, serving salt fish, fungi, choba, pear, eggs, and plantains.

### SALT FISH
*(Salt Cod or Ling Fish)*

2 medium onions, sliced thin
2 green peppers, sliced long and thin
8 fresh green onions, cut in 3-inch long strips, including green stem as far as tender
4 medium tomatoes, cut in eighths
1/4 lb. salt pork
2 lbs. salt fish

Soak salt fish 1 hour in cold water, drain, cover again in water in saucepan, and bring to boil. (Watch pan, as good salt fish will boil over the first time.) Boil for 5 minutes, drain, and repeat 2 more times. The last time (3rd time), boil until fish is cooked but firm. Rinse in cold water. Debone fish and peel off skin. Break in fairly large-sized pieces (about 2 inches) and set aside.

Cut salt pork in 1/4-inch cubes and place in skillet over moderate heat. Cook until grease is removed and cubes are crisp. Add sliced onions and green peppers and sauté with pork cubes until onions are tender. Turn fire high for a few minutes until onions are slightly burned at edges and reduce heat. Add green onions, tomatoes, and salt fish and cook until tomatoes are cooked, stirring and

turning. Add a few grindings of black pepper. Mixture should be moist but not sloppy.

### FUNGI
*(Cornmeal and Okra)*

Use 1/2 package frozen okra or 12 pods fresh okra cut in 3/4-inch pieces and boil in 2 cups water, salting to taste. When okra is cooked, gradually add enough cornmeal, while stirring, to make a heavy paste (amount varies). When cooked, spoon out large full spoonfuls into buttered stainless steel or glass bowl and toss in butter until it makes large round balls about 2 or 3 inches in diameter. Place balls on serving platter.

### AVOCADO AND EGG

Peel avocado and slice in 1-inch strips lengthwise. Quarter hard-boiled eggs and arrange both on serving platter.

### PLANTAINS

Plantains (cooking bananas) are available in many markets nowadays. They are a delightful taste treat.

Cut off both ends of plantains and run knife down full length of 1 side to just cut skin. Insert finger in cut and peel off skin. Cut lengthwise into 3 pieces. Heat small amount of oil and fry until golden brown on both sides. Serve at once.

### CHOBA
*(Eggplant)*

2 medium eggplants
1/8 lb. butter

Wash eggplants, cut off ends, and quarter with skins on. Place in large saucepan, cover with cold water, add salt, and boil until tender. Drain, add butter, chop, and mash with wooden spoon. Serve at once.

## CORAL REEF COCONUT CREAM PIE

**8 oz. basic flan pastry**

Roll out the pastry to a 10 1/2-inch circle on lightly floured board. Lift into a 9-inch flan ring; trim edges. Prick base and chill.

### FILLING:

**2 oz. sugar**
**pinch salt**
**pinch grated nutmeg**
**4 oz. finely grated, peeled ripe coconut**
**1 tsp. vanilla flavoring**
**1 1/4 cups hot milk**
**3 egg yolks, slightly beaten**

Add sugar, salt, nutmeg, coconut, and vanilla to the milk and stir in egg yolks until well blended. Turn into the pastry case and bake immediately in very hot oven for 10 minutes. Reduce heat to moderately hot to prevent filling from curdling, and continue baking another 35 minutes or until filling has set. Cool.

### TOPPING:

**3 egg whites**
**pinch cream of tartar**
**4 oz. sugar**
**1/2 tsp. vanilla flavoring**
**glacé cherries**

Beat egg whites with cream of tartar until stiff, then add sugar and vanilla very slowly, beating constantly. When pie is cool, spread meringue over top and bake in moderate oven for 12 to 15 minutes until lightly browned. Decorate with cherries and serve hot or cold. Serves 6.

## CURRIED PRAWNS IN COCONUT

**1 1/2 lbs. live prawns or shrimp or 8 to 12 oz. peeled prawns or shrimp**
**salt (optional)**
**juice of 1 lime, strained (optional)**

---

## CORAL REEF CLUB
## Barbados

*This magnificent resort has an incomparable beach-front location and a charming dining room that overlooks the Caribbean. The cuisine is internationally famous and includes Continental favorites and tropical specialties.*

**2 tbsp. olive oil**
**1 onion, chopped**
**1 tbsp. chopped chives (or shallots)**
**2 tomatoes, peeled and chopped**
**2 tbsp. curry powder**
**1/2 pt. fish stock or water**
**1 oz. butter**
**1 oz. flour**
**2 small coconuts**

Scald live prawns or shrimp in boiling salted water for 10 minutes. Drain, peel off shell and head, slit backs and remove the black cord. Clean in lime juice and salted water. Heat oil in frying pan, add onion, 1 tsp. chives or shallots, then tomato and curry powder, and cook for 5 minutes without browning. Add stock or water and prawns and simmer over low heat for 15 minutes. Remove from heat. Blend butter and flour together and add in small pieces to prawns, stirring until smooth. Continue cooking 3 additional minutes. While prawns are cooking, halve the coconuts and fill the halves with the prawn mixture. Sprinkle with remaining chives or shallots. Allow one-half coconut per person. Serves 4.

## CHICKEN IN TARRAGON AND ORANGE SAUCE

**6 portions chicken or turkey breast**
**6 oz. white wine**
**1/2 pt. chicken stock**
**1 6-oz. can concentrated orange juice**
**1 pt. cream**

---

**1 tsp. tarragon**
**salt and pepper**

Poach chicken in wine and stock, having seasoned stock with salt and pepper. Add tarragon and continue poaching for 10 minutes. Add orange juice and stir until well blended into mixture. Cook 5 minutes more. Add cream and cook gently for 5 minutes. Place chicken breasts into serving dish and pour sauce over; garnish with chopped parsley. If a thicker sauce is preferred, make a roux with 1 oz. butter and 1 oz. flour and add to sauce in pan. Cook gently until flour is cooked and sauce has thickened.

## CHILLED YOGURT SOUP

**2 cups plain yogurt**
**1 cup cold chicken broth**
**6 ice cubes**
**2 cucumbers, peeled, halved, seeded, and coarsely grated**
**1 cup minced red radishes**
**2 tbsp. white wine vinegar**
**2 tbsp. olive oil**
**1 tbsp. chopped fresh mint**
**salt and white pepper to taste**

In large bowl, combine yogurt, chicken broth, ice cubes, cucumbers, radishes, vinegar, and olive oil. Add fresh mint, then salt and white pepper to taste. Pour soup into 6 glass bowls, being careful to have ice cubes in each bowl. Garnish with more radish slices and fresh mint leaves.

## FLAMING BANANAS

**12 bananas**
**1/2 lb. sugar**
**1 pt. orange juice**
**1 lemon or lime**
**1/2 pt. rum or brandy**
**1 lb. butter**

Place sugar and orange juice in pan and bring to boil, stirring constantly. Add butter and let melt. Peel bananas and cook gently in same pan until tender. Pour into serving dish, sprinkle with a little sugar, and flame with rum. Serve at once.

## CRABBACK

This is made from the land crab that is particularly delicious in the West Indies. It is the meat of the crabback combined with a little finely chopped onion, bread crumbs, parsley, salt, and hot pepper sauce to taste. All ingredients are sautéed in butter and put into cleaned crabbacks. These can be made ahead of time and just heated before serving. Serve with slice of lime on lettuce leaf.

## LOBSTER BROCHETTE

Marinate bite-size pieces of lobster in a little lime juice 1/2 hour before serving. Put onto wooden skewers alternately with equal size pieces of fresh pineapple. Brush with melted butter, pepper and salt, and grill lightly 3 to 5 minutes. Serve on lettuce for garnish.

## HOMEMADE ICE CREAM

Spice Island Inn's homemade ice creams are made with a custard base. Beat 1/2 cup sugar with 4 egg yolks and pinch of salt until sugar is dissolved. Pour 2 cups of scalded cream over eggs, stirring briskly. Strain mixture and cook in double boiler until custard coats spoon. Strain through fine sieve and set to chill. Mix 1 tsp. vanilla and 1 cup heavy cream and combine with first mix. Freeze. To this basic vanilla ice cream, we would add 1/4 cup of nutmeg stew and 1/8 tsp. ground nutmeg or 1/2 cup of guava stew blended well.

---

## SPICE ISLAND INN
## Grenada

*Spice Island Inn is a small hotel whose excellent reputation is based on its fine food and personal service. Fresh fish and many special breads are baked here daily.*

---

## BREADFRUIT VICHYSOISSE

**1 lb. breadfruit**
**4 onions**
**2 cloves garlic**
**1 pt. milk**
**3 pts. chicken stock**
**1 stalk celery**
**4 lbs. butter**
**salt and pepper**

Sauté chopped onions and garlic in butter. When soft and transparent, add the stock. Simmer and add sliced breadfruit and celery. Cook until breadfruit is soft. Cool. Remove celery. Blend and strain. Add the milk while blending soup. Salt and pepper to taste. If too thick, add more milk. Serve very cold with a little chopped chive.

## PIGEON PEA SOUP

**1 lb. pigeon peas**
**2 medium onions**
**1 tbsp. butter**
**3 pts. stock**
**1 egg yolk**
**salt and pepper**

Chop onions and sauté in butter. Add peas, stirring constantly until all are well coated with butter. Add stock and simmer until peas are tender. Blend and return to pan. Salt and pepper to taste. Just before serving, add a beaten egg yolk for thickening lightly.

## CHICKEN BREADNUT

**1 1/2 lbs. breadnuts**
**1 onion, finely chopped**
**3 rashers bacon**
**2 lbs. butter**
**parsley**
**tarragon**
**salt and pepper**
**soy sauce**

Boil breadnuts in salted water until skins are removed easily. Peel and chop finely. Sauté onion in one tsp. of butter until slightly browned; add chopped bacon and continue to sauté. Add the chopped nuts and blend well, adding a little chopped parsley and tarragon to taste. Salt and pepper to taste. Stuff the chicken with this mixture and secure openings with wood skewers or string. Melt the remaining butter and add 1 tbsp. of thick (Chinese variety) soy sauce and pepper to taste. Paint the chicken with this mixture and roast at 300° for 1 1/4 hours or according to size of chicken.

## CHOCOLATE RUM CAKE

7 eggs
6 oz. white sugar
1 tsp. vanilla flavoring
3 oz. sifted flour
2 oz. sifted cocoa
3 tsp. dark rum

Beat eggs, sugar, and vanilla together until frothy. Set in pan of warm water. Sift flour and cocoa together, then sift again over egg mixture, folding into mixture very slowly. Pour into 10 X 14-inch shallow pan lined with buttered wax paper. Bake in 350° oven for 15 minutes.

## BUTTER CREAM

5 egg yolks
1/2 lb. white sugar
16 oz. butter

Beat yolks until well mixed. Make a boiled simple syrup out of sugar and a little water. Add syrup to yolks and mix well. When cool, add butter and mix again. Refrigerate overnight. Remove from refrigerator and allow to become room temperature. Sprinkle a little rum on cooled chocolate cake to soak in. Spread butter cream on soaked cake. Cut cake in 3 even pieces and stack. Spread more cream on sides of layer cake. Melt 2 oz. chocolate fudge frosting so that it may be poured and spread lightly over the butter cream. Press sliced almonds to sides of cake. Serve whole, and slice only amount desired to retain rum flavoring within the cake.

## FRESH COCONUT PIE

3/4 lb. fresh grated coconut
1/2 lb. brown sugar
1 small lime peel (no juice)
1 tsp. vanilla flavoring
1/4 tsp. cinnamon
1/4 tsp. nutmeg
1/4 tsp. allspice
2 oz. currants
2 oz. sultanas
9-inch uncooked pie shell with a little extra pastry

Put all ingredients, with enough water to cover, in saucepan. Bring to boil and cook until most of water has evaporated. Remove from heat and pour into pie shell. Put strips of pastry on top in

---

# VUE POINTE HOTEL
# Montserrat

*The Vue Pointe is one of the best hotels and dining rooms in the West Indies. Extending gracious hospitality toward all, the management and staff consistently affirm the hotel's motto "Our house is your house." The cuisine is delicious and there is an excellent view.*

---

crisscross fashion. Bake in 400° oven for 30 minutes or until crust has turned brown. Serve with whipped cream.

## WEST INDIAN CURRIED CHICKEN

3 lb. chicken, cut into pieces
flour to coat chicken
4 oz. butter
1 large onion
1 small carrot
1 tsp. chives
4 oz. grated coconut
1 tsp. thyme
1 tbsp. curry powder
1 tsp. mango chutney
2 tsp. green pepper

Coat chicken with flour and sauté in butter until golden brown. Remove chicken to an oven-proof dish. In same butter, sauté the onion, carrot, chives, coconut, thyme, curry powder, mango chutney, and green pepper. Last, stir in 4 oz. flour, 2 pts. chicken stock, and 4 tsp. salt until blended. Pour sauce over chicken, cover, and bake in 350° oven for 45 minutes.

## MONTSERRAT GOAT WATER

4 lbs. goat meat or lamb
10 cups water
1 large onion, chopped
1 clove garlic, crushed
4 oz. margarine
4 tsp. brown gravy
1 tsp. thyme
5 tbsp. tomato ketchup
3 tsp. Worcestershire sauce
1 tsp. ground or 4 whole cloves
2 tsp. hot sauce
2 oz. salt
4 oz. flour

Cut meat into suitable pieces. Add water and bring to boil. When boiling, skim and add all other ingredients except the flour. When meat is cooked, dissolve flour in a little cold water and add gradually, stirring constantly. Continue boiling for a few minutes to cook the flour.

## TROPICAL ISLE BROILED LOBSTER

2 oz. butter
1 small onion, chopped
1 oz. chopped mushroom
1 small green pepper, chopped

Sauté all until tender. Split cooked lobster, dice, and add to vegetables. Add salt and pepper to taste. Fill lobster shells with mixture. Brush tops with butter and brown under broiler. Garnish tops with sliced, stuffed olives. Serve with lemon slices.

## VUE POINTE PUMPKIN SOUP

1 lb. diced, peeled fresh pumpkin (about 3 cups)
3 oz. diced, peeled onion
4 oz. diced, peeled carrots
1/2 tsp. dried thyme
1 clove garlic
1 bay leaf
1 oz. uncooked bacon (3 strips)
1 tbsp. Worcestershire sauce
1/4 tsp. black pepper
2 tbsp. ketchup
1 cup water
6 cups chicken stock
10 tbsp. flour
2 oz. evaporated milk

Place pumpkin, carrots, onion, thyme, garlic, bay leaf, bacon, Worcestershire sauce, pepper, ketchup, and water in large saucepan. Add 1 cup chicken stock and boil rapidly for 30 minutes. Pumpkin should be soft and mushy. Remove from heat, add flour gradually, stirring constantly. Mixture will be very thick. Add chicken stock slowly over low heat, mixing well. When blended, strain. Reheat to serve, adding milk just before serving. Serves 10.

## CALLALOO SOUP

*(The leaf of the dasheen plant is called "callaloo." In the Pacific, it is called "taro.")*

1 lb. callaloo
1 lb. soup bones
1 lb. tannias (if not available, use potatoes), peeled and diced
4 oz. butter
1 onion, diced
8 oz. cooked crab or lobster meat
salt and pepper

Place leaves and soup bones in enough cold water to cover. Cook 15 minutes, then add 3 cups boiling water, butter, onion, salt, and pepper. Cook another 30 minutes. Add crab or lobster meat. Serve hot. Serves 8.

## BAKED FISH SUGAR MILL INN

1 large fish (red snapper, dolphin, etc.)
1 lb. sliced tomatoes
1 onion, sliced
1 cup meat stock
1 clove garlic, grated
salt and pepper
flour

Bone fish and cut into serving portions. Season with salt, pepper, garlic, and onions and let stand for at least 1 hour. Dry fish; roll in flour and fry in deep fat until golden brown. Remove fish from pan, pour off excess fat. Save drippings. Cook tomatoes and onions in drippings for 10 minutes. Stir in stock and simmer 10 minutes more. Transfer fish to shallow baking dish, pour gravy over top, and bake in 350° oven for 30 minutes. Serves 6.

## SUGAR MILL INN
## Kingstown

*This inn stands on the foundation of an old sugar mill situated on the coast about two hundred feet above sea level. A beautiful dining room surrounded by tropical shrubs and flowers with a magnificent view of the Caribbean serves excellent cuisine prepared with local fruits and vegetables.*

### BEEF CURRY

3 lbs. diced beefsteak
4 oz. curry powder
1 large onion, sliced
8 oz. butter
2 cups water
salt and pepper
flour

Sprinkle meat with curry powder and let stand for at least 1 hour. Sauté onion lightly in butter, then add meat and brown. Sprinkle meat with very little flour, then pour in water and season to taste. Simmer gently until cooked. Serve with steamed rice and the following as available: olives, grated coconut, chopped peanuts, chopped onions, fried plantain (banana), sliced bananas, chopped tomatoes, chopped cucumbers, pickles, raisins, chopped hard-boiled eggs, chutney, etc. Serves 12.

### STUFFED PAPAYA

2 small green papayas
1 small onion, grated or chopped
butter
bread crumbs
salt and pepper

Cut papayas in half lengthwise. Steam 20 minutes, remove from water, and cool. Scoop out flesh and mash, then sauté in butter with onion. Season to taste. Stuff papaya shells. Sprinkle with bread crumbs, dot with butter. Place in baking dish and bake in 450° oven for 15 minutes. Serves 4.

### GREEN MANGO PIE

4 green mangoes
1/2 cup sugar
2 tsp. cinnamon
4 oz. melted butter
1/4-inch thick unbaked pie pastry

Peel and dice mangoes and steam for 20 minutes. Remove from water; cool. Add sugar and butter. Line a pie dish with pastry and pour mixture into it. Sprinkle with cinnamon. Cover with pie pastry, prick top with fork, and bake 10 minutes in 500° oven, then reduce heat to 350° and bake 40 to 50 minutes. Serves 8.

### BANANA FLAMBE

4 large or 6 medium size ripe bananas
2 tbsp. brown sugar
grated rind of 1 lemon or lime
butter
white rum

Peel bananas and slice lengthwise. Place in buttered pie dish. Sprinkle with sugar and a few pinches of grated lime or lemon rind and dot with butter. Bake in 425° oven until brown. Remove from oven, sprinkle with rum, and flame. Serve while flaming. May also be served with vanilla ice cream. Serves 6.

## BAKED FISH IN WINE

4 fish cutlets
1 onion
1 tbsp. lime juice
salt and pepper to taste
1 large tomato
1 oz. margarine
4 tbsp. white wine or dry sherry
1/4 cup water

Place fish in greased casserole. Slice tomato and onion and decorate cutlets with a little of each, then top with a small amount of margarine. Mix together the tomato, melted margarine, wine, and water and pour over fish. Cover casserole and bake in 350° oven for 20 minutes. Serve hot. Serves 4.

## BANANA BREAD

1 lb. flour
8 oz. brown sugar
2 oz. lard
2 oz. margarine
1 level tsp. baking soda
1 1/2 level tsp. baking powder
4 large or 5 small bananas, mashed
milk if required

Sift flour, soda, and baking powder. Rub in lard and margarine. Add sugar, mashed bananas, and a little milk if required to make dough of dropping consistency. Grease a loaf tin, fill with mixture, and bake in moderate oven 1 hour, then reduce to low heat and continue baking another 15 minutes or more until done.

## STUFFED BREADFRUIT WITH CORNED BEEF

1 breadfruit for roasting
1 tbsp. grated onion
1 tsp. pepper sauce

## GRAND VIEW BEACH HOTEL
## St. Vincent

*This beautiful resort hotel is in Villa Point. Its dining room offers the finest in local and international cuisine. There is a delightful ocean view from the restaurant.*

salt and pepper to taste
1  12 or 15 oz. tin corned beef
2 oz. margarine
4 tbsp. tomato ketchup
2 tsp. Worcestershire sauce

Roast breadfruit. Scrape off all charred outer skin if roasted on an open fire. In saucepan, combine other ingredients and cook over low flame for 7 minutes. Crush beef and mix well into other ingredients. Cut off 1 inch from stem end of breadfruit. Scoop out center of breadfruit and discard. Then scoop out flesh and mix well into corned beef mixture. Stuff shell of breadfruit with filling and serve hot.

## TANNIA CAKES

1 cup grated, peeled raw tannia
1 tsp. grated onion
salt and pepper
1/4 oz. melted margarine
deep fat for frying

Combine tannia, onion, salt, pepper, and margarine. Heat fat until smoking hot. Drop spoonfuls of mixture into hot fat and fry until golden on both sides. Remove from oil and drain on paper. Serve immediately.

## MANGO CRUMBLE PUDDING

4 large mangoes, peeled and sliced
dash of nutmeg
1/4 cup margarine
1/4 cup brown sugar
1/2 cup sifted flour

Place mangoes in greased baking dish. Work remaining ingredients together to consistency of fine crumbs and sprinkle over mangoes. Bake in 350° oven for 25 to 30 minutes. Serve warm with custard sauce or ice cream.

## COCONUT CREAM PIE

1 9-inch pie shell, cooked
1 1/2 cups milk
1 cup white sugar
2 eggs, separated
6 tbsp. custard powder
1 cup grated coconut
1 tsp. almond essence

Combine sugar, custard powder, egg yolks, and 1/2 cup milk in bowl. Boil remaining cup of milk and add to custard powder mix, stirring constantly with a wire whisk. Pour mixture into a saucepan and cook on high flame, stirring constantly with a wooden spoon until mixture boils and is very thick. Add coconut and almond flavoring and cook another 2 minutes. Pour into baked 9-inch pie shell. Cover with meringue. Bake in hot oven until lightly browned. Remove from oven and cool well before serving.

### MERINGUE:

Whisk 2 egg whites until stiff. Add sugar by tablespoons, beating well after each addition until all sugar is used and meringue stands in peaks. Spread over pie and sprinkle with a little brown sugar or grated coconut.

# Index